I0236203

A Principal's Thoughts

By John K. King

Published By
Shades Creek Press, LLC
Savannah, Georgia
Copyright@April, 2016
John K. King

This is a work on non-fiction, and is devised from the experiences and reflections recorded over a set period of time by the author. No part of this book is intended to harm, reflect negatively, defame or damage the character of any person named or referenced within the writings of this book.

All rights reserved. No part of this book may be used or reproduced in any manner, in part or in whole, including internet usage, without the expressed permission of the author.

Disclaimer: I/we are sure that readers of this book may find slight errors or unique usage of wording, grammar, etc. Although we appreciate the reader's keen eye, please do not email or post that such uniqueness has been discovered, for I as the author, have most likely already made those discoveries. *JKK*

First Edition
First Printing, April, 2016
Book Cover designed by Natasha Walsh & John King
ISBN: 978-0-9838376-1-9

Printed in the United States of America
Shades Creek Press, LLC
Savannah, Georgia

A Principal's Thoughts

By John K. King

Introduction

I moved to Georgia in 2001. It was at the bequest of my wife Patricia that we move down to the Savannah area. She was ready to retire from teaching and wanted to move back to the city and to friends that she loved.

We had been married for ten years and known each other for another ten. We had met while married to others and our relationship slowly grew from friends to something deeper and more permanent. Our marriage in 1991 and our work in Prince William County, Virginia required us to juggle step-children, an hour-long commute and challenging jobs. By 2001, Patricia really wanted to retire early and go back to what she felt was her real home. It would prove to be the most important decision she ever made. It gave her time to be with her dear friends; it gave her time to sit on the beach; it gave her time to relax and garden and shop and enjoy life in Savannah.

I just wanted her to be happy. So in early 2001, we decide to do three most stressful things a couple can do: Move to a new town, find a job, and buy a home.

I flew down three times in search of a job in the local public school system. The first time, I met with the Human Resources Director of the Savannah-Chatham Public School System. The second time, I was invited to a panel interview. I went up to a third floor, poorly lit room, where seven people asked me questions related to the principalship, my philosophy of education and why I was moving to the area. With 8 years experience as a principal at the time, I felt like I answered the questions competently. The third time, I was asked to speak with Superintendent Edwards. I didn't know she was retiring and leaving the system, however, seeing her pack boxes while she was asking me questions was kind of a clue. At times she didn't really seem interested in my answers or in the questions she was posing. I finally told that I had flown down to Savannah three times and that my wife and I were definitely moving into town but I just wanted to know if I had a job in the Savannah-Chatham County System or should I begin to look for employment in other systems in the area. Superintendent Edwards looked up at me and said, "Oh you have a job. I just have to decide if it is an elementary or a middle school." I was then asked to go downstairs to the Human Resources Department so I could sign a contract.

A few weeks later I was informed that I would be the new principal of Bloomingdale Elementary School. The school was a Fine and Performing Arts Specialty School. I was excited to have the job. I was a musician and music teacher by training. I had spent a long time studying curriculum so I could lead a building instructionally. Now I was able to do both: I could lead a school instructionally and help with its performing arts program.

In May 2001, I made a fourth trip to Georgia. This time I met the out-going principal Dr. Gretchen Reese and was introduced to the staff. As I walked into the cafeteria for the first time, the staff was involved in some long-forgotten training during what they called "Post Planning". Their school year was over since they started in mid-August. The first thing I was introduced to was Mr. Lawrence giving Ms Kilpatrick a hard time. (He still is.) We had some cake and I met most of the staff and don't remember a word I said or they said. I do remember being excited about being the principal of an elementary school for the arts, of moving to this new town in the south and of moving into a new house in the next few weeks.

My first day as Principal of Bloomingdale Elementary School was in July 2001. A few months into my tenure, the staff watched the Twin Towers collapse during the 9-11 attacks. A few months after that, I began writing a Thought for the Week. These thoughts were meant to be inspiring and encouraging to the staff. It was also my therapy. Writing kept me grounded. I began to send it to the other elementary school principals. They in turn started sending it out to their faculties. I have been writing weekly thoughts now for over eight years although, there is a break there around 2007 that I will explain later.

The Thoughts for the Week became autobiographical, emotional, and soul-searching. They became a backdrop for ten years of trials, heartache, loss and renewal.

In these next pages, you will see what came to pass in my tenure as the principal of Bloomingdale Elementary School. The years 2001 – 2011 have not been boring nor bucolic; they were life-changing and thought provoking. I have attempted to give some historical information around each year's Thoughts. That became a second learning experience as I relived events and re-examined experiences.

I hope the Thoughts for the Week are still inspiring and helpful to those who awaken everyday with the goal of trying to do the best they can for the kids and people around them. It is also a way to show you that a little school in a little town that is part of a large school system can have such an impact on one's life.

John

<u>My First Thoughts – January & February 2002</u>

Thought for the Week – January 2, 2002

This is the time of year when people make resolutions...There is a desire to make positive changes in an effort to make your own and other lives better.

If you look up the word resolution in the dictionary, you find a few interesting definitions. It can mean: To do something emphatically with emotion; To go totally from dissonance to consonance in music; To break down something complex into its simpler components.

During these first initial days of 2002, we need to emphatically find the components of our challenges and resolve them with emotion and enthusiasm. (Notice I didn't use the make beautiful music metaphor).

I wish for all of you the best 2002 you can have. Let the adventure begin

Thought for the Week – January 28, 2002

This past week, our hearts were pulled and our emotions heightened at the news that a baby was found in a dumpster near a car dealership. Baby "Grace" was found in the middle of the night by a man not just doing his job, but doing his job with a caring heart and senses that were aware. Due to his efforts, a little life was saved and generous city was awakened.

You find "dumpster kids" all the time. You listen for them and look for them and open your hearts to them. These kids have been thrown away due to low expectations, special needs, behavioral challenges; parental neglect or we have become the school "du jour" this quarter.

You take them in to your school; you feed them, care for them and love them. (Sometimes that means tough love.) You try to give them the power of success. You will never get the thanks you deserve or get your picture in the newspaper. (At least not for that)

So, I thank you for your gracious heart and caring mind, for your efforts and emotions. There should be no "throw away dumpster" kids.

Have a great week.

John

Thought for the Week – February 1, 2002

Earlier this week, I was using Microsoft Word and I typed in the word "remediation". The word processing program immediately did not like the spelling of the word. It put an ugly red squiggly line underneath it quietly shouting, "Look it up you buffoon!" So, I looked at the word; I thought it was spelled correctly. Knowing that this same word processing program did not like the word inservices (it just shouted at me again!), I decided to check the spelling of the word "remediation" and the suggested correction was the word "redemption".

In the busy-ness of your days and the stresses that you have to take care of, you and your teachers take the time and effort to help your most challenged students. If everyone works as hard as they can and everyone believes in the improvements that can be made, those challenged students can find educational redemption through remediation, time, love and prayer.

Remediation is the support group - the 12-step program for educational success. It can mean tutoring, handholding, tough love, counseling or the use of various strategies until you find the one that works.

Thank you for leading the remediation march down the road of educational redemption. The route taken has many different roads. For some it may be short and smooth. For others, it may be longer with more hills and a rougher terrain. May your students find success along whichever road they take. With you providing the road map, they cannot fail.

Have a great week!

John

<u>2002 – 2003</u>

<u>Thought for the Week - July 26, 2002</u>

Many scientific innovations and discoveries have occurred in the past six years. Many of these have altered the way astronomers, microbiologists, and paleontologists look at their particular sciences.

In the past six years astronomers have discovered several new moons around Jupiter and Saturn. One of the moons has active volcanoes taller than Mount Everest. Even more exciting is the successful landing of a satellite on one of the largest asteroids floating around between Mars and Saturn. This satellite will let astronomers learn more about the makeup of asteroids and their orbits. Finally, astronomers have proven the existence of dark matter in space that has enough energy to speed up the expansion of the universe. (We even demoted Pluto from a planet.)

In the past six years microbiologists have mapped the human genome. They have successfully located and identified the chromosomes that may hold the cure to Cystic Fibrosis, Huntington Disease, high blood pressure and even cancer. They are able to create skin tissue in a dish that will help burn victims survive and they have the knowledge to create nerve cells that may allow individuals with spinal cord injuries to walk again.

In the past six years paleontologists have discovered a hominid skull that pushes the human race three millions years farther back in time. This skull is millions of years older than the famous skull "Lucy" discovered decades ago. They have discovered a fossil of a dinosaur that was 12 inches tall and had tiny feathers! Thus, birds did evolve from dinosaurs.

All this was discovered in the last six years. These scientists took risks; had the courage to do things others wouldn't and were willing to share their knowledge with their peers.

If we are lucky, most of our students, if they start in kindergarten and stay until fifth grade, will be with us for six years. If we can encourage them to take risks and to try things that they have never done before, they can discover and learn more than we ever could imagine. If educators can feel free to take risks and teach in more diverse and exciting ways, imagine the knowledge that could be gained and the successes that could be seen.

In 1996 no one predicted what science would be accomplished by 2002. Our students can make great strides and do great things in six years. We cannot limit them by our own predictions. Let's take some risks and make our classrooms and schools places where we are only limited by our imaginations.

I cannot wait to see what they will discover.

John

Thought for the Week – August 9, 2002

During these summer months, my family had many occasions to get together and celebrate special events. We had to check our calendars to make sure we were at the correct location at the proper time or we were going to be throwing rice at strangers!

Whenever my siblings get together we revert back to our adolescent years. We tease each other, laugh at the stupid things some of us do (usually me), and embarrass each other in front of our grown children.

When we go back home, we are lucky enough to have living parents. We are still somebody's kid. This familial middle management is very comforting and we should cherish it as long as we can.

Soon, students will be coming back and they will be reunited with their school family. We hope that they are getting excited as they reminisce about the fun times they have had in past school years. They too are somebody's kids and they too will get the best we have to give. Why? Because we feel the same mix of excitement and anxiety too!

Let's take our "somebody's kids" and continue to make them somebody special.

Have a great opening week!

John

Thought for the Week – August 16, 2002

Every day we hear new information about businesses who "fudged" their numbers. They called something a profit that really was not or forgot to label something a debt or cost. These businesses wanted to show their stockholders and other businesses that they really were good companies even though their numbers would not show it if they were actually released.

These slights of hand with the books have caused everyone to look at large companies with a jaundiced eye and a wearied mind. We are not sure if we can believe anything they say or any number they can put on a pie chart.

Ironically, in education numbers are everything. We want to show everyone in our community that our schools are good and that we are doing a good job. What proof do we have? The proof is: The numbers on tests, our attendance percentages and the growth shown from previous years.

Don't get me wrong, I am not against looking at test scores. However I promote documenting the qualitative along with the quantitative. How many students have shown educational mobility and have been moved from Early Intervention Program classes? How many students are no longer in special education classes? How many students are on the honor roll every quarter? How many teachers are taking classes or going to staff development workshops to improve their craft? What kinds of needs assessments have been done or will be done in the next year? What do your kids feel about their school? Yes, these are numbers too but they are numbers with a heart.

We don't have the luxury of big corporations. They can say "do over" and give everyone the correct numbers. Our numbers will be correct the first time. We will offer all the numbers and give our community full disclosure of all the great things we are trying to do. I know it will all add up to success!

Have a great week!

John

Thought for the Week – August 23, 2002

I recently asked a first grader what he had learned since the beginning of school. He replied, "I learned never to put a snapping turtle in a pond full of goldfish!" I said, "Not a good thing, huh?" He looked up at me with a sagacity way beyond his years and said, "You have no idea!"

This young scholar had learned a quick lesson and through the carnage has grasped the idea that certain things just cannot be thrown together. They can be respected and liked independently but before they are put together a little research may be needed.

Today we look again at the number of students in our building and more importantly we look at where we have them placed. If we create the best kid-groups possible and we place them with the best teacher for that group – their chance for success will be great. Many people are shocked when they realize we take a great deal of time and effort placing kids. We don't pick up all the cards and throw them down the stairs and see how they land.

Our snapping turtles and goldfish can learn to live together in peace and thrive in the same environment. We just have to continue to understand them and celebrate their differences. Placed in the right environment every child can become more successful. As we learn about our snappers and swimmers, our flyers and plodders, we will help them all be the best independently and collectively.

Have a great week.

John

<u>Thought for the Week – August 30, 2002</u>

For weeks now, national and local newspapers have dedicated numerous lines and pints of ink discussing the possibility of another baseball strike. As one writer put it, "The millionaires are arguing with each other."

I am a rabid baseball fan. I went through many a nine-volt battery listening to games as a kid on a transistor radio at bedtime. What many people call boring, I find full of strategy and sometimes as complicated as a game of chess.

Even as a fan, I am concerned that a discussion about a 'game' gets more press than the daily efforts educators show to their schools, classrooms and communities. What do we have more of a connection with – highly paid men playing a game separated from us by concrete, fences, and tax brackets – or hard working professionals who take the responsibility of educating children and who establish a bond even with the most challenging of families.

These efforts need to be written about and shared. These efforts need to be printed in big large letters and not placed on page 24D near the classified advertisements. If the print media continues to think that this kind of information is not news worthy, then we need to print it and distribute it ourselves. We need to continue to herald our heroes and communicate our crusades to make our kids the best they can be.

Let's keep the positive news flowing so we can battle the daily negativity that is printed about education. The newspaper adage "If it bleeds, it leads," can be changed to "If it succeeds, it leads."

Have a great week.

John

Thought for the Week – September 6, 2002

The other day, a student came into the office holding his stomach. I asked him if his stomach was hurting. He looked at me with a gaze that was a mix of pain and the expression "well duh" and politely said yes sir. I asked him the usual questions you ask a young man holding his stomach: "Did you eat breakfast?".... "Did you buy lunch today?" (It had to be asked.)... "Was it hurting you at home before you came to school?" He answered my survey questions with the same politeness and patience as before and then added... "I think my independex is acting up!"

Sometimes pain can be a great teacher. He didn't really care why his stomach hurt, he just wanted the pain to go away and for someone to care. I was too busy trying to find answers when all I needed to do was comfort and understand. A little later, his independex felt better and he went back to class.

Let's continue to look for kids whose independence may be acting up. Their pain may be loss, or divorce, or loneliness, or academic trouble, or life's hit them with a curve ball. Let's not play 20 questions... let's just be there. You provide much more stability to people's lives than you realize. Yes, you are that important!

Have a great week.

John

<u>September 11, 2002 – A Principal's Thoughts</u>

A year ago this country was injured, threatened and challenged. Many lives were forever changed and many sons and daughters were asked to serve their country to make sure that we did not have to experience the devastation of 9/11 again.

Last May, during the kindergarten and fifth grade promotion ceremonies, we honored our local heroes – our servicemen and women, our police force and firefighters. We thanked them for their dedication and courage.

Today we are here to remember this day not with sadness but with pride and gratitude. Our country has survived. It has become stronger and patriotism has been reborn. Today we sing songs and recite poems to let everyone know that we remember and care, that we support our local and national heroes and that we love our country.

Let us together sing strong, listen carefully and remember sincerely. Let's make a promise to never forget 9/11/01.

John

<u>Thought for the Week – September 20, 2002</u>

I am sure you were as amazed as I was to learn that Christopher Reeve, a quadriplegic, had regained some feeling and use of his hands and legs. Mr. Reeve was seriously injured several years ago in a horseback riding accident and has been a proponent of spinal injury research and genetic engineering.

Now I do believe in prayer and divine intervention. However, I also believe what my mother always said… "The Lord helps those who help themselves!" Mr. Reeve spent years in tortuous physical therapy, agreed to try experimental drugs and never lost his positive attitude that someday he would hug his kids again.

Our kids do not face the same physical and emotional challenges that Christopher Reeve faces. But, some of them with support, educational therapy and experimental strategies can make academic and emotional strides that are equally miraculous.

Mr. Reeve heard from at least one doctor, "Your injuries were too serious; you will just have to accept that they are permanent." Luckily, he ignored them. Let's continue to fight the negativity and work for our own little miracles. When more of our kids find success it will be easy to believe that Superman will fly again!

Have a great week.

John

A Postcard from Savannah

September 22, 2002

I saw the first full moon of the autumnal season this morning. It was a gigantic yellow ball and it appeared to be sitting right on the interstate as I rode to work this morning. It was majestic and awe inspiring.

I have always found school days on a full moon at the very least interesting and at the most anxiety ridden. You never know what is going to happen on a full moon day. After years of experiencing this phenomenon, I can tell when it is full moon day by the activity and volume level of the student body. I usually don't need a large lunar landscape staring at me from route 16 to inform me that another month has passed and I need to prepare for an interesting day.

The days are getting noticeably shorter with the sunrise now around 7:15 a.m. It still stays light here until around 8:00 p.m. but I am not looking forward to the daily loss of daylight until December 21st. At that time sunrise is around 7:30 a.m. and sunset is around the time I am driving home. Going to work in the dark and home in the dark is rough! Of course it is easier to see the full moon that way.

This second year at Bloomingdale has found us being not as harried or hurried and not as stressed. The staff has become accustomed to someone who does not yell and scream at them. They also have become accustomed to having higher expectations for their students while loving them to death. Yes, you can have a high achieving school and a positive climate at the same time. We spent a great deal of time placing the students in classes this year. We met with the grade levels, divided up the children, and placed the best group with the best teacher. We have had fewer discipline problems and I am seeing some great learning activities. When you split up the yahoos life tends to go better........even on a full moon!

The kids have opened up more and seem more willing to share their thoughts and give an occasional hug. The student body for the most part is not concerned about what clothes their wear or who they are trying to impress and their parents don't seem to be status conscious. They care more about fairness and equality than anything else. If you show that you care and that you care equally, they are fine.

I have learned a few things from them as well. I learned from a first grader that "You should never put a snapping turtle in a pool full of goldfish.....you have no idea what that looks like." Another young student when listening intently to the art teacher explain that they were going to use earthy colors including greens and browns, looked up and said "Oh, that is so last year." (Obviously one of the exceptions of the previous paragraph.) I have also learned that kids are the same everywhere and they appreciate honesty and sincerity. They don't mind working hard if they know you're working hard with them.

We just hosted our second annual staff party. We host them in the fall now because nothing could compare to our end of the year galas at NES! One-hundred people came and with the threat of rain, Pat and I didn't know if we were going to have to move people inside or not. The rain held up until the beginning of the next day which was the exact time that the young people left the party. So Pat and I spent until about two in the morning cleaning up the house and putting things back where they belonged. But, It was a great event. The staff actually thanked us this year. I think they were so floored last year they didn't know what to do.

Matthew and Jennifer are enjoying their new married life. Matthew was just accepted as a graduate assistant at the University of Maryland and they are paying for his graduate work and giving him a stipend. That makes me and my wallet very happy. They are looking for a place to live in Maryland that would be between College Park and Washington D.C. (where Jennifer works). Jason is doing well as a Sophomore at UVA. He is taking 16 credits but he seems to be enjoying himself. Patricia is enjoying her volunteer work with the American Cancer Society. She is helping to coordinate a fashion show in October using breast cancer survivors as the models. My dance troupe is going to perform and I will be the master of ceremonies (shocked I know). At the end of October, Patricia and I will be helping to staff a walk/run called "Making Strides Against Breast Cancer." Patricia is also working as a mentor for new teachers.

The sun is slowly rising and I feel lucky that I was able to see that glorious full moon set on the horizon. I felt for a brief moment I was driving alone drenched in the unique lighting of the setting moon and the rising son. A balance between dawn and dusk; the yin and yang of the entire earth focused for just a second on that one spot. Maybe that's why kids are so energized on a full moon. I might as well just go along for the ride. Let's shine as best we can and be glad we are at this place and in this time.

John

Thought for the Week – September 27, 2002

My great niece started pre-kindergarten this year. She is very feminine but still a tomboy. She likes to pick up bugs and be outside and walk through the woods exploring. She does this with dresses and bows on. She's like a cross dressing Grizzly Adams....not afraid of anything and likes to be in charge.

Her mother had the first parent/teacher conference the other day and was appalled to find out that her little girl was trying to tell everyone what to do and how to do it. She is especially fond of ordering the boys around. She is not nasty about it...she just thinks that the world revolves around her.

My niece sat down with my great niece and had the inevitable mother/daughter talk. The rules of school were reviewed along with a reminder of who the teacher was and who the student was. My great niece looked up at her mother and said, "Well if they won't let me do what I want to do...we need to find another school!"

There is always a balance between wanting the students to be independent risk takers and compliance to classroom routines and educational protocols. Neither a teacher nor a parent wants to inhibit a child's natural intuitive nature. However learning how to be socially appropriate at school is part of the hidden curriculum that student's face every day. The teacher has to meet the needs of every child while the students adjust to being part of a group.

It is not an easy thing to do but it is exactly what needs to be done. My great niece will eventually love school because she will be shown how to balance her independence and exuberance with active and exciting lessons in the classroom. Let's continue to do the same for all our students. The world is full of wonderful and exiting differences. Let's enjoy the differences and never try to make everyone the same. What a boring world that would be.

Have a great week.

John

Thought for the Week – October 4, 2002

Tomorrow the American Cancer Society and Savannah Mall will be hosting a Fashion Show in honor of the Voices & Faces of Breast Cancer. Each of the models participating on Saturday is breast cancer survivors.

Around the center court area of the mall they have placed beautifully made placards. Printed on these placards are the photographs and stories of these brave women; each one an example of courage and perseverance.

Yesterday, these women in preparation for the fashion show, met to review last minute details, speak with local merchants on how they can support the event, and select the outfits they plan to wear. One woman had just completed her latest chemotherapy and had to quietly excuse herself from the meeting briefly because she was weak and nauseated. A few minutes later, she returned and with quiet strength and dignity, she remained until the meeting concluded.

These ladies won't just be modeling clothes they will be role models of dedication, strength, persistence and faith. They have an inner glow that is not dimmed with chemicals or surgery. Together, they are a strong, formidable, vibrant group. They will beat cancer individually and collectively.

We can learn a great deal from these ladies. We can follow their example and show stoic strength. We can learn that a collective, energized group can be so much more powerful than individualized efforts. We can see the power of faith and be reminded that nothing can defeat it.

So let's remember them tomorrow and pray for their continued success. Their voices and faces will shine and sing as one: "We've fought it. We've beat it. We've won!"

Have a great week.

John

Thought for the Week – October 11, 2002

The baseball championship series have started. Four teams are vying for a chance to play in the World Series and to be known as the best team in baseball. None of teams playing in the championship series had the best record during the regular season.

One hundred wins is usually the benchmark for a successful year in baseball. The four teams that did reach this benchmark were beaten by the teams currently playing. These teams have something more than a number; something that makes them special. Sometimes we have to look past a numerical score or benchmark reached to see what makes a team successful.

Every school wants to reach their benchmarks. Every school wants to be known as the best at what they do. Schools are also more than numbers. There are many things that schools do to be successful – team building, establishing a positive climate, pursuing productive staff development, and implementing effective teaching practices can have a powerful effect on a school.

Above all we need to continue to match what we do to the students that we have. We will see our students successful and we will teach them to the best of our ability. We will hit our benchmarks but we will do much more – we will have a positive impact on children that will endure long after a numerical score is printed and published.

There are many nay Sayers out there that say we won't be successful and we won't be able to hit our benchmarks. The four teams playing right now heard the same thing and they ignored the critics. They just keep winning and proving people wrong. So shall we.

Have a great week.

John

Thought for the Week – October 18, 2002

Ever since Tony Orlando and Dawn sang "Tie a Yellow Ribbon Around the Old Oak Tree", we have used ribbons to show our dedication and support to causes, beliefs or interests. We wear pink ribbons to support the fight against breast cancer; white ribbons to support Easter Seals; striped ribbons for Christmas Seals; and yellow ribbons in hope of finding lost children and adults.

Next week we will be wearing red ribbons to celebrate Red Ribbon Week in an effort to educate students on the dangers of tobacco, drugs and firearms. We will use banners, stickers, hats, ties, sunglasses and even pajamas to "shake the school house up" and show the kids that we care about them now and we care about their future.

This is not in our curriculum and except for a few health related items; it is not listed in our curriculum. It is an important part of the hidden curriculum and one of the qualitative standards that public schools adhere to.

Some people might think that drugs, alcohol and firearms should not be addressed by schools. They believe that parents should be relied upon to teach their children about living safely. However, it is the schools that in the last 20 years have had too many incidents involving drug abuse, alcohol or gun related deaths. We don't want to take the place of parents but we can offer them support by speaking in one voice and showing that we care.

So let's wear our ribbons proudly next week. Let's not be afraid to take the time to educate our students in this quality hidden curriculum. Maybe someday we won't have to wear other ribbons that remind us of lives wasted or children hurt.

We wear ribbons to show that we hope for a better future….we teach for the same reason.

Have a great week!

John

Thought for the Week – October 25, 2002

Next Thursday we will open the 2002 Holiday Season with Halloween. As a child, I remember this being a one-day event or even a short evening where the kids in the neighborhood would dress up in costumes and go around the neighborhood for one reason only....To get free candy!

In recent years Halloween has become a major commercial venture. It begins right after Labor Day and it is second in sales only to Christmas in the amount of money spent and profit made.

Dressing up as a cartoon character or fictional being is a way to push our fears away and deal with reality. We have threats of war, economic concerns and terrorism in our own country. Even the day to day stress of making a living and taking care of kids can be fearful.

All of us need to have an opportunity to gain strength and bravery via make believe or donning a mask for a short while. When kids and adults have the opportunity to be something or someone else they will drop their guard for a while, laugh and relax. We tacitly tell everyone that it is okay to be different; okay to take risks; okay to try something else.

So let's encourage and applaud all the Scooby-do's, Sponge Bob Square Pants, Ninja's, and Fairy Princess' we will see next week. We may not like the commercialization of Halloween, but extending the length of time to play dress-up is not a bad thing. Sometimes we are so intent on being ourselves that we never reveal the real us. Maybe by wearing costumes we reveal more of our real selves.

Next week let's join the kids and try it – just once for fun. We might discover something about ourselves while we dress up with our students.

Have a great week!

John

Thought for the Week – November 1, 2002

The very busy month of October has just ended and once again the goblins and ghosts have put their costumes away for another year. Today, we will see many co-workers attempt to give away excess candy to anyone and everyone they see. What looked so good yesterday is now looked upon with disdain and disgust. We will hear people say, "Save me from this….If I have one more miniature Milky Way I am going to get sick….Don't put any of your candy on my desk. I am trying to give away the stash I have!"

It is interesting how opinions can change overnight. The anticipation of an upcoming holiday or special event is in some ways more enjoyable than experiencing the actual day. Once the day is over, we are quick to return to our normal schedule and go back to our comfort zone.

It is like that with change in education. We know we need to adjust how we teach and what we teach. We need to alter how we lead so we can encourage new ideas and increase the enthusiasm for what educators do. It is so easy to fall back to our educational comfort zone and wait and see how change turns out for someone else. Change is scary because you don't know exactly how to get where you want to go. It is like using an old map to try to find a newly built school.

If we can have the same anticipation and enthusiasm for educational change that we have for holidays and maintain that energy and excitement, we will have a better chance of going forward and not slipping back into less effective traditional ways.

Change does not have to be scary like Halloween. It can be like a present yet to be opened or an event yet to be shared. Like all things important, it takes preparation, support and courage. Let's take the risk and think about ways we can make things better. Our schools will be the present that will amaze, excite and encourage all who open it and take a look.

Have a great week!

John

Thought for the Week – November 8, 2002

Monday we commemorate Veteran's Day. There are only two dates on our calendar that we do not celebrate an event but remember our losses and the sacrifices of others. Veteran's Day and Memorial Day are set aside for the American People to stop, pray, and say thank you for the freedoms that have been purchased by the toil and blood of men and women who served in the armed forces.

As the years go by, we are losing many veterans who survived the onslaught of Pearl Harbor, the Battle of Midway, the liberation of France and other horrifying battles that occurred during the years we call World War II. Many of the veterans are now in their 80's and we are losing a primary resource that could explain a time that our children and grandchildren could not even comprehend.

These were the days of black outs and food rations; of curfews and lookouts; of soup kitchens and war bonds; of letters that informed families that a loved one would not be coming home.

Many of these veterans came back home and took advantage of the GI Bill and became educators. They had a chance to mold a major change in education as a nation decided how to respond to Sputnik, beatniks and hi-fi's. Many of these veterans/teachers taught us! They had a major impact on our lives and in many cases we didn't see it at the time. Tom Brokaw called these veterans "Our Greatest Generation". It is easy to agree to this moniker.

So, take the time this weekend to remember the veterans of war and the veterans of the classroom. We need to take the time and thank them. If we could talk to them and say thank you, they would say, "We did what we were supposed to do and what we had a responsibility to do."

They sound like educators, don't they?

Have a great week.

John

Thought for the Week – November 15, 2002

A young student asked me the other day, "Why are buses yellow?" Wanting to be the ever helpful educator I answered, "So cars and trucks can see them on the road and that will help keep the students safe." The student looked back at me and asked, "Then how come fire engines are red and not yellow?" Feeling like I was losing a Trivial Pursuit game with a six-year old, I hesitantly continued… "In some cities, fire engines are yellow. I think the red is more traditional. If you look at old books they almost always seem to show red fire engines." Like a good chess player the young student had already planned his next move. "If yellow is supposed to keep you safer, then how come I don't see more yellow cars on the road?"

We spoke a little longer and I exhausted most of what I knew about traditional colors and safety. I didn't even bring up the fact that the yellow is the least favorite consumer color for a car and that red is the hardest color to see at night. The student seemed to enjoy our conversation; I was mentally exhausted.

How many times in our classroom and school do we have these kinds of conversations? How many times do we actually listen to this kind of questioning? Do we take a few minutes to stretch their minds and our own; to create an educational relationship with the child, or do we shut their thinking down because we need to complete an activity or lesson? Learning should be something we do with the students not to the students.

I know you are remembering when you were in high school and you could get this one teacher off task instantly by asking an inane question. (There is always at least one in every high school.) That is not what we are talking about. We want children to feel comfortable to ask questions and be intuitive. We have to monitor the amount of time it takes and sometimes say, "Hold that thought, I will be right back to hear your question."

Give educational conversation a chance. It might open up a whole new world to you and your students. Every time the six-year old looks at me he just shakes his head and mumbles, "Yellow buses, (sigh)". I guess some answers will take longer but all questions are worth answering.

Have a great week.

John

Thought for the Week – November 22, 2002

Earlier this week, I got up at four in the morning, turned on the coffee pot and bundled myself up in two jackets, a hat and a blanket. I grabbed a lawn chair and with the precious coffee in hand, I went outside to watch the Leonid Meteor Shower.

It was an amazing thing to see. This is not Star Wars. The streams of light come in and streak in all directions and they make no audible sound...A silent symphony of light; a dance of fireworks in the deep, high sky choreographed by God!

I was thankful for being there; thankful for the show. I sat in solitude and I felt warmth in the cold. This warmth gave my heart strength and my soul renewal.

What are you thankful for? Do you look up for the lights that stream and show briefly in your sky? Everyone shines sometimes. Are we aware and still looking up when they do?

Enjoy your Thanksgiving time. Look for your shooting stars. The impact and effect lasts much longer than the visible light. Let's take the time, enjoy it and feel the warmth!

Have a great week and a great Thanksgiving!

John

Thought for the Week – December 6, 2002

The holiday season is the only time of year where we change the look of our house, the clothes we wear and even the songs we sing or listen to.

Some people get wilder than others. My house has so many lights outside that airplanes can use it as a marker as they prepare for landing. Last year cars drove by and drivers honked their horns. I wasn't sure whether they were saying: "Nice job!" or "What were you thinking?" The idea is to have some fun; to do something different; to take a risk and add to your electric bill.

Lights have special meaning to all religions who celebrate at this time of year. The lights on a Menorah, the star atop the Christmas Tree, the candles of Kwanzaa all communicate one thing........hope; The hope of a safe tomorrow and the hope of continued prosperity.

These lights illuminate our dreams and bring our most heart-felt wishes to the surface. These hopes and dreams shine as bright as any decoration and for a brief moment we are not afraid to share them with our friends and family. In fact, the lights seem to shine brighter when more people are around them. Their energy seems to be matched with the power of love.

So, get the knots out of the garlands, plug in the lights and see if they work. (Or go to Wal-Mart and pay a couple of bucks for a brand new set. I have already done that.) Use any color you'd like and light a path that celebrates the past and looks with hope toward the journeys to come. Think of it as House Dress-up Time! I'll drive by and honk the horn in celebration!

Have a great week!

John

Thought for the Week – December 13, 2002

At this time of year, children are looking forward to the holidays with great anticipation and excitement. They are curious as to what they may find under the tree and inside fancy wrappings.

During these days of curiosity, there is a multitude of light: A portion of it from the lights on the tree; some reflecting off the wrapping paper and the ornaments; others created brightly from the eyes of children.

This waiting period is the best part of the holidays. It is almost anticlimactic to open the presents and reveal the surprises. We are happy to receive them and the love they contain, but we are slightly saddened that the excitement is over.

Wouldn't it be wonderful if everyday throughout the school year children would feel the same excitement and anticipation as the walk through the front door of a school? If they could feel the same wonder and curiosity about what would happen that day and what new things they would discover?

If children could look at each school day as a present to be opened, the future would be as bright as a child's eye or a bejeweled ornament. The students would be disappointed at the end of the day because they had to leave this loving place of wonder and excitement.

It is not folly to think of schools in this way. We are only limited by how much we believe in ourselves and believe in our children. We have the possibility of shining like a star in the desert….Lighting a path that illuminates the future!

Have a great week.

John

Thought for the Week – December 19, 2002

The other day, kids were arguing in the cafeteria about whether Santa Claus was real or not. There is always one in the crowd trying to burst the beliefs of others and they seem to take great pleasure in trying to convince them. They ask questions that would make a lawyer proud… "Have you ever seen him?.... Did you notice he uses the same wrapping paper your parents used?... How does he bring toys all over the world in one night?"

After that barrage, one of the kids looking beaten but not bloodied looked up at me and asked? "Do you believe in Santa Claus?" Without hesitating I answered, "Absolutely!"

The most wonderful thing about Santa Claus in this age of cynicism is that he gives without asking for anything in return. We leave for him, milk and cookies (obviously not lactose intolerant) or a snack for his reindeer (depending on what country you live in). We aren't billed later and he certainly does not knock at the door because his delivery is C.O.D.

I believe in Santa every time I hear kids sing out strong with brightness in their eyes that glows like a star atop a Christmas tree. I believe in Santa every time a child tells me how excited they are about seeing a relative who is coming to visit. They smile the same smile shown when they are about to open a present. I believe in Santa when kids are tolerant of each other and walk hand in hand and try to help each other. I believe in Santa when adults are surprised when a gift comes their way from the last person they would think of. I believe in Santa when people take the time to appreciate their blessings rather than count their inconveniences.

The believers at the table looked at the heretic and said, "See, I told you he was real!" I hope he stays as real for you and he is for them. As the preacher once said, "If you need proof, what's the point in faith…If you have faith, you don't need proof!"

Have a blessed holiday season and the most joyous of new years.

John

Thought for the Week – January 3, 2003

Western society loves to celebrate and to party hearty. We love to move from one special event to another with an anticipation unequaled in the history of mankind. In just the last few months, we have lived through, (some of us just barely), Halloween candy, Thanksgiving feast(s), Holiday festivities, New Year's Eve parties and any number of "smaller" galas during the days in between.

If you are thinking we are done now for a while, let's take a look at the next few months. First, we should properly celebrate Martin Luther King's Birthday. We should celebrate how far society has come, (even if some politicians are still living in the dark ages. My father told me a long time ago, "The good old days, weren't all that good."). In February, it is Valentine's Day and in March, it is (of course), St. Patrick's Day. Even a recent edition of the newspaper printed a Vox Populi stating, "Now that the holidays are over, we can prepare for St. Patrick's Day!"

Celebrating is not a bad thing. It brings people closer together, it reduces stress and makes us evaluate our lives and it gives us a chance to reconnect with friends and family members. This reconnection renews our souls and fills our hearts; it gives us the energy and strength to succeed in our everyday lives. It is this power of friendship and love that binds us together and makes us stronger.

Is it possible to celebrate each day like this? Can we find educational reasons to party hearty? If celebrations lift up our souls and renew our spirits, think of what we can do for our students if we celebrated each individual academic victory or each classroom success. We don't need party favors or wrapping paper. We don't really need pizza or popcorn parties. All we need is a few cheers, a few smiles, a few handshakes or a few high fives. In this way, we aren't just commemorating a day, we are celebrating progress. What better reason is there?

Let's make each day a celebration. Have a happy new year!

John

Thought for the Week – January 10, 2003

When I drive around this beautiful county, I take notice of gasoline prices or what may be on sale at different convenient stores. I like to comparison shop from behind the wheel. Something I call five speed window shopping.

Recently, while I was checking out how high the gasoline prices have increased, I noticed sitting behind a gas station, was a lovely, old brick building. It was not a large building but the brick was dark deep red; the kind that make up early 20th century structures. It had character and strength that had not been diminished by years of storms, heat, humidity or progress.

What amazed me was that I had never noticed the building before. I had driven that way hundreds of times before and never once did I look past the brightly colored gaudy convenience store to see what else was there.

We can do that with people too. Sometimes, we can only see the loudest or the most flamboyant and not notice the quiet one in the back or the ones obscured by others who are more comfortable with themselves. These quiet students can have the strength, beauty and stoicism of that old brick building. Like that old building, they wait quietly to be noticed; to be included; to be understood.

Let's look for the quiet ones today. Let's make them feel welcome. We may discover something that is beautiful and magical. They're out there; just waiting to be seen.

Have a great week.

John

Thought for the Week – January 17, 2003

During his acceptance speech for the Nobel Peace Prize, Dr. Martin Luther King Jr. stated his hope for a world in which all people would come together and create a "Psalm of brotherhood."

When you analyze the meaning of these words, you find symbolism and straightforwardness. This is one of the things I admire about Dr. King. He had an amazing way of writing for oratory and for thought; poetry for social change.

A psalm is a joyful ode or a song of celebration. A brotherhood is a group of people dedicated to a common cause. Dr. King was hoping for a day when an entire world could celebrate an equality of thought, an equality of deed, and an equality of potential; a world in which your future was not pre-determined or limited by your creed, color or pedigree. He looked for a world that would celebrate change and offer each individual an equal opportunity to find success in their pursuit of happiness.

Our worlds are smaller but not any less complexed. We have students of all different backgrounds and with varying levels of support and it is very easy to create a bell curve of success. We want everyone to succeed but we see their limitations instead of celebrating their differences.

Let's work to make our little worlds a place where everyone can hear a psalm of brotherhood. A mantra that encourages all children to believe that they can succeed and that who they are and what they are is special and wondrous.

Let's also sing about the differences we bring to our worlds each day. We need to model how to celebrate differences by supporting and understanding our own. We are not talking about a utopia or an ideal world that can never exist. We can create it in our classroom and in our own school by our thoughts, words and deeds.

Let's sing a little today.

Have a great week!

John

Thought for the Week – January 24, 2003

When I was a small boy, my parents and especially my mother would try to teach me what I needed to know to survive and be a successful adult. I call it basic training. The rules she would review with me and my siblings may seem funny or corny to some now but, it is something I can't forget or ignore.

We learned things like: "If you opened it, close it. If you borrowed it, give it back. If you do something wrong, apologize for it. Whatever you do, do it the best you can. Treat people older than you with respect and people younger than you with patience." My favorite one has to do with cleaning my room… "You can stare at it as long as you want, but it won't happen by itself!"

We hear about educational change all the time and how these changes need to be made to help our students to find success in the 21st century. We may be preparing them for jobs that haven't even been created yet. This makes the changes even more challenging and in some cases very scary. We are going to have to take some risks. The one thing we do know is… "We can stare at it as long as we want, but the change won't happen by itself!"

We have to give our students the basic training in sharing information; working cooperatively; sharing without being competitive; making conclusions from the information giving; and listening when others are speaking. We also need to balance that training with basic training in literacy and numeracy. Without the balance our students won't be ready for future employment and future thought.

Without these changes, our students will not be successful in the real world. Without the balance they will never see how tradition and innovation are connected. They will never see how technology is important but so are the skills needed to speak intelligently on a subject and to work cooperatively in a group for a common goal.

So let's help our students get their basic educational training. For the 21st century they need more than the ABC's and the 123's. They need to be given choices and the time and the materials and the support from fellow classmates. They need to feel free to take risks and to learn from each other.

Change takes time but most important things that have an impact on society do. Let's stop staring and start changing.

Have a great week!
John

Thought for the Week – January 31, 2003

We have had some very cold temperatures in the last several weeks. Everyone has been outside covering plants and dripping faucets in the hope that both would survive and be fine when the weather warmed up again.

Even with these efforts, I noticed that some of the plants still are freezer burned and I will have to nurse these plants back to respectability before I can have guests visit my garden. For days these plants were sitting on a table with numerous blankets and towels on them. It looked like the laundry had taken over the back porch. I thought they would be protected and do fine. I believed that my efforts were good enough to help these plants survive. I was amazed to discover that some of the plants did well and some are in deep distress.

I do know that their root system is fine and that after cutting the plants back, (some may get buzzed pretty low to the ground), they will come back and grow and thrive again.

We can get into a comfort zone and feel that everything is moving along fine and our efforts are good enough to help our kids succeed. Sometimes it is necessary to look under the surface and make sure things are going as smoothly as we hope. Occasionally, we have to change what we do to get the desired results and we have to individualize our actions to help individuals find success.

Let's continue to work toward finding ways that include all different types of learners. If we try to cover all of them in the same type of curriculum blanket we may end up disappointed when the cover is removed. We can give them what they need to be successful in challenging times. Different types of actions are needed to fit the various needs of the students. You can do this. Believe in them and they will grow.

Have a great week!

John

Thought for the Week – February 7, 2003

Less than a week ago, this nation lost seven people of great courage, great vision and great intellect. We all lost them.

Ironically, many of us didn't remember or notice that Columbia was in flight. The news media and our culture has made space flight as common place as the birth of triplets. Sports scores are plastered all over the front page but news from space is relegated to page 24A.

However, this tragedy made us stop, regroup and learn about seven people lost; seven families devastated; seven continents humbled. We were reminded of the fragility of life.

These seven souls knew the risk and understood the risk. Risk to them was a necessary by-product of the scientific process. They did what they wanted and died believing that what they did was worthwhile.

People of the scientific community are usually labeled atheists. All seven astronauts had a faith and a relationship with their God and they were not afraid to show it in their actions and in their daily routines. You might say that space flight allowed them to have a closer relationship.

As each parent was interviewed on television, they all said the same thing. It didn't matter if they were in Texas, India or Israel. They all stated with pride that their children died doing what they loved… helping science evolve and helping their country grow.

We are reminded of course of another tragedy twenty years ago. Christa McAuliffe was to be the first teacher in space. Instead she and another six souls lost have taught us to persevere and to continue to take risks.

So two tragedies connected; fourteen souls who took risks are now together. God's choir has gotten a little larger this week. Let's look up and hear their quiet song.

Have a great week.

John

Thought for the Week – February 17, 2003

I was away last week. I went up to Virginia to take care of my mother while she was recuperating from heart surgery. Actually, my wife and I were taking care of both of my parents. The surgeries caused both of them to adjust their schedules and their activities.

They are an amazing couple. They have been married 57 years and they are totally dedicated to each other. My father wants the love of his life back to 100% as fast as possible. The whole thing has been kind of scary for him. My mother on the other hand has taken the whole thing in stride because she wants to live longer and live stronger. The 87 pound woman is no weakling. I know I wouldn't have bounced back from heart surgery as fast or as quietly as she has.

She is not allowed to pick up anything over five pounds for another four weeks. So we made enough food for several weeks and taught my father how to turn on the washing machine. No, he didn't know how because that was her domain. You don't usually get my mother and her appliances. This is one of the adjustments I spoke of earlier.

So for a week, my wife and I played the role of "tweeners"….Adult children who have adult children of their own and are now taking care of their parents for a while. It is a weird role. All of a sudden you are taking care of people who took care of you. You suddenly realize that your parents won't be around forever and this time together is precious and special.

You also realize that hereditary traits and family traditions are good things and that you can still learn some great things from 75 year old people. Grace, dignity, hard work, patience, dedication and love are not corny, old-fashioned terms and laughter can help all of us deal with growing older.

Families have an inner strength that you can feel whenever its members get together. This strength is built by time, love, trust and blood. You forget about it and you don't realize that you've missed it until you visit and feel it again. This strength is an unbreakable bond. It cannot be weakened by time, distance or age. All family members benefit from this strength. It is always there; we just need to remember to feel it. We did and my mom is getting better every day.

Thanks for allowing me to share my parents with you.

Have a great week!

John

Thought for the Week – February 21, 2003

This weekend, one of the cable stations is presenting a documentary about African-American entertainers who performed in the early to middle part of the 20th century. These men and women were legends and people all across the country were buying tickets to see them in person and audio equipment to hear them at home. They were the standard bearers of dance, music, art and drama. They had perfected their craft and were the legacy of hundreds of years of oral tradition, practice and learning from their elders. People watched them; revered them; adored them.

However this was the early part of the 20th century. These same wonderful performers who played for standing-room-only crowds….weren't allowed to stay in the same hotel or venue they were performing in. Some places quietly displayed their ignorance and prejudice by having signs posted saying – WHITES ONLY. Some places were not as tacit in their intolerance and gave the performers a certain amount of time to change and leave before the police to escort them out.

To add insult to injury, these performers that were loved by everyone on stage were paid less than their white counterparts once they left the spotlight at the end of the evening.

Slowly through the years, we have seen improvements. We still have intolerant people who live in ignorance but we should use them as an indicator of how far society has progressed and as a reminder of how far we still need to go.

Education has always been and remains the great equalizer. Educators can give all students a wedge that can be used to open the doors of inequality. Student can be given the tools to succeed and the vision to not accept anything less than a spot at the head table; equal pay for a performance; or equal seating in the audience. Educators teach tolerance by being tolerant; fairness by being fair; equality by believing that all students will succeed because some of our elders and teachers expected nothing less.

Educators are in charge of the future. They can give their students the power to succeed and the skills to overcome history.

Have a great week!

John

Thought for the Week – February 28, 2003

We lost a great educator yesterday. Mr. Fred Rogers was an American Icon; he was a man of simple beliefs who always had the same message: Children should be respected; children should be loved; children should celebrate learning.

He was a man of grace and quiet dignity. He developed "Mr. Rogers' Neighborhood" because he did not like what children were watching on television. For thirty years, his show invited children to use their imaginations, understand their feelings and open their minds. The format was simple and repetitive yet deep and well-written and it became part of our culture. Recently, one of Mr. Rogers sweaters was donated to the Smithsonian. In true Fred Rogers' style, he wasn't sure what all the fuss was about.

However, Mr. Rogers was a trail blazer for equality and understanding. During his show, guests would come by to share things with his 'friends'. Among them were dancers from Harlem, long-haired musicians, poets, opera singers, architects and builders, people of all ethnicities, and handicapped adults and children. He was also the first to hire bilingual assistants to ensure that all children could be reached. He did this without fanfare or headlines; he knew it was the right thing to do.

Mr. Rogers' Neighborhood has even been lampooned by Eddie Murphy, Steve Marten, and even Johnny Carson combined his persona with John Rambo's to create Mr. Rambo's Neighborhood. You know you have made an impact when comedians can use you for a laugh because everyone in the audience knows who you are!

So today the train to make believe land won't be running; there is a black ribbon hanging on the door of Mr. Rogers' house and his "neighborhood" is grieving today. However, his quiet, respectful life's work of empowering children with the use of love and simple songs and stories has impacted the lives of thousands of children.

He created a way of teaching that made us feel as comfortable as the tennis shoes he put on to begin each episode. So let's show our respect by liking people today for being "just the way they are" and "have a snappy new day". He wouldn't want it any other way.

Have a great week!

John

Thought for the Week – March 7, 2003

Last Friday evening, as we were leaving our house to do some errands, we spotted a young, happy yellow Labrador retriever running around our neighbor's yard and heading for a very busy Victory Drive.

Not wanting the do to endure a death by Michelin, we encouraged the dog to come to us, (which it happily did). Now this dog had a choke collar on but no identification tags. She was obviously well taken care of and she obviously owned by someone who was painting their house a nice color of green since there were two or three faint splotches of paint on her. This was because she was a normal, curious retriever.

Being an owner of two dogs, my wife and I knew that the first step was to put the dong, (now known as Precious – because she was) in our fenced-in back yard, let our dogs out and see if they would play with each other or show teeth and pretend to kill each other. Our two dogs had been on alert since we called Precious to us and had been whining continually for the previous fifteen minutes. So, we let the dogs out and in less than two minutes, they were running around the yard playing with each other like they had known each other for years.

Later that evening, we called animal control and the local police department to report a missing dog. Being dog lovers, we know someone would be looking around for *Precious*. We placed our two dogs in their usual sleeping areas and allowed Precious to sleep on the couch leaning against me so she wouldn't whine and be scared.

Early the next morning, her owner called and was grateful to find that we had her dog. She explained that she had moved in down the road and was painting her house and that *Sweetie*, (figures), had jumped over the fence while she was at work. She was planning to build a tall stockade fence to keep Sweetie from escaping the homestead again. Our dogs watched as their new friend happily bounded home with her owner – we had done our good deed for the week.

It is amazing what animal lovers will do to protect them. They don't ignore stray animals; in fact, animal lovers will take them in, take them to supportive organizations, and even pay for their recovery. However, when we see a child running around without supervision or improperly clothed, we think of them as vagrants, runaways or even criminals. These young people didn't "get out". They may have been pushed out, kicked out or left out. Just like Sweetie, they are precious and just like Sweetie they deserve extra time, thought, commitment and support.

How many stray children do you see every day? How many could use a little support? How many have one constant – us! Let's help make their school the homestead they don't want to escape from. Let's remember that all our Sweeties can be precious too!

Have a great week.

Thought for the Week – March 14, 2003

The rain and the warmer weather have combined to awaken plants, trees, and lawns. What we thought was dormant or destroyed after numerous nights at or below the freezing mark has shown great resilience. They are proudly showing off their vigor in the form of beautiful white blossoms of the dogwood trees, bright red and pink blooms on the azaleas and the many hues of green seen in lawns all over the area.

This rebirth invigorates us and renews us; it gives us hope and restores our belief in the world. The colors of nature awakening fill our senses and lift our souls.

It also might be reminding us of our allergies and filling our senses with a little more than metaphors. Things that have impact and importance tend to have something that balances them out; something that makes them more complicated.

The most beautiful of roses is surrounded by thorns. (I know you can get thorn-less roses but that is just not right!) The tallest and strongest oak tree sheds leaves and acorns eight months out of the year. The plants that are presently blooming in a myriad of colors and combinations are producing enough pollen to make even the least vulnerable blow their nose and scratch their eyes.

The third quarter is now over and a very fast school year is quickly coming to an end. This is the time of year when conclusions wished to be reached and one chapter of a student's or teacher's life is seen to pause and wait for a few months to start again. Why can't the fourth quarter be used as a time of growth, excitement and anticipation similar to what we feel when our gardens come to life? Instead of looking at testing as one of the signs that the school year is ending, let's use the time around the tests to push our kids a little more, excite them about the world around them and give them a chance to blossom. They need a chance to show off their beauty and to show how strong and able they have become.

We forget in the spring how far we have traveled with our students. We forget how much they have grown and how much they have learned. Don't be afraid to step back and gaze upon the many different types of beauty and combinations you have in your room or school. Be proud! You have tended them and nurtured them. They couldn't help, even in the smallest way, to grow!

Have a great week!

John

Thought for the Week – March 21, 2003

This year we have worked hard to find ways to engage students in their own learning. We have seen the benefit of having them work with each other and supporting each other as they learn new things. We have seen teachers use the training they have received to take risks and try new things to help their students succeed. We have seen and felt the change of climate in the classroom. The excitement of learning has returned to the teacher and the taught.

We have also prepared to send our sons and daughters in the military to war. We support them by counseling, comforting, and supporting their families. We talk with them, encourage them and at times, hug them. We know that the stress they are under is unlike any other and we also know that for seven hours a day we can give their children a little normalcy.

The two things listed above – teaching and caring – are the two things educators do better than anyone else. You cannot teach with caring and there is no better teacher than showing young people what matters by example and action.

We are asked now to consider how we can do this important job with larger class sizes, fewer supplies, and minimal support and with a belief from some people that we are a wasteful group.

I find that a perplexing commentary. I do not know any teacher or administrator who has not spent their own money on their classroom or school. I have not met any teacher or administrator who is not willing to find ways to save and scrape and reuse and recycle to give the students the things they need. Just put on any table in any school a box of old crayons, pencils, paper, even toilet paper rolls. In ten minutes the box will have been taken and put to use in a classroom. I do not know any teacher or administrator who has not written and submitted grant proposals to find ways to help bring to their schools the things they need for student success.

As I get older I become more like my father. That is not a bad thing. I just get surprised when I say the things he used to say to us and I swore I never would! Two came to my mind today: "There is no such thing as a free lunch." And "You get what you pay for." Our kids, our programs and our school district are worth an investment from the community. This investment will pay wonderful dividends. The cost of not investing will be devastating and long-lasting.

I know all of you are worth the investment. As we pray for our military and understand the cost of peace, let us remind our community that an educated populace is not a choice, it is a necessity.
Have a great week.

John

Thought for the Week – March 28, 2003

Recently in a fourth grade classroom, students were reviewing the causes and effects of the period of United States History known as Western Expansion. In small groups, the students discussed and listed what they thought were the major developments and talking points of this period (WOW).

The students came up with a comprehensive and interesting list. Some of the effects listed were: An increase in the number of people living in St. Louis; An increase in the number of towns; A need for workers, builders, food, law enforcement, teachers and services; A need to push Native Americans farther west; A need for more resources so these new towns and homesteads could survive.

Cause and Effect is a big part of our history. We can just about teach anything related to social studies, science and even mathematics using the term cause and effect. Students also find it an easy concept to understand. They can relate to the idea that if they do something it will create a reaction. If they study hard for a test, it is likely that they will receive a higher grade. If they attend baseball practice religiously, they will see themselves improve as an athlete. If they punch the biggest kid in the school, they might lose some teeth. Kids have no trouble understanding cause and effect.

It is time for other people to understand the concept of cause and effect. The schools can tighten their money belts and work with a more austere budget. We can continue to find new ways to bring revenue into the schools with more grant money, business partnerships and even PTA bake sales. We can continue to show our community and our leaders that we are not wasting money but using it for materials that help our students find success. But just as those new cities needed support 200 years ago, schools need the necessary support to be the greatest resource a community has.

Our students will continue to discuss cause and effect and will continue to be engaged in thought provoking honest discussions. Next year, there will probably be a larger number of kids in that classroom but they still will be discussing important concepts and they will be learning. I hope that those who look in that classroom and hope and want students to be successful, will have given them the resources to at least make success possible. That is the effect we all wish to see.

Have a great week.

John

<u>Thought for the week – April 4, 2003</u>

There are no songs for education. If you know of any please let me know. We have war songs, (Battle of New Orleans, When Johnny Comes Marching Home, The Green Berets). We have peace songs, (Give Peace a Chance, Where Have All The Flowers Gone). We have songs of perseverance, (We Shall Overcome, A New Day is Dawning). We have love songs, care songs, we love our car songs, but I cannot think of a song about education.

Of course there are plenty of educational songs. Hap Palmer, the Muppets, Mr. Rogers' and Sesame Street have given us plenty of those. I am talking about songs that make a point; songs that remind everyone how important education is to society; songs that may have a political or social message; songs that make you think.

Here is what I think it should sound like as I use the music to Eve of Destruction (My apologies to Mr. Morse."

<u>Eve of Instruction</u>
They say our class sizes, they are a'growin
The money's not there and people are grumblin'
We are cutting budgets but now our efforts
We're treating it like a spectator sport

And you tell me over and over and over again my friends,
We must believe we're on the eve o instruction.

We've written letter and had our meetings,
They've been honest and we've shared our feelings.
The parents are willing to pay more money,
For something they believe in; they're not running

And you tell me over and over and over again my friends.
We must believe we're on the eve of instruction.

And now our leaders, they make tough choices,
Some go their own way, some listen to other voices.
They pray for guidance to do what's right,
Remember the kids, they're too young to fight.

And you tell me over and over and over again my friends.
We must believe we're on the eve of instruction.

Teachers still teaching; youngsters still learning,
       They feel the stress and dark clouds are looming.
They know they will save every nickel and dime,
       When did the lamp of learning become a dollar sign?

And you tell me over and over and over again my friends.
       We must believe we're on the eve of instruction.

Thought for the week – April 11. 2003

For the past several days we have watched in amazement the bravery, tenacity and strength of a young soldier named Jessica Lynch. We admired her bravery as she fought against the enemy. We were awed as she held on to life while sufferings numerous injuries. We were humbled by her strength as she quietly asked about her fellow soldiers as she was being transported for treatment to Germany.

We need these kinds of victories in our lives. It balances out the horror of war and eases the pain of hearing about a young man or woman who won't be coming home. We feel the emotions right along with the families and we celebrate or mourn with them.

We hear a great deal about how selfish a people we are. We are told that we are only interested in ourselves and our own. Educators are told that they don't care enough or don't invest enough time. In an era of simple perspectives, people are evaluated by the simplest of terms. Caring means success; agreeing means you are a good person; disagreeing makes you a bad person; lower taxes means life is good; higher taxes means life is bad. If life cannot be summed up in ten words or less, no one is going to read it or believe it.

We have many mini Jessica's in our schools. We have seen them also work with bravery, tenacity and strength. They have represented their school well as a visible sign that the school is successful. This is living, breathing accountability. Our Jessica's are nurtured, supported, loved, watched and prayed for too. They are our daily heroes and they strengthen our resolve to continue in this noble profession.

We will continue to pray for all the Jessica's in the world. It is the least we can do.

Have a great week.

John

Thought for the Week – May 2, 2003

Earlier this week parts of Georgia and the Carolinas were jolted by an earthquake registering almost 5 on the Richter scale. People were more shocked that Georgia would experience an earthquake than the earthquake itself. This type of earth burp is supposed to happen in California and other areas of the "left coast". We expect Mother Nature to be fair: They get the earthquakes; we get the hurricanes.

Seismologists will tell you that the continents are still expanding and there is a need for the earth to make adjustments as this expansion occurs. Most of the adjustments made are mini-quakes that we cannot feel at all. These occur all the time and it is a good thing they do. Otherwise, the only way the earth would have to let off steam would be huge devastating earthquakes, volcanic eruptions and in their wake, tidal waves. The destruction would be incredible.

Letting off steam is a good idea for educators too. We have to share ideas, thoughts, concerns and even fears with each other. We don't do that well. We do a good job of sharing complaints or the problem de jour. We are not skilled in voicing our ideas about new ways to help students, sharing our thoughts about teaching strategies, listing our concerns about how large class sizes will be next year and conquering the fears that come with budget cuts. Like the earthquake, we hoped that these educational rumblings would happen to other jurisdictions.

Scientists are learning more and more about earthquakes. They may never be able to predict where the next one will take place but they hope to become knowledgeable enough to help keep people safe.

Teachers and administrators need to keep reading and learning about what is going on around them. They need to know how they can participate in the positive process and how they can help their own little world expand and improve.

You are the epicenter of change and progress. Believe in what you do. You can move mountains!

Have a great week!

John

Thought for the Week – May 9, 2003

One of the lead stories on the national news this week focused on the Georgia High School that sanctioned a white's only prom. This was the same high school that last year made headlines because they were promoting their first integrated prom.

This year the high school decided to host two proms: An integrated prom at school and a white's only prom off campus. I guess they felt that if it was held off campus it would take the heat off the school system and the school's administration. In reality, it appeared they wanted to exclude others from the prom and wanted to exclude others from the location.

Even the Fox Show, The O'Reilly Factor made it their lead story on Monday evening. Bill O'Reilly, who is the self-appointed conscience of the world, (now that Bill Bennett is in gamblers anonymous), said "It is amazing how young people are allowed to go to war together, fight together and die together, but aren't allowed go to proms together. This is just wrong!"

These types of stories always make the headlines. The daily efforts and successes of schools and teachers everywhere aren't front page material. Bill O'Reilly wouldn't have a show about teachers who have made a difference. It wouldn't be considered a news worthy item. So, the whole educational establishment is judged and represented by a hand full of snap shots that show us at our worst.

Every day, we welcome, teach and care about students from all different areas, backgrounds, religions, and capabilities. Some have needs so great that we bring together as many professionals as possible to help them. We want to find inclusive solutions rather than exclusive strategies.

Every day we see improvement. In some, we see quiet, small gains; in others we see great strides. In both cases, it is because of loving, hardworking teachers who care enough to come and do their jobs even when the talking heads and newspapers continue to tell us how bad we are.

We need to blow our own horn and share our successes with anyone who will listen. To stay positive and to be proud of what we do. There is progress being made. Every time a teacher gives a hug and love is shown to a child, a bond is formed and learning can take place.

On this Friday of Teacher Appreciation Week, let's remember that teaching is an honorable and worthy profession. Let's not base our self-worth on snap shots of unthinking people.   Let's show them our volumes of daily, weekly and yearly accomplishments.   Let's show them the hours of meetings that we have attended to help one child; the home visits; the phone conferences; the conferences held very early in the morning or very late at night.

Let's never forget how inclusive we are even when we don't get credit for it.

Have a great weekend!

John

Thought for the Week – May 14, 2003

I saw a bumper sticker the other day. It said, "Change Happens!" Interestingly enough it was on a 1966 Ford Mustang that was long overdue for an oil change and a tune up.

It is amazing what we feel about change. We look at it as a negative; something we are forced to do; something we have to endure. We are comfortable in our normalcy because we think we know what will happen, even before it will occur. We like to prepare for and control our changes.

Famous rock groups from the 70's are making new music and performing live again. The Eagles, Fleetwood Mac, and REO Speed wagon have all gone on the road to packed houses full of people who want to go back in time. They want to forget for a brief moment that many things (like our waist lines) have changed.

Change is as constant as time. It can either be a vehicle to help us grow or it can wear us out as we try to keep it where we want it to be. Change will go around, behind or over us. We cannot stop it. We cannot ignore it.

At this time of year, we need to take the time to notice how much our students have changed and how much they have grown. We need to remember how they acted on August 11, 2002 and how much they have matured. Even your most challenged students have improved and they have learned something from the love and care given to them.

It is easy to worry about the budget and class sizes for next year. Those types of changes are always with us and we always have something to worry about this time of year. However, we have a duty to our students to tell them `how much they have changed; to celebrate their accomplishments; to encourage them to smile and be proud too.

Change is not a bad thing. We want to see positive change in our students every day. We want to know that the change we are going to see will be due to hard work, planning, and vision. Our cars need a new bumper sticker. It should read: "Change should happen!" The future can be fun and exciting.

Have a great week!

John

Thought for the Week – May 26, 2003

This weekend, our school community lived through another heart breaking experience, the funeral of Ashleigh Moore.

I say "our school community" because her death has and will affect us if we just look through the tears long enough to see.

Ashleigh was 12 years old. She belonged to all of us. The elementary school remembered her growing up and becoming a helpful, happy fifth grader. The high school she would have attended understands what kind of young adult she would have become. The middle school, her daytime home, knew her best, knew her heart and knew her soul. Their prayers are our prayers; their pain is our pain.

I was amazed to see Ashleigh's family. They were so strong and they talked to all the young people and parents about cherishing their time together. These amazing people can put our lives into perspective. I know if I lost a child, I would not be able to do what they did.

We have the same tenuous, uncertain relationships with children that parents have. Teachers and administrators are not given guide books on how to solve all problems or what to say and when to say it. Parents are not given a handbook and warranty when a child is born. Educators and parents have that one strong bond that should bring them together: We don't know all the answers, but we will do our best because we love our children.

Like a shooting star that we stare at with awe, Ashleigh light here on earth was bright but way too brief. We wish we could stop time so we can reflect and collect ourselves. However, time is cruel, it just keeps moving on and it forces us all to walk with it.

> For everything there is a purpose even though we don't know why,
> Things happen for a reason for God's up in the sky.
> Don't worry about tomorrow, don't worry about yesterday,
> There's a new angel in heaven, who will daily show us the way.

John

Thought for the Week – May 30, 2003

This is the time of year when kids of all ages pay good money to dress up in uniform medieval dress for the privilege of walking across a stage to receive a diploma.

This rite of passage is accepted, expected and respected by everyone youngster to oldster. Even the coolest of cool high school student will gladly put on a long flowing un-cool robe and equally un-cool square hat with a tassel and think he is still cool! (He is!)

Throughout the years we can remember robes and tassels coming in every color of the rainbow: The pastels of the 70's, the bold colors of the 80's, the traditional dark robes for the boys and white for the girls of the 90's. Today, we see that even with uniformity the individual can still shine.

Students now don the graduation uniform and look for ways to comply with the dress code while dressing up the outfit. They glue balloons, tennis balls, teddy bears or other toys to their hats. The more artistic will draw and paint the school mascot on their robe usually on a spot not seen until they stand up or turn around. The more loquacious write poems or messages on their hats or robes so every video camera can record their feelings about the rain forest, politics or which school they plan on attending in the fall.

It is important for people of all ages to let their hair down by dressing up. You really cannot relieve the stress of life without doing something different; without shaking things up.

We see kids dress up like this every year but the kids use it to measure their lives. The graduation ceremony sections off a part of their life and allows a new section to begin. They only get to wear a cap and gown if they have completed the necessary academic criteria and mastered the curriculum.

We remember our graduations as we revel and rejoice in theirs. We remember every "hi mom" or "I fooled you all!" written on a cap. We remember every smile and every tear on the face of happy graduates. Let's throw our caps up with theirs and cheer along with them. They are a reflection of our work. Let's be proud of what they have accomplished and see what they do next!

Have a great summer!

John

Thought for Ms Oliver – June 2003 (Ms Oliver was my boss from 2001 – 2003. I was invited to speak at her retirement party and was told it was casual dress. I came in a golf shirt and slacks. Everybody else came in suits and ties and long gowns. I have never believed anyone saying I could dress casually again.)

It is time for another mature adult (translation: older adult), to retire. Retirement used to mean rocking chairs and knitting; assisted living and assisted will writing; straw hats, larger shot glasses and stronger eye glasses.

Retirement has become a rite of passage; something celebrated like your 50th birthday, your first kiss, your wedding or weddings, the birth of children, graduations and job promotions.

Retirement now means: golfing and gardening; grandchildren and great grandchildren; spending your children's inheritance without guilt; parties and traveling; new vocations and new avocations; new challenges and new adventures.

As Assistant Academic Services Officer, Ms Oliver has qualifications to do many things successfully. Ms Oliver's experiences alone give her the capabilities of finding success in a number of different and new careers.

Ms Oliver could be the new coach of the Washington Wizards basketball team. With her experience in making the worst situation look good, she might even be able to help this horrible team at least look or sound better than they actually are.

Ms Oliver could work at the complaint department of any major department store. There is nothing they can yell at her, show her or throw at her that she has not seen or heard before. She will just smile at them and say, "No ma'am, you obviously don't understand the way this works." Or "What you are going to have to do is this."

Ms Oliver could be the next Mayor of Savannah. She is used to working with bureaucracy, letters to the editor, angry people, nutty constituents and co-workers and idiots who write weekly thoughts thinking their cute. I'd vote for her but I like her too much.

Ms Oliver could put the Savannah Symphony back on its feet and run it with a profit. Her understanding of budgets and the budgetary process and how to work with people (even artsy people), could mean a new symphony with a new attitude. Of course her knowledge of budgets and the budgetary process makes her a good candidate to work at the sewage treatment plant too!

Ms Oliver could work as a psychiatrist's assistant. Her knowledge of counseling, active listening skills, soft-spoken manner and experience working with "special and exceptional people" would be a blessing. She would also be working right next to someone who can prescribe medications. She didn't get that perk with her old job.

Ms Oliver could also write a book about all her experiences, all the people she has met and known throughout the years and the daily events that happen at 208 Bull

Street. Just the threat alone might bring in a few bucks from people who do not want you to put anything in writing.

Ms Oliver needs to take her time and go over her options. She needs to relax and reflect for several weeks before making a decision on what to do next. She might also want to get unlisted number so people don't ask her, "So what are you doing with yourself?" or "How retirement going?" or "You mean you haven't decided yet?" These questions only come from people who cannot retire yet and hate the fact that you can. Remember, smile at all times, it drives working people crazy.

Ms Oliver has earned the right to relax, reflect and renew. She has earned the right to smile and to gloat and to be euphoric about the chance to do something else before she dies.

We hope that you enjoy every minute. We will miss you and we wish we could go with you. Happy retirement and find a little time each day to think of the people you left behind, close your eyes and just laugh.

2003 – 2004

Thought for the Week – July 25, 2003

While families are on their annual beach vacation, they find themselves walking with toddlers and young children in search of sea shells.

We all know that every strip mall from Atlantic City to the Gulf of Mexico sells large, shiny, perfect shells that came from the Pacific or other areas no where near the east coast. We could easily buy as many as we wanted and show them off to the neighbors. However, it is the thrill of the search that makes it so much fun. We look forward to it and feel like we have accomplished something. It is as if we are making a connection with our primordial ancestors; that ooze that made us.

No matter how old we get, we never lose the urge to pick up shells. We select shells of all different sizes, shapes and colors. Some are damaged or marred in some way but we keep collecting them and happily place them in jars, buckets, pales or pockets. We take them home, place them someplace special and look forward to next year when we will do it all over again.

School is like that. Every year kids come to us excited about what they will discover. They come to us in all shapes and sizes; some with blemishes or tough histories. We enjoy having them and making them better. Like looking for that perfect shell, we look for the perfect strategies that help all students succeed. We walk together and look forward to discovering new things each day. We keep coming back because we know they are there. They need that connection and we need it too.

Let's help them keep that enthusiasm and excitement. Let's give them wonderful days and memories so they want to come back again. Let's show them what a noble and wonderful profession teaching is. Let us work to make every day something to look forward to.

Have a great week.

John

Letter to the Editor – September 5, 2003

I have watched a great deal of baseball on television lately and I am astounded at the number of people who pay a lot of money for seats behind home plate. I am more astounded at the reason why they bought those seats – They want to be seen calling someone on their cell phone asking that person to watch them on television. In other words, they paid good money to call and wave at someone sitting at home. They're not even watching the game! They are waving at a camera. I am having a hard time watching the game because I am watching them too! To make matters worse, there are more of them than you think. Watch a game sometime and you will see what I mean. How many video-fanatics do we need?

Recently, more articles have been written questioning the cost and benefits of No Child Left Behind. How are we really helping kids when the assessments have not kept up with the goal – student achievement? These assessments are designed to show what students have mastered, what they have improved on and what still needs to be done. However, people are only focusing on the test scores or an attendance percentage or the number of schools that have been labeled as failing based upon a number.

The viewer at home watching a friend wave and smile while holding a cell phone is missing the game being played on the field. The reader of test scores and newspaper articles is only getting part of the story of what is working in schools. They need to look at all the educational strategies implemented and the curriculum that has been mastered. They need to visit schools and see what is going on. Both the viewer and the reader look busy, but they are missing the great performances all around them. They are looking at one thing rather than the whole. They are so distracted by the waving and the pointing, they are missing the positive, exciting things that are going on around them.

Let's back up and continue to look at the bigger picture. Let's enjoy the teamwork and applaud the improvements we see everyday. Let's not miss the important things and don't be distracted from our goal – successful students!

John K. King,
Principal, Bloomingdale

Thought for the Week – September 12, 2003

Another Patriot Day has been commemorated and many of us reluctantly are asked to remember that awful day two years ago. Everyone's life changed that day and 9/11 has been etched in our nation's chronograph right next to December 7, 1941 and November 22, 1963. We will always remember where we were, what we were doing and how we felt.

Each generation from the Greatest to the Baby Boomers to the Gen-Xers have been molded and tempered by these solemn events. In each case, these generations have been asked to grow up fast, to do more than their share, and to do whatever it takes to keep a great nation alive and strong. The challenge was taken and the job continues to be done.

Educators need to take up the challenge as well. Doomsayers and gloom-makers are quick to predict the demise of public education. They start every paragraph with a negative statement or generalization. These comments must be answered with a quick, measured response.

Following World War II, the GI Bill allowed more young people to attend college than ever before in the history of this country. The Camelot days of the Kennedy administration was followed by a committed war on poverty, the first Elementary and Secondary Education Act and PL 94-142.

How can educators fight terror and respond to 9-11? We can offer hope by being a safe haven for all children. We can offer strength by providing the best curriculum possible. We can offer a bright future by answering every negative comment with an invitation to come and see what our young people are doing and how we believe that education is one of the cornerstones of a free and strong nation.

That is patriotism at its best!

Have a great week!

John

Thought for the Week – September 19, 2003

Earlier this week, as we were preparing mentally and physically for the possible arrival of another hurricane, a third grade child grabbed my hand and asked: "Are we going to have an evaporation drill because of the hurricane?

Now this turned into a teachable moment even as we found the humor and innocence of it. A question born from concern can lead to introspection and reflection.

Listening and reacting with respectful humor is very important in the world of education. We can get so hardened and scarred that we do not watch and listen to things going on around us. We can be so busy planning for a catastrophe that may or may not occur that we fail to enjoy and persevere with a positive attitude through this challenging yet wonderful profession.

As the wind dies down and we put our hurricane boxes away at least for a little while, let's look into our students eyes, and listen to what they say. They grow up so fast and their youthful honesty evaporates quickly.

Have a great week!

John

Thought for the Week – September 26, 2003

At a meeting this week, we discussed and tried to come to consensus, (hard for principals to do), on this question: "What beliefs do you hold that you would get fired for?"

It is an interesting question. When you first think about it, you may shy away because we need to work and pay bills and we like to eat. We may even think that politics always comes into play when you make a decision. Even some would just look at the person who posed the question and think, "What does he mean by that?"

A bigger question might be, "What do I believe in more than anything else and what overarching tenet guides every decision connected to my profession?" It is a question of philosophy; it is our belief system that elevates a job to a profession.

Maybe a better question is, "What creates the fire in you to do your profession better than others?" To ensure and guarantee success, we know that a profession comes with long hours, strong convictions, amazing energy, and the will to pull others along with you toward that final destination.

Let's light the fire and let's believe that we can be the difference in people's lives. Don't let showers of negativity douse the fire inside of you and the people around you!

Have a great week!

John

Thought for the Week – October 3, 2003

Several people I know are involved in different weight-loss programs. They all promise great results with little work. Some promise that we can lose weight while eating, (that's my favorite), and each one claims to be the best way to get back to that fictional weight that we used be (back when we were 18). From low-carbs to low fat; from fruit drinks to shakes; from high protein to coaches as close as the nearest phone, we have been bombarded and sold on this 21st century snake oil that will miraculously help us lose weight with little or no effort.

Testing is education's weight loss program. It promises that it will show quick results and success if we just continue to do it. It has become the standard measurement for every child, every school, every local education agency, every community, and every state. Now, we want to force success by tying promotion/retention to test results. The belief is: "If we continue to test, we will find success."

Teaching and testing should not become synonymous. We should continue to find ways and strategies to promote long-term learning and to measure real educational success. We need a balanced approach in this test-crazed era we live in.

Good teaching matched with test-wise-ness preparation will give our students the best possibility of mastering not only the test but also the curriculum. Using testing as a prescriptive strategy will give us more information and show the students what they have mastered and what they still need to do. We realize that non-educators are pushing this "test to success" mentality. As always, we need to take a deep breath, find strategies to help our students succeed, and support each other as we make our way through this amazing time in the history of public education.

In the future, due to testing, our grade levels may gain weight by having more students for more years than we thought they would. I believe there will be some changes in the testing logic as we progress. They will trim it down and the weight that it carries will be adjusted. Until then, let's do what we do best: Think it, plan it, deal with it, pray about it, talk about it and do it! We are lean, mean teaching machines. Nothing would shock them more than if we succeed. Let's nourish each other with the belief that we can and we will.

Have a great week.

John

Thought for the Week – October 9, 2003

During this time of year, there are many mornings in which our vision is obscured by the heavy fog covering the area. We have all heard of accidents and severe pile-ups that can occur in weather like this. Scientists have discovered that when we drive in fog, our optic nerve and our brain wants more visual information to make out the terrain, curves and length of a highway. To get our brains to receive the needed information, drivers will actually accelerate and drive too fast to physically react to the changes in the road. After severe accidents in the fog, drivers have said, "They didn't realize they were traveling that fast." This is a dangerous paradox: We need more information but we may crash before we get enough information to know that we needed to slow down.

When we use testing to determine if a child should be promoted or not, we are making a similar decision. We want more information and we want to be able to tell everyone from parents, to politicians how well we are doing, but we may be on a collision course toward factory-outlet teaching and away from reasoning. By the time we get the correct information, we may have already hit the brick wall or slid down the slope called No Child Left Behind.

Should we despair? Should we succumb to teaching the test? No! Students need a balanced approach that teaches them to think and gives them the skills needed to show what they know on standardized tests. They need test-wise-ness but they need also to think at a higher level. There are not a lot of jobs out there where you fill in bubbles all day.

So what is the solution? It is another paradox: By slowing down, taking a deep breath, teaching the curriculum, and providing test-wise-ness and test practice, our students can balance testing with learning. We want all of our students to be successful – not just in test taking, but in life.

Otherwise, our daily, slow successes will be obscured by the fog of test results and numerical scores that will never show the individuality and talents of our students. Let's see clearly and move carefully through the testing highway. Let's not miss the view. There are great things to see in our classrooms every day.

Have a great week!

John

Thought for the Week – October 16, 2003

The chilly mornings of autumn are upon us and the smell of falling leaves, marigolds, and asters fill the air. It takes us back to a time when kids could bob for apples and make apple sauce or candied apples without teachers and parents being afraid of law suits. Back then (not that long ago!), teachers and parents would create classroom and family traditions and kids learned that hot things might burn them but they could also create some wonderfully tasty things. We remember names of classmates or teachers when we get a quick whiff of nutmeg or cinnamon. These traditions are important. They teach us not only how to do things but they teach us how to be and how to enjoy simple things.

When I feel a chill in the air, I remember my first job as a youngster. I delivered the early morning local paper. I would get up every morning, deliver 100 papers, and be home in plenty of time for breakfast before school started. I wouldn't ride a bike to do this. I would walk and deliver each paper individually and put it on their front porch or inside their screen door. My father told me, "Service matters." I believed him especially since he helped me deliver the Sunday paper (which was huge) so we could get to church on time. I also got to know the neighbors and their dogs, which would eventually let me deliver papers without their teeth showing (the dogs, not the neighbors).

Take time today to go outside and smell the scents of autumn. What does it remind you of? Where does it transport you back to? By retracing these memories, you can help your students find ways to remember what is important and what makes a tradition.

Years from now, when your students or children breathe the crisp air on a fall day what will they remember? What fond memories will they have? Let's teach them ways to remember the important things and let's use activities that they will never forget. We have the knowledge, talent and power to affect everyone we teach. Like a cool breeze, we can make them stop, take a deep breath and remember!

As for me, I am going to go get some apples. Fresh apple sauce and biscuits sound good to me right now.

Have a great week!

John

Thought for the Week - October 24, 2003

I was in Boston last weekend to see my grandchildren. It was one of those quick turn around visits people take when they have too much on their schedule but they want to see relatives, especially little ones, more than once a year.

The city of Boston as well as the rest of the New England area was in mourning. Once again, the Boston Red Sox found a way to lose the American League Championship Series and they would not be going to the World Series. Worst than that, they lost to the hated New York Yankees. This was a team that only needed five more outs and they would have a chance to win their first world championship in over 80 years! People were crying. They took off from work. They called into every talk show in town. No one was on the road and it was a Saturday morning!

One woman called in to a radio station and said, "I will never do this again. My house is dusty and dirty and clothes need to be cleaned and ironed and my yard is a mess. I have spent the last two weeks on an emotional roller coaster with this team. I will never invest this kind of time and energy again! The loss is too great!

Now I love baseball and the World Series is an important part of each autumn. However, it is still only a game played by men and designed to entertain and be a stress reducer. (Try telling that to a Boston Red Sox fan right now.)

What amazes me is that people will invest the time and emotions; they will cry tears and get angry; they will call anyone around them to celebrate a team victory, or mourn the underachieving utility infielder. However, they will not invest the same time or emotions for an educational system that is responsible for the future of the country. They will not call a friend to tell them about something wonderful going on in their school. They will not call politicians or talk shows to ask them if they had visited a school lately or were they just basing their opinions on the never ending mantra – "public education is in trouble."

We need sports and other diversions to give us mini-vacations. They help us get through the stress of work and family. They give us a chance to yell and sweat through every play and every game. We need to be avid and rabid fans of the game. We also need to be avid fans of what we do for a living. We invest too much emotion, energy, time and sweat not to celebrate each educational victory and mourn each loss. It is another way education becomes a profession not just something someone does because they liked school when they were small.

All Red Sox fans will eventually recover from this loss and by Sunday the World Series will be over for another year. The slogan "Wait 'till next year" will begin to echo from every team who didn't play in October. We can't wait until next year. Every minute, every class period, everyday counts. Let's cheer each other on and continue to work to make this year the best yet!

Have a great Red Ribbon Week!

John

Thought for the Week – October 31, 2003

This week, I had the honor of attending my nephew's graduation ceremony from the Police Academy in Atlanta. He was one of 27 young men and women who answered the call to protect and serve their community. They looked impressive in their uniforms and I said a short prayer asking for their protection and safety.

The mayor of Atlanta spoke briefly but poignantly. She said, "Thank you for becoming public servants. Never forget the importance of your profession nor the responsibility that accompanies it. I am proud of all of you." Following her address, the senior officers joined her in a standing ovation for the new officers.

Educators are also public servants. Our profession also has importance and great responsibility. Many people have forgotten what public service means. Just as the police have to enforce rules and laws sometimes to the chagrin of the public they are sworn to serve, we as public servants have to look at what we do to provide the best service to our students and co-workers. Being a public servant does not mean that you continually alter your philosophy or ethics. Being a public servant does means that you have to build an ethical professional philosophy that gives you the strength to provide the best service for the people. This philosophy provides the foundation for everything we do, say or teach to others.

Today let's be reminded of what it means to be an educator; a public servant; a community leader. It is not an easy profession. Just like those young officers, we answered a calling to do something extraordinary. Let's be proud of what we do and let's continue to say short private prayers for all public servants.

Let's be proud of serving the public!

Have a great week!

John

Thought for the Week – November 7, 2003

It seemed appropriate this week that an election was held to determine the next mayor of Savannah, (not fully decided just yet), and a vote was finally held to extend Superintendent O'Sullivan's contract for another three years.

The mayoral candidates focused on a need for change; a different direction; a new kind of leadership. Most educators wanted continuity; a chance to continue down the same road; an opportunity to see success.

It also seemed appropriate that a run-off election would have to be conducted to reach a final consensus for mayor and a unanimous vote from the school board would never be seen.

No one is going to agree with any one person all the time. That is what makes us individuals. However, it is important to disagree with people in a respectful and understanding manner and not just disagree because you don't like something about them. Looking beyond philosophical or ideological differences is leadership, not partisanship.

As educators we try to find and cultivate the best in every child, co-worker and parent. We look beyond differences and encourage their growth and improvement. We hope by example we can show that people can think differently about things but live and grow supported by each other. This is more challenging than it seems in an era of negativity, my way or the highway thinking, or "let me tell you what you think" talk shows.

Good leadership leads to slow and steady progress. Supported leadership leads to a work force that will work hard and fight hard for the success of all people that enters the school house door. Tenacious leadership breaks through the walls of negativity, individual agendas, and the expectation of "business as usual" once the smoke clears.

Leadership is also a flow chart. It has to flow from the top down and from the least experienced employee up. It must flow laterally from support personnel and people elected to oversee and create policy. It needs to flow out of every classroom and main office with a belief that it will make a difference and it will be heard.

One leader was voted in for a few more years. Another leader is waiting in the wings until the final count is tallied. Let's do our part and lead our little piece of the world the best we can!

Have a great week!   *John*

Thought for the Week – November 14, 2003

Education Secretary Ron Paige visited the Savannah area earlier this week. He spoke about No Child Left Behind and the need for administrators, students, and parents to feel a sense of "urgency" about these new guidelines. It was an appropriate choice of words.

The Webster's definition for urgency is: "A need or necessity for action or deed." It does not say panic but it does not say to ignore it either. The educational landscape has changed and we need to accept it, plan for it, and ride through it. Urgency is also not cowering in a corner afraid to do anything because someone is waiting to stomp on your attempts at creating an educational environment that assists students in mastering content while passing gate-key tests.

If you have ever taken the time to stand dominoes up on their ends carefully, (| | | |), you know that one move or flinch could knock one domino over and all the others would subsequently fall as if connected by an invisible chord. However, if you lay a domino down between each standing one, in this pattern (_|_|_|_), they cannot be knocked down; they are supported from both sides.)

As educators and administrators we need to give support and be supported from all sides. If we fail to do this, we will end up in a blame game of who was supposed to do what and when they were supposed to do it. Worse yet, we could play "if only": "If only the _(fill in the blank)_ would do __(fill in blank)_ we would be successful!" We cannot let NCLB make us cynical, caustic, impatient, or despondent.

Educators need to support all their children, even the weakest or the least able. Educators need to be supported by their administrators and encouraged to try new things to help their children succeed. Administrators need to be supported by the school system and encouraged to provide different staff development opportunities and different learning opportunities for families. The School System needs to be supported by the public. Not the ones who write in the paper, but the ones who we work with everyday.

With this two-way support, we cannot be knocked down. We will have the opportunity to be change agents and we will take the challenge and make the necessary, needed improvements.

This is the time to be prepared not scared. There are incredible people all around us. We need them and they need our support. Let's see what we can do together!

Have a great week!   John

Thought for the Week – November 21, 2003

Yesterday, at the WOW (Working on the Work) training for principals, I had the privilege of meeting and listening to a cadre of teachers who were the trailblazers for their respective schools. Each educator was eloquent and sincere in their use of the WOW philosophy and their belief that it leads to a different type of teaching and a successful student body. One teacher called it, "Being a practicing educator."

Being a practicing educator should be considered equal to a practicing physician or a practicing attorney. Each one should create a picture in your mind of a person constantly working at their craft, trying to help and serve each other.

When we think of a practicing physician, do we think of Marcus Welby? (I am showing my age now.) Do we think of the physicians on the show E.R.? I think of Dr. Byrd who was our family physician forever and if he told us to drink turpentine we would have done it. I think of my current family physician who gets tired of hearing the stereotypical description that all doctors are milking the insurance companies and they don't care about patients anymore.

When we think of a practicing attorney do we think of Perry Mason or Matlock? Do we think of LA LAW or LAW and ORDER? I think of a friend of mine who is an attorney and a very generous person with his time and his money. He truly tries to find ways to help people and he is always studying to keep up with the ever changing legal system. He gets tired of being stereotyped as an ambulance chaser and being out "just for the money".

When we think a practicing educator do we think of Ms Brooks or the Room 222? Do we think of Mr. Holland's Opus or Boston Public? I think of Mrs. Guthrie my fourth grade teacher who pushed me and would not accept anything but my best. I think of Mrs. Woods, my sophomore English teacher who taught me how to write and helped me fall in love with the written word. They are for me the epitome of the professional practicing educator. I also think they would be tired of being stereotyped as overpaid, under-trained, and can't do anything else individuals.

Our challenge is to be a practicing educator. To constantly work at improving the educational system and the daily activities that go on in our schools and in our classrooms. The only way to fight the stereotypes created by ignorance, is to battle ignorance not argue against the stereotype. Every time a student succeeds because we tried something new and encouraged new thinking, the stereotype is hit hard. Every time a teacher is given the freedom to try new things or discuss new learning, *the* stereotype takes another blow. It is a constant battle but it is constantly rewarding.

As we get close to another Thanksgiving season, let's join that cadre of teachers as a practicing educator. Let's use that terminology when we have conferences and when we talk at assemblies.   To practice medicine, law or education is to accept one of the highest callings a person can receive…..The calling to serve!

Have a great weekend! I am thankful for all of you!

John

A Thanksgiving Thought – November 25, 2003

What are we thankful for?

We are thankful for our daily challenges;
        It is God's way of saying what we do is important.

We are thankful for our friends, our co-workers, our students;
        They give us the strength to continue the good fight.

We are thankful for everywhere we have lived with;
        Those experiences help us to understand each individual student.

We are thankful for everywhere we have worked with;
        Each experience makes us a better teacher and gives us new friends.

We are thankful for each challenged student;
        They teach us as we teach them.

We are thankful for our parents and our family;
        They keep us grounded and think of us as gray-haired children.

We are thankful for our children;
        They give us the daily reasons to teach; to learn; to believe.

We are thankful for everyone around us;
        We need each other to help each other.

We are thankful for each day, each class, each teacher, each co-worker;
        They make us who we are.

We are thankful that we are called teachers;
        It is what we were called to do.

We are thankful!

Thought for the Week – December 5, 2003

This anticipatory time of the year is represented by candles. We see them with fiber optics, adorned on wreaths, huge inflatable ones tied down on a front porch, electrically powered ones attached to windows, and even old fashioned ones that have wicks and that you actually light with a match.

Candles are an important part of many religious and secular remembrances this time of the year. They are a symbol of the miracle of oil lamps burning for eight days during Hanukah. They are a thanksgiving for a good harvest and for the unity of all people during Kwanza. They represent a guiding star that shone brightly one night so long ago during Christmas. They are a beacon in the window and a remembrance of our youth and of celebrations completed and celebrations yet to come.

Candles are powerful yet delicate. They provide light and warmth and yet they can be extinguished with just a puff of air. They shine with wonderful colors and can fill a room with precious aromas and yet they will burn down and go out faster than we expect leaving us saddened at their departure. That is why we purchase more and burn more this time of year - they are our ghosts of past, present and future holidays.

Let's light more candles this holiday season. Let's use them to remember that we can bring light and warmth to the people we work with and the students that we teach. Let's us remember what the light of a simple candle means to us and what it can mean to someone else.

Candles are important to all of us. They mean hope; they mean light; they mean faith; they mean joy!

Have a great week!

John

Thought for the Week – December 12, 2003

I saw a rainbow the other day driving home from school. It was a welcomed sight after viewing the torrents of rain that fell from mid-day through the late afternoon.

It was a beautiful, distinct prism that jumped out from the dark clouds that loomed behind. It looked powerful, yet delicate; imposing and wistful; distinct yet holographic. A wonderful quirk of nature that allows us to see all the separate colors that collectively makes our reality and our world.

We are all rainbows. We are made up of separate events and happenings that have shaped us into who we are and what we are. Like the many colors of the rainbow, we are as diverse in our thinking, our feelings, our beliefs, and our philosophies. These differences come together to make our schools and offices a rich place where our diversity becomes a strength and that strength helps all to succeed.

Our students are still building their rainbows. You may not be able to discern the different paths they will choose that will become the colors of their lives. We must remember that we are part of the rainbow and we have the power to play a part that shines for them. We also have the opportunity to build and add to the personal rainbow of anyone we meet.

Let's remember the rainbow and know that we only notice it after stormy darkness. Let's try to notice all the rainbows around us and revel in their beauty. Remember, you have the power to help people shine!

Have a great week!

John

Thought for the Week – December 19, 2003

In a few short days, we will once again celebrate the birth of an individual who never accepted the minimum from himself or anyone around him. Throughout his life he asked questions and pushed men and women to be better and to do more than the minimum. He continually preached, taught and demonstrated that the minimum was not acceptable. Maybe that was why he was called "Teacher".

Giving your maximum in everything you do is not easy. You may get minimal returns in the beginning and you may not see the return on your efforts for quite some time. Teachers may not see how much their students have mastered until a year later when their present teacher tells you what a great class it is. Learning is a linear process it does not start in August and stop in May; it starts at four years of age and hopefully continues throughout a lifetime.

Getting the maximum out of others is also a challenge. It starts with each of us demonstrating that anything less is not acceptable and that excellence is expected. The mantra in every classroom should be that if your name is on it, then it should be your best work.

You are tired because you have given your maximum. You may not see the return on your investment yet, but you will. Get some rest and know that your efforts do make a difference. Excellence takes a maximum effort; excellence is never easy.

As we celebrate the birthday of the greatest teacher of all, let's believe in what we do, and why we do it. Let's believe in the people around us and let's look past our fatigue and continue to work toward excellence. Maximum effort will yield maximum results.

Have a great holiday season and may 2004 bring you happiness, peace and joy!

John

Thought for the Week – January 9, 2004

My wife and I attended a funeral yesterday to show support for a teacher who suddenly and tragically lost her husband in a car accident on I-16 earlier this week. In an instant, this teacher's life and the lives of her two children were changed forever. For all three of them, things would never be the same. Their world would never look the same or feel the same; it was irreversible.

The church was packed with family and well wishers. Also in attendance were school administrators, teachers, specialists, custodians and other staff members who had taken the time to drive over an hour to be there. They were there to show their love and care; to share in the loss and the heartache. It is what educators do.

At the conclusion of the final prayer at the gravesite, the two little children bounded from their mother and ran to the arms of their teachers who were also in attendance. These wonderful educators had a difficult time containing their tears as they held their students. Yet, they wouldn't have been anywhere else that day or at that time.

Teachers and administrators do make an impact with their students. You are the constant positive force that does not waver, does not falter, nor end, no matter the tragedy, hardship or challenge. You provide more strength than you know and more love than will ever be acknowledged.

There will always be children who in times of crisis will look for the strong, familiar face of their teacher. They know their teacher will provide for them the strength they need to carry on another day. Let's be there for all of them. It is what we were called to do.

Have a great week!

John

Thought for the Week – January 16, 2004

What do you think of when you hear the word hero? Do you think of costumed crusaders who help the downtrodden and the abused? Do you think of members of the greatest generation who landed on Normandy and fought in the Pacific to rid the world of a tyrant? Do you think of everyday people who fight a daily battle with cancer or physical disabilities and quietly, stoically succeed one day at a time? Do you think a hero makes their community or the world change even if it is just a little bit?

This weekend we remember the life of Martin Luther King Jr., a true hero. With quiet determination, Dr. King fought for equality for all people. He battled to destroy the tyrant named segregation and he changed the world through his belief in non-violent demonstration. He died too soon; too young; but his death couldn't stop the changes that he started. He focused a generation to work toward social, political and educational activism.

We can see the results of Dr. King's work in college classrooms where not only are the students as diverse as this country but the instructors are as well. We can also see the first fruits of Dr. King's dream in the board rooms of major corporations, and the head coaching offices of college and professional sports teams. There is a long way to go but the world has changed since 1964.

As educators, we know that the dream has not been fully realized; that a great deal of work still needs to be done. We also know that Dr. King was not only a preacher but also a teacher. Everyone who ever met him or walked with him has said that they learned something from him.

A true hero does not have to wear a costume, or be conspicuous or loud. They just have to dedicate themselves to continue their daily march toward success. They have to continue to believe in their dream and pray for the strength needed to make it through another day. A true hero ignores negativity, fights through the phalanx of ignorance and never tires of working toward the prize: equality in mind, equality in thought, equality in life, equality in faith, and equality in destiny. Let's remember, let's hear the march and let's join them!

Have a great week!

Thought for the Week – January 23, 2004

We have always been fascinated with time. Stephen Hawking, noted physicist and author has stated that there is the possibility of traveling forward in time (who would want to), but traveling back in time would just be too difficult.

We have songs about time: Time In a Bottle; Time, Where Did You Go; Does Anyone Really Know What Time It Is?; etc. We have movies about time: The Time Machine; A Matter of Time; A Moment in Time; Time Traveler; etc. We have time-outs, time pieces, and egg timers. We have digital clocks, LCD clocks, wind-up clocks (for when the power is out), analog clocks, cuckoo clocks, grandfather clocks and even Mickey Mouse clocks. We even have watches and the time pasted on the bottom of the computer screen that I am typing on right now.

Time is important to us because is connects our activities, our challenges and our successes to a moment that cannot be repeated and once it is past, it may never be retrieved. That is why it is easier to look forward than to look back. What we may do is easier to see than what we have done or what may not be undone.

This week we celebrated the 100th day of the school year. In those 100 days we have focused ourselves and our students on the coming challenges of testing and the needed mastery of material that comes with new federal guidelines. To that end, we are receiving daily reminders of the time we have left to prepare our students.

It is truly an amazing time for educators. We are counting up the days to celebrate what we have accomplished while we count down the days we have remaining before we are evaluated two-dimensionally with paper and pencil.

Some people find the counting down reminders annoying. Some of our constituents think it self-serving that we count the 100th day. They think we are just counting the days until we can have another break. They need to understand that important things are timed.

Presidents are measured by what they do in their first 100 days in office. In 58 days, we will be judged by our test scores. In 100 days from now, we will be in the middle of June preparing for the next countdown for success to begin.

Time waits for no one; Time is fleeting; It is just a matter of time; Time marches on. Let's not be afraid of time. Let's use it to our advantage and not waste a minute.

Have a great week. *John*

Thought for the Week – January 30, 2004

Captain Kangaroo passed away last week. We have lost another connection to our past; another educator gone from out sight; another memory fading from when the world was presented to us on a black and white television screen.

Time magazine gave tribute to Bob Keeshan (the Captain), as a trailblazer who always worked and competed on commercial television until cartoons and the need for ratings moved him to public television in the 1990's. The Savannah Morning News eulogized him as a man who used simple things to teach us about safety, friendship, the need for fresh air and understanding. He also showed that you can have an effect without saying a word. The Bunny Rabbit and the Dancing Bear taught us many things silently and respectfully.

I remember watching that show and waiting for the omnipresent ping-pong balls to fall out of the sky demonstrating once again that the Bunny Rabbit, or Mr. Moose had tricked Captain Kangaroo again. I remember him taking time to read a book, explain what was read and encouraging everyone to read every day.

As I got older (not more mature, just older), it wasn't cool to watch the Captain. He was considered boring and was replaced with fast moving, colorful cartoons. The advent of the color television helped produce Technicolor Saturdays, but the things presented had no soul; no heart. There was more laughter, but the learning was gone.

The most amazing thing about Captain Kangaroo is that he kept true to his philosophy through years of different sponsors, various networks and numerous producers. He didn't have a problem with education as entertainment as long as it had substance and meaning. Sounds like a master teacher to me!

Some of you may not remember the Captain but he was a pioneer. He was the first. He treated children with respect and understanding, was able to laugh at himself and wasn't afraid to use television as a teaching tool long before anyone else.

Unlike puppets and Muppets who can have replacements handle their voices and movements, there is no replacing the Captain. He touched many lives, made many of us smarter, kinder, and better. The best tribute we can have is to try to do the same for our kids today and everyday!

Have a great week!

John

Thought for the Week – February 6, 2004

For the last two months, NASA has been enjoying the afterglow of several successful space missions. The Mars Orbital Spacecraft has sent geological information about mars since early December 2003. The Spirit Rover landed on Christmas Day and has successfully rolled slowly over Martian soil and has discovered smooth, rounded pebbles, like the kind you find on the sea shore. A second rover landed on the opposite side of the planet and has successfully begun it mobile explorations.

This is an amazing story for a space agency that had, until these last few months, experienced failure after failure. They lost 7 brave people in the Columbia tragedy. They have had numerous deep space satellites break down after lift-off, self destruct or they are just a useless piece of space debris the size of a Volkswagen. They persevered through months of bad press, restructuring, self-assessments and adjustments.

Through it all, no one at NASA ever stopped believing in their cause. They knew that every scientist, specialist and teacher who had lost their life, would take the chance again and become an astronaut. They knew the risks of what they wanted to do with their lives and the benefits of their efforts.

Educators do the same thing. They live through bad press and erroneous information. They are always in the middle of some assessment, restructuring activity, revision, program or self-study. They see success everyday but understand that most of it will go unnoticed because it is below the "bad news" radar of the media. Still, educators know the risks of what they do. They know the challenges they face and responsibilities they share. They wouldn't have it any other way and they are proud to be called teacher.

Like the good people at NASA, we have to keep the faith and do a job that most don't understand and everyone's likes to criticize. We must continue to believe in ourselves and support each other because our only support group is us!

Every payload specialist, scientist, pilot and educator-astronaut started their journey in a classroom. Every minute in preparation for space flight is spent learning, and mastering techniques needed for survival in a dangerous place. Every teacher began their journey in a classroom as well. Every lesson taught is a lesson refined; every teacher changes and grows everyday.

We will learn new and exciting things about Mars in the coming weeks. Much of what we thought we knew has been totally revised. The pictures and information coming to us will be amazing. Let's also be excited about what we learn daily about our students. Let's continue to revise and change and be amazed at what we see.

Many journeys will start and continue today. Let's enjoy the ride!

Have a great week!

John

Thought for the Week – February 13, 2004

Valentines Day is upon us once again. Children (and some adults), look forward to having another reason to eat candy. Teachers and parents remind children to bring signed Valentines for every student in their classroom, (whether they like them or not), and men drive around or go on line hoping to find a better gift than last year. How many candy, gold, silver or diamond hearts can one person receive?

The heart has become synonymous with Valentines Day. Even jewelry companies think that a gift purchased from them will go "Straight to the heart"! Our gifts or our actions can be interpreted as soft-hearted or heartfelt. Or we can mess it up completely and become Hard-Hearted Hannah from Savannah.

We can have hearts of gold, hearts of glass or hearts of stone. We can have the heart of a warrior, a sacred heart, a heart filled with gladness or even a heavy heart full of sorrow. We can hear people tell us to "have a heart". We can feel bad when people call us "heartless" for forgetting their birthday or saying something they don't agree with.

In ancient times, people believed that the heart was the center of everything. The soul and all that makes us human was stored in the heart. The heart was our mind, soul and essence. It is what made us different from anything else on earth.

As educators we do many things daily from the heart. We don't really expect thanks for that; we do it because we care and we love what we do. We are heart broken at times when we worry about struggling students or families in crisis. Our hearts are filled with joy when a child masters something for the first time or survives a situation and learns to thrive.

So take a moment today to accept the little cards, and candy hearts and maybe even a hug or two. In a world where very few people thank you for what you do, it will do your heart good today to hear "Happy Valentines Day!"

Have a great week!

John

Thought for the Week – February 20, 2004

Reality shows are the rage of the 21st century. People enjoy watching supposedly "normal" individuals compete for prizes, get voted off exotic yet rustic locations, eat things that were never meant for human consumption, cheat on each other, cook, or even fix up and clean up their houses.

Television production companies love shows like these too. They are relatively cheap to produce, there is no need for a live audience and stations can show repeats, (I mean encore presentations), as often as they wish. Most people don't care if they have seen the same episode several times. They love watching other people!

This relatively innocent and inexpensive voyeurism has network executives thinking of how they can raise the bar for that next new reality hit! As long as people keep tuning in, the networks will continue to try to find that next cheap fix for the reality show junkie.

The philosophy of a greater hit for less money has oozed over into the world of education. Everyone wants to have well-educated children, high test scores, clean and upgraded schools, the best technology possible all for less money than was allocated the previous fiscal year. Several factions, (usually not stakeholders in the system), are shocked when school systems state they cannot function with an ever decreasing flow of dollars. The expectations for success and the Holy Grail known as test scores are still there but you are really a successful school division when you can do it on the cheap!

I propose a new reality show. It will be about a group of adults who have to work together to help a group of children succeed academically, socially, emotionally and physically. Every week the number of adults and the total funding is reduced until after several weeks there is only one adult left working with the least amount of supplies. If the lone survivor leads the children to success, the reward will be that the show would be renewed, but there would be more children to work with next year and less funding again! I doubt if the networks would buy it. It is a little too real and little too scary.

Let's continue to work hard and be proud of our own reality show. Many people can fix houses, eat disgusting things for points, fall off high places, or even get fired by Donald Trump. Few people can do what you do!

Have a great week!

John

Thought for the Week – February 27, 2004

In a few short days, we will complete Black History Month for 2004. This month has been a time for ethnic dinners, plays, reflections, readings, discussions, fashion shows and even musicals. These activities are designed to educate all people about the African-American community past, present and future.

During this month I am reminded that many people of color were not given credit for ideas, innovations, inventions and writings. Benjamin Banneker's almanac gave Colonial era farmers important weather and science information. He needed a foreign patron to make it happen. Garrett Morgan's traffic light and oxygen tank are usually credited to other people who had similar designs but were patented much later. Langston Hughes was considered for too many years a lesser poet and writer and contributor to the Harlem Renaissance. He is, in reality, one of the finest poets of the 20th century.

The people mentioned above and many others were finally recognized and memorialized many years later. Some were forgotten about for years. They were lost in the abyss of ignorance, disinterest and disrespect. They were unnoticed though they shined like stars adding wonderful things to the world.

Educators are sometimes ignored and forgotten too. They invent, build, write, create, hold up and help forward. Many do their job in extreme anonymity; nobody sees what they do, nobody knows what they do, few feel what they do. Just like Banneker, Morgan, and Hughes, they have an inner strength that gives them the fortitude to work hard everyday and to believe in what they do. Educators like this realize that they succeed every time a child learns a little be more, understands a little bit more, and retains a little bit more. Recognition may not come to them verbally; it will come to them mind by mind and heart by heart.

Let us remember all the innovators, and risk takers and poets and designers that reside in your school or office today. They are there working quietly. They just need to be discovered again, for the first time.

Have a great week!

John

Thought for the Week – March 5, 2004

Earlier this week, I was driving home and I was traveling behind a very new SUV. I continue to be amazed at how big these Sports Utility Vehicles are becoming. Every year they get bigger, taller, wider and more expensive. In fact, if I owned one, it would never go off road; I would buy an old army surplus jeep for that. I would be afraid of hitting something with a very nicely equipped battering ram.

This particular SUV that I was following stopped at an intersection and didn't move for close to three minutes. I couldn't see what was going on in front of the vehicle because of the tinted windows. I also couldn't see because I had to stop so quickly that I was basically studying the finer points of the spare tire tastefully bolted to its rear door.

I assumed that there was a fender bender or maybe a malfunctioning traffic light or maybe even just evening traffic slowing us down. I finally decided to step out of my car to see how long the wait might be or offer assistance or just turn around and find an alternate route. When I looked beyond the SUV, I saw nothing but open road and green lights! It seems the person driving, (unseen due to the tinted windows), had stopped to look for something! I returned to my car and drove around the SUV muttering something like, "Only in Savannah!"

Every day we are bombarded with catalogs, e-mails, snail mails and other correspondence offering the latest educational fad that will help our kids succeed faster, better, and higher. Each one seems to come with some new accessories that are guaranteed to make our lives and our students lives better. Just like leather seats and cup holders, these new add-ons are supposed to induce us to buy and use their product.

We can get so caught up with the pretty packaging of new software programs and learning games that whistle and applaud that we don't notice that we have stopped moving altogether! We get so intense on finding and using the latest instructional fad that we don't take the time to step back and look around to see if we are still on the same road and moving in the same direction.

It is nice to have new things: New cars, new computers, new software, even learning games. However, the most important thing you give the students and each other is time. No matter how it is packaged, when time is given it shows commitment, caring, understanding and compassion. You can still move forward when spending time instructing a child and helping each other. Sometimes it is good to travel slower so you can see the view. Don't get behind something that slows you down or inhibits your vision. Take the time to get out and look around and see where you are going. You will find that it was worth your time and your student's time as well.
Have a great week! John

Thought for the Week – March 12, 2004

A few days ago, our SCA officers and their teacher-sponsor spent an hour in the afternoon cleaning out and weeding a little garden in our courtyard. This is Zachary's Garden, a memorial to a student who died several years ago in a car accident.

The students did a wonderful job of weeding and cleaning up the area. They were careful not to pull up the newly grown plant shoots or flowers when they were weeding. It was a very time consuming and meticulous job. The young people took their job very seriously. They knew what it represented; it was a labor of love. They could envision what the garden would look like after all the weeds and overgrown grass (the best grass is in the garden), was removed and new mulch was placed delicately around the plantings.

To give up your time and to help make a project successful is sometimes the best therapy a person can have. In an era of selfishness and self-gratification, it is important to strengthen ourselves and each other. We need to look past the weeds of ignorance and the overgrowth of negative opinions and continue to work in our individual educational gardens.

Sometime this can be back-breaking work. It can seem that the weeds and thorns take up so much of our time that we are hardly seeing any progress. However, like the SCA officers, we need to envision what our gardens will look like and redouble our efforts and work quietly and efficiently toward our goal.

Have fun working in your individual gardens. Some of them may need more weeding than others and more care than people understand. Always know that your efforts will lead to the beauty of success and a bouquet filled with pride, understanding and a belief that all things are possible!

Have a great week!

John

Thought for the Week – March 19, 2004

I love parades! I enjoy watching and listening to the bands as they strut down the street.   I reminisce about the hours of practice it took to play, march and move seamlessly in a straight line for miles. I remember how tiring and yet exhilarating it was.

I enjoy seeing the military units that tacitly remind us that freedom is not free. I enjoy seeing the tractors and animals that remind us of our agricultural heritage and future.

I find people riding uncomfortably on the back of convertibles hilarious. They wave and smile and they have no idea who we are. A friend of mine has a rule: No matter who it is in the car, they pretend to know them personally. They will yell something like, "Donnie, great to see you again, how's the family?" Donnie will stop waving and look and sincerely say, "Everyone's fine, good to see you!" You can see the look on his face trying to place these mythical constituents. I have even seen one politician lean over and ask his wife, "Who are those people?"

Parades are part of what makes us who we are. We need celebrations and floats; bands and beauties; cars and costumes; pomp and politicians; dancers and divas. These celebrations give us a chance to cheer for ourselves and to enjoy what we have.

Education needs parades! We need to celebrate the little victories and not move on too quickly to the next, "crisis de jour". We need to blow our own horn and march down the streets of disbelief and let people know that we are making progress. The community needs to remember that a free and appropriate public education is one of the cornerstones of freedom; it is true freedom! Like the people sitting on the back of the convertible, we must ride high and point to the good things that we are doing. We need parades!

If we can have an all day event to commemorate an Irish Bishop, (which by two-o'clock in the afternoon most people had forgotten that concept), we can certainly take some time to celebrate each small success and each concept learned. We need to not feel guilty for parading our accomplishments in front of those who know us and don't know us; those who respect us and those who do not.

Sound the trumpet, strike up and band, smile at the camera and give yourself a pat on the back. Education needs a parade and it starts with us!

Have a great week!

John

Thought for the Week – March 26, 2004

The Northern Pacific Ocean is one of the least traveled placed in the world. Only science vessels, naval ships and rarely seen tankers ever venture there. Amazingly, it is also one of the dirtiest areas of ocean on the planet!

Due to ocean and wind currents, careless sea-goers and irresponsible ocean liners, this area of the Northern Pacific is littered for miles with floating plastic bottle tops, lids, trash bags and other assorted flotsam. It is a thick as a landfill and it takes up an area that matches the state of Texas!

This debris is not just floating there. It is being eaten by fish and fowl and they are dying at an alarming rate; poisoned or choked by the ingested plastic.

Environmentalists feel that there is a need to clean up this area. They believe that even an area as large as this one can be cleaned with a comprehensive, focused, and well-designed plan. This plan would include cleaning up the existing area, regulating how large ships dispose of their waste materials, and incentives for businesses to help in the clean up/maintenance plan. The science community's first step was to inform the people that this problem exists. A solution cannot be found until people know there is a problem. It would be easy not to try because of the size and scope of the issue.

Educators know that creating and maintaining change can be as challenging and overwhelming as cleaning up an environmental disaster. We might not even want to try new things or innovations because we think the problems or issues are too great. Some of us may think that change must come from somewhere else; that we are too small to make a difference.

We have a comprehensive, focused and well-designed plan for educational change. Every time we try a new strategy and meet the needs of a child, we show that we are not afraid of change. We are not afraid to say that what we do matters. We are not afraid to believe that the life our students live with us for 7 hours a day can have as much impact as the way they live the other 17. We are also willing to inform and communicate with the public about what we do, why we are doing it and what differences we are making.

Educational change is as demanding as environmental clean-up. It sometimes requires a stubborn, sustained, unyielding presence that only accepts what right and best for each child, each classroom and each school. It can happen; we just need to believe.

Have a great week! John

Thought for the Week – April 2, 2004

Many people think baseball is a boring game and not a demanding sport. They think that it is a bunch of guys scratching and spitting who sit around a long time between hitting and catching. They look at the façade of the event rather than the foundation of the sport.

Baseball involves thought and strategy equal to a chess match. Every move a manager makes will have an impact two or three innings later. Where to place the fielders, how long to keep the pitcher in; how to line up your batters; when to start warming up your relief pitchers; what to say to players who make errors; when to complain to the umpire to excite the crowd or your team – these are all part of the hidden mind game called baseball.

If you think I am exaggerating, remember the 2003 American League Championship series between the Boston Red Sox and New York Yankees. The Red Sox Manager left their ace pitcher in too long and the Yankees won the game and advanced to the World Series. Due to his decision, the Red Sox Manager was fired and the entire town of Boston went into mourning. Strategy and timing do make a difference.

Many people think education is boring. They think it is something you do to kids. They do not see the strategies, planning and work involved to teach children. They think we just ask them to open a book and the content is miraculously learned.

Every decision an educator makes, just like a baseball manager, has an impact later that day, later that week, or later in the life of that child. We don't make decision capriciously; we try to take all our experience and knowledge and make the best choices possible for our students.

Baseball teams have 162 games to show who made improvements from last year, who made the right decisions and who will be, once again, looking for next year. Educators have 180 days to show that they have made the right decisions, used the correct strategies, and utilized new training and new ideas.

Neither education nor baseball is boring. It is an intense calm movement toward excellence. Let's continue to use the strategies we know are correct, the high ideals that we know are a must. I know that if we continue to do the things we know are right we won't have to say, "Wait 'till next year!"

Have a great week!   John

Thought for the Week – April 8, 2004

If you go downtown any day throughout the week, you will notice that the spring crush of tourists has already begun. You can tell the tourists are from the north because they are so excited that the temperature is above freezing and they are already wearing shorts and shirts that say Savannah on them. You can tell the tourists are from the south when they are wearing jackets in seventy degree weather that it is too cold and too breezy.

In both cases, the people are excited to see the historic areas, the river front, the old churches and squares, the golf courses, the universities, and even the malls! They take picture after picture of each area hoping to save a snap shot of the way the light comes through the live oaks and dances around the beauty of the area; the experience of riding a horse drawn carriage following the ghost tour; the boat ride to Hilton Head; the experiences of a Savannah Sand Gnats game; the food enjoyed at most restaurants.

There are many sights, sounds and tastes people come to Savannah to experience. They read brochures that list the best places to go, best restaurants to eat in, best places to stay. They go home with memories of a diverse, busy, beautiful, intense town; a town that feels little but acts large; a town that can offer anyone a variety of activities, employment and enjoyment.

A selling point for any area should be the school system. It should be on the list of important sites to visit. It should be part of what makes the area great! Tourists may not take several pictures of a school in our district, but they should be made aware of the exciting things that are happening, the strides that are being made, and the accomplishments that have already been documented. We need to create our own brochures inviting people to visit our schools in the same way businesses lure the tourists to their shops and eateries.

This is a tourist time and tourists leave with an indelible impression of the towns they visit and the places they stay. They tell their friends the best parts and the worst parts of an area. Stores and restaurants gain customers by word of mouth, advertisement and reputation. Schools should promote what they are doing, encourage people to share the information with the community and invite people in to see for themselves what great people can do. Businesses don't wait for other people to do the work for them; neither should we. If we don't promote ourselves; who will?

Have a great week and a great spring break! You have earned it.

John

Thought for the Week – May 7, 2004

Showing appreciation for something can take many forms. It can be demonstrated visually with a pat on the back or a round of applause. It can be shown privately in the form of a note or letter. It can be represented physically by the sharing of food or gifts. It can be addressed orally in song or verbal praise.

We don't show appreciation enough. Our culture is trained to find fault and expect the least of individuals, groups or even cultures. We stereotype rather than celebrate; we label rather than laud. It is also difficult for us to accept praise or thanks. We don't do it well.

Showing appreciation is divided into two distinct parts: First, someone has to acknowledge and share their appreciation for a person or group in some demonstrable way. Second, the person or group must accept the appreciation and be grateful for it in return. Appreciation is only as powerful as the connection between the two individuals, groups or parties. It is this emotional hug that lifts the souls and fills the hearts.

This week, we thank educators for their year of hard work, dedication, and ability to get up each morning and do their job! Educators are always grouped together, stereotyped and spoken about as if we are one big organism. However, you have worked hard and you have fought the good fight and you are tired!

Please take the time today to accept the appreciation of others as they praise you for all that you do. Please also take the time to go to a fellow educator's room and thank them for being a peer; for working alongside; for being who they are.

No one knows what you do except a fellow educator. Thank each other, lift each other up, and appreciate each other for what you can do. You do what few can; you teach!

I applaud and appreciate all of you. Have a great week!

John

Thought for the Week – May 17, 2004

Around the country this week, politicians and other notables will be celebrating the landmark Supreme Court decision – Brown v the Board of Education. This decision overturned the idea that separate but equal in education was reasonable and constitutional.

Much will be written about how this ruling has affected schools, or how things haven't changed in our society. We will hear about how busing worked or didn't work. We will hear about white-flight to the suburbs or the increase in private schools since the decision. Many will even question whether the decision had an impact at all.

For me, what has changed in the fifty years since the Brown Decision is that our classrooms have become more diverse. Even in a classroom that is mostly white or mostly black, there will be students from all different backgrounds, religions, family units, economic levels. Some will come from out of town; some will have family roots here for generations. Some have moms and dads in the military and they will be moving somewhere else soon; some have moved from school to school trying to find that "perfect" educational system. We have students from Latin American countries and even from Europe. Diversity is there; we just have to look.

Our school faculties have become more diverse as well. We have teachers from Canada, United Kingdom; we have teachers from every state in the union representing every major religion. In fifty years our world has changed and we have seen it in board rooms and faculty rooms.

While we listen to pundits and commentators decide what impact the Brown Decision has had on society and education, we need to just look at our students and our school one more time. See the different levels of maturity, the different backgrounds, the various accents, and the variable support from home, the different needs that must be met.

Our teaching strategies have become just as diverse as our population. Success will be found as we celebrate the differences and support the heterogeneity of our schools. By working together as students, they will learn to live together as adults. Let's see how we look fifty years from now!

Have a great week!

John

Thought for the Week – May 21, 2004

Certificates, diplomas, and awards will be distributed soon. Students of all different ages and heights will dress up in cap and gowns, smile, get their picture taken shaking someone's hand, and receive a piece of paper.

But what a piece of paper it is!

To kindergartners, fifth graders, eighth graders and high school seniors, it is a key that unlocks the door to the next level of education. It is a visible sign that we can move up and we should move up to the next challenge in our lives. It is a way for the entire education community to say, "You are ready. We have prepared you. Go and make us proud!"

To all students, awards, recognition and applause is important to put the year in perspective and show them how far they have traveled educationally. The exceptional child may never be on the honor roll, but he may have worked harder than ever in his life. That should be acknowledged and celebrated. The student leaders who keep the young ones safe should receive a big thank you for the work they do. The students who quietly always do the right thing should not be ignored even though you spent 97% of your time on the louder portion of the student body.

This is a time to celebrate the progress that has been made. It may have taken some a long time to reach a minor goal. Others may have surprised you with how far they have come. Either way thank them for who they are and where they are now.

Look around these next few days and thank the teachers and specialists and paraprofessionals that have helped you in your journey as well. They may have supported you through a tough time, stretched you with a new idea, or even challenged you to prove to them that all your students could be successful. Thank them all, pray for them quietly, and look forward to working with them again.

Over thirty thoughts for the week have been prepared for you throughout this school year. I hope they have helped you and supported you through another challenging and worthwhile year. I know you are tired and you need a well-deserved rest.

Please read some, write more, smile often, and rest occasionally. Before you know it, we will be back for another year as professional educators. Why not? They need us and no one else can do what we do!

Have a great weekend; great ending of school; great summer!

John

Thought for the Week – August 6, 2004

My six-year old grandson stayed with us for three weeks this summer. It was fun and he reminded us that young children were created by and for young adults. We are still recuperating

My grandson is a bright child, (of course), curious, and full of questions about the world around him and everything in it. In fact, he talks incessantly. One night, I went to his room to check on him and he was even talking in his sleep! He is definitely an oral learner. He also thinks he cannot read.

My grandson is not a phonetic learner and yet he is in a public school in Boston that professes a strong belief that phonics instruction works for all students. I believe that phonics instruction is an important part of a good language arts program but phonics does not work for everyone; sometimes other strategies have to be used in tandem with phonics or independently.

What amazes me is that my grandson, at the tender age of six years, has already deemed himself a reading failure because he sees reading success measure by how well he does during phonics class. In other words, he is basing his self-worth on a program that does not fit his learning style. Remember, this is the child that would rather talk it to death than sound it out. He will talk for an hour, (or more), about the cat down the street but has difficulty reading c-a-t.

In a few days, your classrooms will be filled with children who came with different backgrounds, experiences, and pre-conceived ideas of what school is all about. How many of them have already decided that they are failures because of a single strategy or evaluation system. If learning is a life-long process then we must find ways to help all students master the curriculum and learn if there can be many roads leading to the same destination.

My grandson will learn how to read. It will take different verbal and vocabulary building strategies. He will be encouraged to take risks and to realize that phonics is not his strength but it is also not the only way to learn to read. He will learn that he does not have to be great at everything; no one is. He will learn to believe that he is a special, unique, wonderful person. He will have a support system that will guarantee success.

Let's work so all our students can be seen as individuals. They have strengths and weaknesses and some may even talk your ears off! They are why we do what we do. When they succeed, they give us confidence to keep going and to believe in what we do.

They need us. Let's get started. Have a great week!   John

Thought for the Week – August 13, 2004

For the past two days, we have been glued to the television watching the weather channel to see how the weather duo, Bonnie and Charles, would impact this area and the start of the school year.

Hurricanes are amazing things. They start as a tropical ripple, become a disturbance, then a depression, a tropical storm and finally a hurricane that is categorized from #1 - #5. They begin as a chop in the water and end up 500 miles wide with the power to evacuate cities and change people's lives. They become historical events remembered with awe at just the mention of their name.

Soon another school year starts. It also will start with just a little ripple or disturbance in time. Some may even be depressed because summer vacation has ended. Some may storm into school ready to learn and looking forward to seeing old friends and making new ones.

You have the power to energize schools and change people's lives. The things you do can build up to a point that no matter where your students live or how they live, they will succeed. If you believe in yourself, they will believe in you.

No one can stop a hurricane. They can only ride it out and adjust to it. When you put all your energy and force into what you do, no one can stop you either. They have to ride it out and see where you take them.

Lead well and take them where they have never been before.

Have a great week!

John

Thought for the Week – September 2, 2004

In the 21st century, technological innovation is moving faster than ever before. Things are moving so fast that the computer system you buy today will be obsolete in 18 months or less. The nano-technology is so amazing that is sounds like something out of a science fiction novel. The smaller the computer chip becomes, the more data it will hold. We have cell phones that remind us (or me) of Star Trek. We have smart cars that do everything for us except drive us to where we want to go. (I will be the first in line to buy that car.) The technology is amazing and yet overwhelming at times.

I still remember as a child having one phone in my house and it was on a party line. You could have impromptu conversations with a neighbor if you picked up the phone at the wrong time. I remember when a cell phone was what they called the pay phone at the police station. I remember when there were only four television channels and seven radio stations to choose from. I remember when people talked to each other and not to something.

Recently, a man was released from prison after serving a twenty-year sentence. Someone asked him, "What was the hardest transition he had to make when he rejoined society?" He replied, "I can't get over all these people talking to themselves with their hand on their ear."

I am not against technology or the comfort or convenience that it brings to society. However, nothing takes the place of a face-to-face conversation. Nothing can substitute for a handshake or a pat on the back. It forces you to listen better and to form a deeper, more thoughtful relationship.

Making a quick phone call or dashing off an e-mail is faster and more efficient. It is also colder and less personable. It is always easier to convey a dissenting opinion when you are not looking into the eyes of your debate partner.

So take the time today to have some conversations with real people in real time. Who knows maybe we will learn to appreciate people as much as the new technology that is being unveiled everyday.

I apologize in advance for sending this to everyone via e-mail. I don't miss my typewriting. The word processing program is the greatest invention since cable television!

Have a great week!

John

Thought for the Week – September 10, 2004

I saw three hummingbirds yesterday. They were barely visible flitting quietly from flower to flower in the filtered sunlight of a late summer evening. I had to concentrate and watch carefully to see their neon green bodies against the dark shadows created by the trees. It would have been easy to miss them or ignore them. It would have been easy to spend the time on something else; maybe something more important. However, sometimes a quiet, reflective, watchful moment is worth the time.

Three years ago tomorrow, our lives were changed by an act of terrorism. This country and world has not been the same. The term 9/11 was added to our national lexicon. It brings on an instant memory. It induces a quiet, prayerful reflection.

It would be easier to ignore this painful anniversary. This nation does not like feeling vulnerable or helpless. We don't want to remember those dark days and numbness we felt.

We need to remember the heroes. We need to remember how people worked together unselfishly to help each other and support one another. We need to remember the people of New York who gathered up their children, climbed up to the roof of their buildings and prayed. We need to remember how our elected officials gathered together and sang God Bless America. We need to remind ourselves that we are still here and it is not a bad thing to remember the things that shape our lives.

Three years, three hummingbirds. It is amazing how the littlest things can carry the biggest message.

Have a great week!

John

Thought for the Week – September 17, 2004

After 25 years, the nation's top interviewer, Barbara Walters is retiring from the entertainment industry. Whether you consider her work fluff, irrelevant, hard-hitting or part of television history, her leaving brings a level of sadness and disappointment. She has been around so long she has become part of our history too.

Many of us remember her long before her interviews became the appetizer or tease before the Emmy or Academy Award shows. For years, she co-hosted the Today Show with Hugh Downs. This was long before Jane Pauley and Katie Couric. This was when the Today Show won Emmy's as a news program and not an entertainment program. Ms Walters later left the show because the network executives wanted a more entertainment type format (and she wanted more money). Several years later, she and Hugh Downs would be reunited as the first hosts of 20/20. It was an effort to compete with 60 minutes and other news "magazines".

During her career Barbara Walters was lampooned by Gilda Radner of Saturday Night Live. Her Barbwa WaWa skits are classics and we remember them every time Ms Walters is on the air. We also remember how Barbara Walters would say Haiwy Weasoner when working with Harry Reasoner on ABC's World News Tonight. She has been around so long we look at it as a personality trait rather than a personality flaw.

Twenty-five years form now, what will we be remembered for? We may not have the television exposure (thank goodness), but we certainly will have the longevity, the stubbornness and compassion for the job equal to anyone, anywhere.

Someone will become the new king or queen of the prime time interviewers. It will probably not be the same. The questions may be better and it may be presented in High Definition but it will never be able to replace the original.

Let's be the best and most original we can be. Let's be irreplaceable. In this time of complexity and accountability, we need to show that we are the best and we will succeed. If we do that, future teachers will enter the profession, but they have to learn from the irreplaceable, unflappable, original experts – you!

Have a great week!

John

Thought for the Week – September 24, 2004

I attended a funeral this week for a young man who died way before his time. Through no fault of his own, a traffic accident took him prematurely from his family, his university and his friends. There would be unfulfilled goals, unmade promises and even problems that would never be confronted or solved.

Stacy Webb had just started college at Atlantic Armstrong State University on a golf scholarship. He was excited about playing for his local team. He was excited about meeting his teammates and starting the next chapter in his life.

Last Friday evening he was taken too soon; the reasoning or plan behind it is too complicated for us to understand. The world keeps spinning, the sun is shining, the air is cooler, and it does not seem fair. The world should stop for a second, the sky should cry momentarily and the sun should dim for a short while. However, our lives go on and everyone is asked to move on; live on; carry on.

Sometimes we think more about things than we think about people. We are more concerned about the what's in our lives than the who's. We spend more time worrying about getting something rather than building or keeping relationships. In the end that is all we have. We will be remembered for our relationships and how we lived our lives together with our family, our friends and our co-workers. The stuff is left behind.

Stacy Webb in his short 18 years had built many relationships and made a positive impact on many people. His death reminds us that everyday is precious and every person you meet is worth your time.

Let's take the time to build our relationships with the people around or rebuild connections that have eroded away. Let's not take the people in our lives for granted.

We can stop our own world for a while with a conversation. We can dim the lights for a moment by calling an old friend. We can cry for a moment in prayer or song. It is our relationships that give us strength. It is our calling to provide strength to those who feel pain or suffer a loss greater than can be imagined.

Don't let the things in our lives get in the way of what matters – us.

Have a great week!

John

Thought for the Week – October 1, 2004

One of our teachers has been recalled to active duty in the National Guard. It is a difficult time for him, his family, his students and his school. He is showing responsibility; doing his duty; answering the call. He is leaving because although his students need him and his family needs him, his country needs him more.

This is a difficult time. It brings the world and all its challenges very close to home. It brings the concept of safety and security to the forefront. We are not talking about keeping a school or campus safe anymore. We are talking about keeping our city and nation out of harm's way and continually free to pursue our dreams. Ironically, some men and women literally have to give up their freedom and their pursuits for a while so that we can maintain ours.

Steven Hill is a teacher, a patriot, a true hero. He loves seeing students learn and grow but he loves his country more. Patriots do what they are supposed to do and they give up things that many of us would not give up. Steven made a commitment to the National Guard and as an officer and a gentleman, he will fulfill his commitment. Heroes do that. They work quietly and with a constant belief that what they do will make a difference.

Please join me today in thanking Steven and all the other teachers who have been called back to service. There country needs them but they will be missed. We look forward to the day when they come back to us and are rejoined with their school families. May God give them strength and be with their every step.

Have a great week!

John

Thought for the Week – October 8, 2004

The long humid days of summer are over and the cool days of autumn are here. I certainly welcome the change in climate but I never look forward to the shorter hours of daylight. I enjoy my sunshine. I like the bright colors of an azure blue sky mixed with the green of a freshly mowed lawn surrounded by the orange and pink blossoms of lantana bushes. It is a view to be savored by the senses. It is a vision that is eventually lost as the sun moves on its yearly journey and equinox stealthily arrives in the midst of late summer activities.

Autumn brings its own aromas, sounds and visions. The fallen leaves change the look of the lawn and have their own unique smell and sound differently as you step on them. Chrysanthemums and marigolds and asters are in bloom and they add a rustic beauty to any yard or porch. Less humidity brings a feeling of a wide open sky that encompasses us as it stretches out as far as the heavens and back.

During this amazing time of the year, I tend to reflect on present goals, evaluate the status of various home and work projects, and begin to make plans for the upcoming year. In twelve short weeks, 2004 will be over and we will be starting anew and we will be amazed at how fast the time has passed and how much more we wish to do.

Let's use the time wisely and spend our time productively and sincerely supporting each other as we do the important work that we do. Our enthusiasm should not diminish as the leaves begin to fall and the growing season ends. Let's breathe it in and let it enfold us like a cool autumn evening. Let us be grateful for each day we have with each other. They are a blessing and as precious as each cool autumnal day.

Have a great week!

John

Thought for the Week – October 22, 2004

The passing of Christopher Reeve was a sobering reminder of the fragility of life. Even though individuals with his type of paralysis have a five to seven year survival rate, it was still shocking to hear of his death. It was too soon; it was like losing a friend.

Since his sudden injury almost a decade ago, Mr. Reeve never slowed down in his efforts to raise awareness about spinal cord injuries and raise money to research possible new technologies and new procedures to assist quadriplegics and paraplegics. Even as his speech labored due to the use of a respirator, he would speak to members of congress and local community groups about his new challenge and his new goal. Mr. Reeve left the world of make believe in Hollywood where anyone can play one and became a true, strong, real American hero.

If our life instantly changed as dramatically as Mr. Reeve's did ten years ago, would we have responded the same way? Would we have taken up a cause? Would we have become a public figure even with our discomfort and limitations? Sometimes we fight the simplest, little changes because we want things to stay the same. Change sometimes happens whether we want it to or not. It is how we handle the change that makes the difference.

Christopher Reeve always had the goal of walking again. We will always remember him playing the man of steel with his handsome smile and unwavering love for truth, justice and the American way. In many ways, throughout the latter part of his life, he became a fighter for people who could not fight for themselves. He walked a walk that many of us would not have accepted and did a super job. His acceptance of change changed us all!

When we think of super heroes, we envision brightly colored costumes, supernatural powers and good triumphing over evil. We think of comic books and cartoons. Mr. Reeve lived, fought and endured in the real world so others may have a better life in the future. He never stopped working, moving, fighting, and believing in a better world and a better life for others. If that isn't a hero, what is?

Have a great week!

John

Thought for the Week – November 5, 2004

This weekend we will experience autumn for the first time this season with the accompanying smells and activities. The dew on the grass will be more visible. The leaves on the ground will be more aromatic. The world around us will seem smaller; cozier; closer.

I love the seasons here in Georgia. Each one is identified by its level of humidity, which leaves or pollen is flying around, which flowers are blooming and how much time we spend watching the weather channel to check to see if we need to pack up the backyard again.

Even though you live in the same place, the landscape around you changes dramatically as the days get longer then wane toward a new calendar year. The angle and intensity of the sun varies and is identified by the length of the growing season that is so wonderfully long in this part of the country. The harvest is celebrated via county fairs, fall festivals, chili cook-offs and oyster roasts. It is hard to believe it is the same place that was dripping with humidity like a rain forest just a few weeks ago.

It is fun to face the world in three-month intervals. No matter whether you enjoy the heat or the cold, you know that in around ninety-days, it will be changing again. You know that your view of the world will change every quarter without even leaving your home.

In the middle of a cold morning, we forget for an instant what it felt like to mow the grass on a 100+ degree day. It gives us a chance to look at the world refreshed. It reminds us how rapidly time passes; how quickly each year moves on.

Let's take time today to walk outside and look at the world in its freshness. Let's breathe in the clear, cool air. Let's enjoy the moment and not let the stress and speed of the day keep us from this one brief reverie. It won't be around long; enjoy it!

Have a great week!

John

<u>Thought for the Week – November 12, 2004</u>

On Wednesday, the school board exercised one of its responsibilities – the retention or release of a superintendent. Unfortunately, it is unclear whether this exercise will be in the best interest of the district or the students. At this time of uncertainty and amidst accreditation concerns due to the behavior of a few board members, it is not a good time, in my view, to look at a change in leadership. It would have been selfless to find a way to work together; selfless to change and adjust to what the commission found to be improper; selfless to put the children first.

The newspaper and certain members of the community may feel that this change was the right thing to do. They may even justify it as a bold and necessary move that will help heal the rift between the school board and the school system. Our non-stakeholders, who always speak of a better future for our students but for a cheaper price, are probably happy that the superintendent and the school board have parted ways.

Yesterday we commemorated Veterans Day. We remembered those heroes who made the ultimate sacrifice to keep our country safe and our freedoms intact. We also took the time to thank our living veterans for their hard work and dedication in protecting our country.

Today we find that our superintendent, a retired veteran of the arms forces is now a released veteran of this school system. We should thank him for his efforts in both arenas. Both jobs take courage, intelligence and a will to survive. I know he will move on and find success in whatever future endeavor he seeks.

As for us, we will move on and keep working hard. The future is unclear but our goal is the same and each caring and giving educator will make it happen. I just wanted to walk with him a little bit longer just to see how good it might have been.

Have a great week!

John

Thought for the Week – November 19, 2004

The word leadership has become overused and under demonstrated. We want strong leadership and then we complain that it is too harsh, too progressive, and not pragmatic enough. We want counseled, careful leadership and then we complain that it is too slow and not bold enough. We are very picky about leadership.

There are so many books out there on leadership, you could spend all of 2005 reading and studying each one and still not come up with the one right way to lead. Many of the books have researched the way other leaders have found some measure of success. Others suggest what you should not do. Still others give you pointers on how to lead change; be a change agent; build capacity for change; lead for lasting change. Although all of these are nice mottos, you need followers to make it happen.

Leadership is the act of convincing people to adjust their own personal agendas in an effort to work together for a common goal. Leadership is the art of compromise and collaboration. It is not the practice of digging ones heels in until everyone agrees with your ideas. When you do that you do not have followers, you have compliers and yes people. They are not part of the team that makes things happen, they are people who happen to be grouped behind the so-called leader.

Without followers a leader has no one to lead. Without followers a leader is left trying to move mountains or make structural changes totally alone. They can raise their voice and stomp their feet and claim to be the way to success, but ultimately, no one will be there to listen.

True leadership is hard work that respects the ethics of the organization and fights for the common goals they came together to accomplish. It is not pleasing everyone all the time. It is not battling people all the time. It is establishing, communicating, teaching and living a message that says we need each other and we will work together to ensure that success is not optional, and that if we believe and truly work together, it will be inevitable.

Have a great week!

John

A Postcard from Savannah December 1, 2004

It is hard to believe that the first semester will be ending for us here in Savannah Georgia. It seems like we just started school and until a few weeks ago the humidity camouflaged the coming of autumn and the holiday season. Now, the weather is cooler and drier and the sky appears bluer and the trees a more vibrant green. Soon 2004 will be over and I do not think I will miss it once it is gone.

On June 24th, Patricia's birthday, we received a call early in the morning to inform us that our school's data clerk, Gail Sullivan, was killed in a head-on car collision the night before. Gail was a wonderful person and was a great friend and confidant to many of our young teachers. That day, we were going to leave on our vacation to visit the grandchildren and our friends in Nokesville and other places in Virginia and Boston. We weren't able to leave until the next week. Even though it was good to see the little ones, our truncated vacation had a somber edge to it. You don't know how much you rely on people until they are gone.

We have a new data clerk named Lynda Shields. She is working out wonderfully and the staff has made her feel welcome. It has been an adjustment but I think she will work out well.

My mother continues to have difficult health issues. Osteoporosis has caused her right hip to be in continual pain. The medication the doctors put her on is not working and she has developed a dark spot on a lung that no one seems to be able to identify. I asked her if I could talk to the doctors and be her advocate. She politely told me no and she would continue to deal with it in her own way. I just cannot understand why a doctor cannot find a medicine that will at least take some of the pain away. However, she is a proud, stubborn, soft-spoken southern lady. In other words, what she says – goes. We just wait and try to support and do what we can. We will be visiting them sometime in 2005 but right now we don't know when.

In October, our nephew Peter, who is a policeman in Atlanta, was severely injured chasing a car thief. He was running through the woods after the thief when his head hit a tree, he broke his neck, and hurt his shoulder. For a short while, they thought he might be paralyzed. After a lot of prayer and waiting, he improved and has slowly recuperated and last week he started driving again! Peter is a true miracle and the power of God is surely present in him. We spent four days in Atlanta spending time with Peter to help him and feed him. His mother was able to come from Cleveland after that to be there for the longer haul. We hope to see him during the holidays

Also in October, Emma's (our close friend here), mother in-law collapsed in her home and was found to have an obstruction in her large intestine. It almost killed her. But she has slowly recovered and is now recuperating at Emma's house. Patricia and I have offered our physical and moral support to them and we hope she continues to improve.

In November, Patricia's step-father died suddenly. So, Patricia had to make a quick trip to Albion, New York to be with her mother and family. Millie, Patricia's mom, has once again lost a husband. We hope that she will take the opportunity to travel to see her children and grandchildren more and stay away from the cold north. She is 78 years and in very good health. I hope she does decide to become mobile. She can travel from Cleveland to Florida and be gone as long as she wants.

In November, we also learned that our daughter in-law's mother, Elaine, is in the final stages of a very chronic, debilitating disease that will claim her life in no more that six months. So, we will be ready to travel to Boston when we can to support the family.

During the fall semester, the ever rocky relationship between the school board and superintendent, ended when they bought out his contract and released him. Most of the teachers and administrators were very upset about this change. I have worked for several superintendents and he has been the best I have ever worked with. He listened. He was collaborative and he made necessary changes that have helped us improve. His idea of using benchmarks and standard based instruction has helped us a great deal. It is new stuff down here but we were doing in the VA a long time ago. He also allowed us to map the curriculum and institute portfolios and math journal writing. He will be missed and now members of the community are pushing for the recall of school board members. It will get messier before it gets any better. I am glad I am out here in the western area, where it is way too far for people to go to ask my opinion.

We decided (can you tell why?) not to travel this year for Thanksgiving. We needed some time to get some work done on the house (like clean it) and put up our decorations. We enjoyed the long weekend and celebrating thanksgiving with friends down here in GA. It was time to catch up and take a deep breath before the holidays.

We have concerts coming up tomorrow and next week and some training that I need to be involved after that and before you know it, it will be holiday break time. Patricia and I are looking forward to the beginning of 2005 because the last half of 2004 has been very challenging.

The students and staff here continue to improve. Because of the growth out here in the western end (you can't build east), we are up to 650 students. Every room and area is being utilized for teaching and storage and offices. We are going to have to adjust our magnet numbers (people we take from out of district) before next year. We cannot get any bigger without major problems. The staff is getting better and bigger all the time.

We just found out that we have two national board certified teachers! We also have two teachers who will finish their doctorates this year. The staff is continuing to get to the level they need to be so that the students can continue to improve. I have been facilitating staff development in differentiated instruction. Patricia will offer training in algebraic and geometry beginning in February 2005.

The kids are doing well. Matthew continues his doctoral program at the University of Maryland. They are now listed among the top 25 philosophy departments in the country. I told him that was because he was there. :) Jason will be graduating in May from UVA with an environmental science degree. He has done very well. During the holiday break, he will be snorkeling with manatees off the coast of Florida. A group from Virginia Tech asked him to be involved and they are paying him to help in the research! The grand kids continue to grow and be a lot of fun when we see them.

I am playing music a lot now. I am in charge of the choir at my church. We joined a little Lutheran Church down the street from where we live. It is a great community and we have a great deal of fun and it is great to sing and play again. At school, I am teaching third grade strings and recorder to the fourth graders. I have to keep my hands in it, even with the principal-ling I have to do!

Well, I know it has been a while and I hope now you know how busy we have been. If you add the three times we had to move everything from our back yard and porch because of the possible hurricanes (4), it has been a very busy time.

Please know that I think of you often and have NES pictures on my office wall and I see you guys everyday! I wish for you the best in 2005 and I hope to see you guys sometime soon. No matter how many things we have to do or how many miles are between us, our friends mean more to us than anything else. We miss you and love you all.
We hope the New Year brings you joy, peace and happiness.

John

Thought for the Week - December 3, 2004

I was called to jury duty this week. You forget about the formality and the slow pace of the experience until you go through it again. You realize the importance of the prospect of sitting on a panel to decide someone's future. You bring to it all your baggage and personality quirks that are usually left hidden or pushed way down in your individual psyche. It is not one of most enjoyable experiences. That is why they call it a duty.

In an organized yet random way, sixty-five people were brought together and from them lawyers and judges and the defendant would choose twelve jurors and two alternates. These fourteen people would be thrust together to listen, weigh and discern whether a person was responsible for a crime. Quite frankly, if we were the defendant, we wouldn't want it any other way.

During this long process, the day starts with people using cell phones, reading books and magazines or writing (like I am doing now). As the day progresses, groups start to form and conversations begin. We are communal animals and most of us like to talk. The educators spoke about the latest news. A mechanic was giving free advice to two people about why their car was making that horrible noise. An oncologist spoke of the latest treatments for cancer. A few professors were complaining that they had to get back to SCAD. Mothers worried about how long the day would be and if child care would be an issue.

Within four hours time, short term relationships were established (at least until the duty was over). Some business cards were exchanged and even some people found out that they knew a friend of a friend who worked with them a few years ago. These relationships provided the larger group comfort and support.

How often in our lives do we take the time to maintain relationships with people we see and work with everyday? We will go to a strange place with strange people (some stranger than others), and in a very short span of time establish friendships and find out how many children they have. Sometimes we overlook the people around us because they are so easy to see. They provide us daily comfort and support and yet we take very little time to say thanks or acknowledge their daily assistance.

During this holiday season, please know how much I appreciate your daily efforts and the things that you do as we take this journey together. Let's take some time this week to talk with the people who quietly and efficiently support what we do every day. We should thank them not out of duty, but because that is what colleagues do!

Have a great week!   John

Thought for the Week – December 17, 2004

Yesterday my office was full of bicycles donated to needy families. Our counselor's office was full of toys and clothes. Our freezer contained turkeys and canned food was bagged and ready to be distributed. Teachers were busy planning and buying gifts for those students who were not looking forward to a very happy holiday season.

Educators are generous people. They do not get enough credit for their gracious hearts and giving personalities. They are rarely identified with generosity and the selflessness that epitomizes this time of year. They do not want you to notice the tears that are shed over the needy in the community. Teachers are problem solvers. They find a way to make it better; improve a life; show a child they are loved.

During this past year, many random acts of kindness have come our way. In many cases we have been too busy to notice them. We get distracted by testing, in-services, school board side shows, and newspapers that describe the macrocosm of the educational system.

All of us need to remember the microcosm of a teacher in a classroom, a paraprofessional helping a handicapped child, a specialist hugging a teary-eyed student, and an administrator that smiles and doesn't mind getting hugged thirty times a day or giving high fives and pats on the back.

Compassion and love is best shown in the quiet actions that you do on a daily basis. It gives the little ones consistent comfort and support. Without it, our children just survive. With it, our children thrive and succeed.

I thank all of you for your daily contributions to the noble profession of education. What you do cannot be described in a textbook or a lesson plan. You care; you love; you worry; you pray.

I wish you peace and joy during this holiday season. The generous and compassionate need rest too!

Happy New Year!

John

Thought for the Week – January 7, 2005

An earthquake of biblical proportions spawns a massive tidal wave that leaves a wake of destruction and death from Thailand to Sri Lanka. The number of people who perished in that moment in time is staggering. Over 150,000 people have died or are lost and presumed dead. That is five times the number of students who attend our schools every day.

This incredible event made poor countries poorer. It destroyed an already challenged infrastructure that will take years to rebuild and heal. It reminds us of the fragility of human life and the realization that living in a global society means helping and supporting all countries in need.

Relief is coming from a variety of sources. Elementary school children are gathering food, clothing and money. Local churches and universities are hosting prayer vigils and collecting donations. Celebrities and government officials are pushing for faster assistance and the development of a tsunami early warning system.

Americans and especially educators cannot sit by and watch others in distress. We are not made that way. We find comfort in helping others because that is what we were taught to do. Loving and supporting our neighbors in times of need is a responsibility we take very seriously.

At a recent church service, our congregation remembered and recalled by name all the people we knew who had passed on during 2004. We do not belong to a big church, and yet, the sharing of names went on for 10 minutes! I and many of my friends and relatives were not upset about reaching the end of 2004 and we are looking forward to a new, more prosperous 2005.

Our own personal losses and the immense loss of life due to the tsunami put our own daily little inconveniences in perspective. Our own little world may not be perfect, but we are here and we can and will make a difference in 2005. The little things we do every day will make an impact. We should not wait to help and assist others. In an instant, it can be taken from us.

Let's continue to help the ones that need our help the most!

I wish for you joy peace, love and the time to experience it in 2005.

Have a great week!

John

Thought for the Week – January 14, 2005

Martin Luther King Jr. would have been 76 years old this year. Unfortunately, we cannot picture in our minds how he would look at that age. He is forever young; seen always as the strong leader, talented orator, thoughtful preacher and martyred hero.

As a child, living near Washington, D.C., I remember the speech. I remember the crowd and I remember how he spoke. I had never heard anything like it. (My preachers were not as talented.)

Martin Luther King Jr. left a great legacy that challenged all people to work together for total equality and peace. His brilliant strategy of non-violent protests focused the nation to see the inequalities and the need for change. This was not a quiet revolution. He and many others would be arrested and abused. However, he would never waver from his philosophy even when close-minded retaliation was harsh and intense.

Martin Luther King Jr. would have been around the same age as my father. The world has changed a great deal since that dreadful day in 1968. But his words echo on and are just as eloquent as the day I remember four years earlier as I sat with my father in front of a small black and white television listening, watching and being in awe of how he put words together.

Have we fulfilled his dream? No. Are we closer? I hope so. Ironically, his words continue to give us hope and strength as we strive to give all our children the greatest equalizer. We as educators can continue to work toward a society that judges people equally and fairly. We can continue to build a society of young people who can do anything they dream of because they have been taught well and have learned much.

We are part of the dream. We just have to remember.

Happy Martin Luther King Day! Have a great week!

John

Thought for the Week – January 21, 2005

My dog celebrated his thirteenth birthday this week. He has aged gracefully with his black hair becoming tinged with white and his jowls looking like a gray beard on his Labrador face. Even down to his feet and the tip of his tail, his coat has become a mixture of colors from black to brown to gray to white to almost transparent.

King, (my wife named him), has been by my side since he was small enough to fit in my hand. He is 80 pounds now, down from the 100 pounds he held easily in his prime. He runs a little bit slower, sleeps a little bit longer and louder and takes his time when he is called. He is the elder statesmen in the house. At 91 human years, he can take all the time he needs.

Time passes fast when you have a dog. Their clock ticks much faster and each moment therefore becomes more precious; more valuable. They give unconditional love and loyalty and they do not ask for much in return. No matter how tough a day you have had, they greet you at the door and they treat you like you are the most important person on the earth.

I have had other dogs and I have mourned their passing and I still rejoice in their memory. Their time with us is fleeting but their time with us is pure joy. Even though it hurts to lose them, what we gain from them as our lives intersect makes it worth it.

I hope the "old man" is with us for many more years. However, I hope I age with as much grace and dignity. I also hope to remember to forget my age occasionally and do something silly. He likes chasing squirrels he will never catch and playing tug of war like a young pup.

It is true that you cannot teach old dogs new tricks. You don't have to. You can learn by just watching them and cherishing every moment.

Have a great week!

John

Thought for the Week – January 28, 2005

Some scientists and many science fiction fans have been enamored with the idea of parallel universes. This takes Einstein's theory of time and space and pushes the idea that there is a possibility of multiple earths in multiple dimensions living parallel but not mirrored lives. Trekkies call this, "Infinite diversity in infinite combinations."

To believe that there are several earths with several kinds of us is intriguing. Somewhere out there is another me who took the job I turned down several years ago. There is another me who wasn't afraid to ask the dark-haired girl out in high school. (Her name was Tia and she was out of my league.) There is another me who didn't lose his younger brother to cancer way too soon.

However, we need to remember that if we believe in parallel universes, we must understand that there may be other crises and wrong decisions there also. We cannot assume that our "other" lives are better than the ones we have. That is why it is science fiction and not reality TV.

We are who we are because of the decisions we have made and the experiences that we have had. Life hones us and shapes us; polishes us and molds us to be the best we can be. We may wish for a utopia out there in some other dimension, but the challenges of this life is what we were made to face.

As educators you can look at some of our students and wish for a better parallel life for them. You know of their challenges and hardships. You wish you could take them away. What you need to remember is that you are a very important part of their universe. You are a major force in making them who they will become.

Years from now they will marvel at how well they have done and how much they have grown. They may not remember you by name but they will be living in a better time and place because of what you do in their world now. You are beyond parallel!

Have a great week!

John

Thought for the Week – February 4, 2005

I received my first "A" in math when I was in college. Before that major landmark in my life, math had always been my nemesis; my downfall; the mill stone around my neck. I loathed math. In high school, my geometry teacher gave me a passing mark because she really didn't want to see me again. I frustrated her because math didn't come easily. She couldn't understand why I didn't understand. She truly thought that if I just worked harder, the understanding would come. She was a nice lady but not an exemplary teacher.

The reason why I finally earned an "A" was because the instructor kept working with challenged students like me continually until we understood the algebraic concepts completely. (He was differentiating long before it was cool.) He wanted everyone to get it. By the middle of this required course, I even looked forward to going to class. I wanted to conquer something that had been so unattainable.

Recently during a training session, our small group was divided into teams and given a rather challenging geometry problem to solve. Some of the groups had people with math backgrounds who jumped at this opportunity like guys at the all-you-can-eat buffet. My team was not so lucky. The three of us tried valiantly to remember the geometric concepts and formulas but in reality we became very frustrated. Our math phobic buttons were pushed and all those bad emotions surfaced again. We were just handed this problem. We were given no review or guided practice. It was not a pretty sight.

The instructors understood our frustration and they were making an important point. One said, "It is not that you don't know how to do it. Really, if we had taken some time to review and do some pre-work with your team, you would have been successful. You are really only fifteen minutes behind."

How many times do we expect students to know something without the proper review or instructional focus? How many times do we get frustrated because our students just can't learn something? Maybe the pre-work hadn't been done and maybe they are just fifteen minutes behind the group that innately knows the material and is ready to move on.

In the years since my first "A" in math, I have focused on trying to learn different strategies to teach curriculum in a more effective way. That college professor gave me my first opportunity to be successful in my worst subject. He did that by helping and pushing me so that I could make up those fifteen minutes.

Simply, that is what great educators do: They take the time to make up the time so all students can be successful!

Have a great week!

John

Thought for the Week – February 11, 2005

There is something living in my shed. It could be any number of things. It could be one mouse or several, one rat or the whole clan, a squirrel looking to move from his tree top condominium, or even a possum or raccoon. I have never seen the animal, but I still know it is there.

I know there is something in there because animals from all over the neighborhood have been coming to the shed to investigate. Not only are my two dogs spending more time amongst the lawn mowers and plumbing supplies, but I have seen four cats peruse my shed and I don't think they were admiring the new table saw I received as a gift for Christmas.

I probably should investigate and find out what kind of animal has taken up squatters rights in my out building. However, I find it much more interesting, (and less messy), to watch the animals and see what happens. It sure gives the dogs something to do. The animal doesn't harm anyone or anything. It is not like a family of raccoons has found their way up to my attic. Then I would have to do something immediately and permanent.

Finding out what kind of animal it is would be kind of anticlimactic. There is a little mystery there; a reason for a little imagination. Until it is caught, scared away or meets a natural death, there could be a puma up there.

Sometimes in our own lives, signs point to the obvious. Students may come in a little more anxious, a little more worried or scared. There could be a few more tears or they seem needier and want continual reassurance. They could even be more or less obnoxious than usual. Something is there. We know it because we see the signs.

Let's take the time to observe and read those signs. There are times when you should wait and prepare to help. Other times they may need immediate and intense support. The challenge is to figure out which to do and when to do it. However that is what educators do best!

Have a great week!

John

Thought for the Week – February 18, 2005

A new addition to a family is celebrated in many ways. Phone calls are made, pictures are taken, and e-mails traverse at the speed of light all over the country to inform friends of the important event. Huge wooden or plastic storks are placed on the front lawn and pink or blue helium filled balloons dance in the air from their semi-secure spots on mailboxes, cars, door knobs, trees and the aforementioned storks. It is grandiose exhibition to acclaim the happiest of times.

What if the new addition to a family is twelve years old? You celebrate it differently but just as loudly!

Andrew is a twelve-year old who was abandoned by his parents at the age of eight, had numerous learning problems and was very hyper-active and impulsive. He never spent more than five months in any foster home. He was challenging to say the least. When my friend and pastor met him over a year ago, he was taking several medications, was slightly overweight and had no muscle tone.

In a year, Andrew joined a swim team, is off all medications, hosted the first birthday party of his life, was baptized and as of last Monday, officially adopted. I am proud to say I was a witness at his baptism and final adoption hearing.

When asked by the judge to state his birthday, Andrew replied, "How about today?" The importance of the day was not lost on this young man. The impact on his future was felt by all in the room. Now Pastor Steve is called "Dad" and he smiles whenever he hears the word.

Now Andrew has a long way to go. He is attending a school that is helping him fill in the gaps of his education and he still acts younger than his age. However, the power of family and love is an amazing thing. He has come so far in so short of time. There is no limit to where this child can go and be in the future. The child who was once lost has been found and it should be celebrated and made known.

In our busiest of times, we can sometimes forget the importance of families. We can take for granted the support and strength that we gain from them. We forget the times our family supported us, helped us and gave us love.

The power of family: All you have to do is watch Andrew and his Dad. They have been blessed and both have received a great gift – each other.

Have a great week. John

Thought for the Week – February 28, 2005

I was back home last week to visit my aging parents. Those of us who are lucky enough to have parents still living know of the challenges of being a "tweener". We have adult children and older parents and we are trying to balance between the two. The plus is that you are always somebody's child when your parents are still on this earth. You still feel a little younger, (as long as you don't look in the mirror), and all your siblings look older but you haven't changed a bit!

The greatest challenge is offering advice in a way that is not rejected automatically. Members of the Greatest Generation have to think about things, muse about them, and ruminate on them prior to making a decision. Baby-boomers are known and respected for quick thinking, risk-taking, make-a-plan-and-go philosophy. I bet you wondered why the generation gap occurred when it did! We are very different and what happened so quickly in a generation has never been seen before. We will probably feel it in about ten years when our kids get further along in the twenty-first century.

Our parents are stubborn, resourceful and strong. These are attributes that kept them going during the rough times of the Great Depression, World War II, rationing, gas lines, Watergate and the new millennium. Their bodies may have become frail and their hearing has become impaired, (sometimes by choice), but their resolve and independence is still going strong.

So we wait and help when we can and we hope they are around for a long period of time. As we support them as their children, we are reminded that we can still learn a great deal from them. No matter how frustrating they are at times, they have lived through more than we can ever hope to experience. They are stubborn and strong for a reason – they survived!

I hope to be around for as long as they have been. I hope to be as strong and resourceful as they have been. I also hope to drive my kids crazy! It just seems the right thing to shoot for. My parents wouldn't want it any other way.

Have a great week!

John

Thought for the Week – March 4, 2005

There seems to be two powerful trends in early 21st century television programming: Reality-based shows and Crime Scene Investigations.

The first tends to try to create a pictorial history that places the viewer in someone house, living room or other parts of their domicile. We then see everything in that person's life. They may place the scene on an island, in a house owned by "big brother", in fancy restaurants where a bachelor or bachelorette decides whose heart to break, or even connected to a house that is about to get a big and expensive "make over".

The second tries to fascinate you with the exciting world of forensic science. It shows you how interesting autopsies can be and reminds you that there never has been nor never will be a perfect crime. It has simulations and experiments and tries to finally convince you that all the math and science courses you took for granted could really be useful in a crime fighting heroic sort of way.

I am not criticizing these shows, in fact I like some of them. What I question is the need to have ten shows just like them on every day of the week. When a television show becomes a hit, instead of the popular "spin-offs" of the 70's and 80's, (I know Joey spun-off of Friends. I will give you that one.), we create several of the same type. We may even have characters from one assist in the establishment of another. Success builds and promotes duplication.

We need to do that in education. There are many teachers who are doing innovative and exciting new things. Instead of sharing them so we can duplicate them, they are afraid that they will look like braggarts. They will be concerned that they will be perceived as stuck-up or trying to impress the administrator.

Like the most popular television shows, we must promote the professional sharing of ideas, strategies, activities and assessments. Nobody knows everything and we can learn so much from each other and adapt what we learn to make it new and better. All of us have the same goal: We want all of our students to succeed. We should celebrate new learning, like the people on CSI are proud when they catch the bad guy.

Our reality is not resolved in a sixty-minute television show. Our greatest fear factor is not sharing with others or not allowing ourselves to learn from our peers. We should all work toward an instructional make-over that creates the type of learning community that guarantees that all of us become a survivor of this great race.

Have a great week! John

Thought for the Week – March 11, 2005

The words spring break brings with it memories and reflections of years past. Some of us think of trips taken. Others think of family get-togethers. Some think of religious traditions. Others think of working full time for a few days to make extra money for college or to pay a bill brought on by youthful zeal.

Spring break is also identified as an important mark in time. We know that when we reach spring break, a majority of the school year is over. We know that we need to rest up to make that final push with the students. We need to prepare for all those fateful letters of the alphabet – AYP (Adequate Yearly Progress), NCLB(No Child Left Behind), CRCT(Criterion Referenced Curriculum Testing), and EOCT(End of Course Test). It is how we will be valued and assessed. It is how we will be compared and studied. I think we need a break from all that too!

During spring break, enjoy the beginning of the growing season. See how the flowers and plants start their cycle again and remind us how colorful life can be. Everything is so much greener and the colors are so bright. It renews us and gives us hope.

Our growing season started months ago. Our cycle will be coming to an end in a few quick weeks.

Let's rest, renew, and get ready. It is a journey worth taking.

Have a great spring break.

John

Thought for the Week – April 1, 2005

More snow has fallen in Boston this year than in any other winter in recorded history. More rain has fallen out west than in the last five years. So much rain has fallen in desert areas that seeds, dormant for seven years, have germinated to create a sea of yellow and red blooms. There have been flooding in Australia, seventy degree days in Wisconsin in February and the coldest St. Patrick's Day in forty-five years in Savannah.

Why is this happening?

People always try to find reasons for why things happen or why things don't happen. We are not comfortable with vague answers like: "That's the way things are" or "No one knows for sure". We are not comfortable with a chaos theory that can blame all of this strange weather on butterfly sneezes somewhere off the coast of Africa. At the same time we do not trust experts who want to give an hour long presentation about global warming, the increase in the use of fossil fuels around the world and how if California gets hit with a big earthquake, Nevada may have water front property.

We don't want all of that. We want a simple explanation. There is a cause and effect to everything and we just want to find out what it is. Simplicity is comforting to us; routines keep us going; we don't like change. The weather is supposed to be warmer in March and deserts are supposed to be deserts.

It is sobering sometimes to realize how little we do control. We can't control the weather and we certainly aren't real good at predicting it. We are good at adjusting and taking what each day brings and making it as good as possible. We celebrate little victories and quickly forget bad days or bad situations. The resilience of mankind is amazing. We make the best of situations because that is what we do and that is how we survive.

As the warmer weather comes and the growing season expands, let's enjoy everyday and cherish the time. Who knows, maybe we will celebrate New Year's Day 2006 in shorts on the beach!

Have a great week!

John

Thought for the Week – April 8, 2005

I know it is spring. I know because my dogs chase anything that moves. I guess they believe that they are keeping the yard safe from creatures 1/50 their size. I really cannot complain about it. The doggy aerobics has given my 14 year-old lab the exercise he needs and it gives my younger dog something to do.

Occasionally, they actually catch something!

Several days ago, I saw Roxie the wonder dog, (the younger one), walking around the yard with something in her mouth. In the past, she has caught toads, or rocks she thought were toads. So I asked her to drop it. It was a bird! She either snuck up on it or the bird was already dead when she found it or she actually bird-dogged the bird.

I went into my shed and donned a work glove and grabbed a trash bag to prepare for the process of removing the starling from my grass. As I leaned over to pick up the bird, it rolled over, shook its head several times and quickly flew away! Roxie watching the whole drama, looked at me, sniffed loudly and walked away.

I was surprised that my ADHD pet actually caught something. I was appalled when I thought she had killed the poor thing. I was amazed that the bird actually wasn't dead. I was surprised when it flew away. I wasn't surprised when Roxie got disgusted with me and walked away.

How often in your everyday life does something routine become extraordinary? How often do we take the time to look? How often is a prayer answered; a miracle seen; a smile quietly shared? Sometimes amazing things happen in the silence of a beautiful morning or a child sleeping. It does not have to make a lot of noise to be worth noticing.

I will continue watching my dogs chase real and mythical creatures. As for Roxie, she got over losing the bird in no time at all. She is now chasing squirrels and trying to climb trees. I would say she is incapable of finding success, however miracles do happen!

Have a great week!

John

Thought for the Week – April 15, 2005

A high school reopened this week. Students went back to class and they received a thirty-second sound bite on the evening news. Just a few weeks ago, the school became another example of an angry student violently taking the lives of other students and educators. It was another Columbine; another senseless loss of life.

The question is: Have we become desensitized to it? Has the novelty worn off because the occurrences have increased? Do we talk about and listen to talking heads question the responsibilities and listening skills of teachers, counselors and administrators?

In a recent parent survey, (mine), several parents raised concerns about kids bullying other kids. A very supportive parent recently told me something her fifth grade son shared. He said, "You wouldn't believe what kids say to each other when an adult is not around. It can make me angry and very hurt."

Just watch television any night and see how even cartoon characters treat each other. They yell at each other, make fun of each other, ridicule each other and then they take the last two minutes to reconcile. Situation comedies do the same. They are just cartoons with real people. Try to be safe and watch CNN or FOX news and you have self-acclaimed experts yelling at each other, ridiculing each other, stating that the other one does not know what he/she is talking about. Do you see a pattern here?

One thing is certain: We need to listen to our students and react if we see them become more insular, angrier or hurtful to their peers or teachers. We must help them and support them prior to them feeling that the only way to handle a real or perceived problem is by violently hurting themselves or others. We must also be a positive example to them. We must be positive in our comments. We must praise and encourage and not fall victim to the negativity that is the cash crop of the air waves.

Little things do matter and what we say can have a bigger impact and save us from another image of students trying to cope after a tragedy. We do not need to see another impromptu shrine of teddy bears, candles and ribbons. We do need to keep working to help every child know that they will never feel lost or alone. We need to keep hugging them to show that we care. We can't afford to wait to console them after a loss.

We have the power to make a difference. Let do it one child at a time.

John

Thought for the Week – April 22, 2005

The first week of testing is now complete and the biggest part of it is done. During the past three days, we have focused on Reading, Language Arts and Math. Now we wait to finish the test and then we wait to get the results. Who says there's no prayer in public schools?

If you are like me, you have reviewed everything that has been done this year to prepare the students. You have even second-guessed yourself after seeing and administrating the test. You find very few items on a strategy you spent two weeks on. You discover that you didn't spend enough time working on something else. You analyze and criticize and have already made instructional adjustments for next year.

Don't judge yourself too harshly. I know these tests are important and we want the students to do well and we want our schools to be successful. However, we want our students to know more than what the test asks and we want to be evaluated in multiple ways not just by the test. We need to judge ourselves, each other and our students in multiple ways as well. We don't want to make the mistake of trying to do one thing well, testing, rather than educate everyone well.

I am not trying to minimize the local, statewide, and national significance that these tests hold. However, our goal as educators is to take these kids as far as we can and teach them to think at a higher level. If we do that, the testing will be an affirmation of what the kids know and not an ordeal that shows what they don't.

Take a deep breath and believe in yourselves. Ask your students what they thought of the test. I asked some and mine and most said, "It was easy." If nothing else we have taught them confidence and given them self-reliance. Those two things will help them in life after all this testing is done.

Have a great week.

John

How many times have you been asked lately: "Is your school safe?", "Are your bathrooms monitored properly?", and "What are you doing about bullying?" Many adults and community members will share with you the wish for the good ole' days, when kids would treat each other respectfully; when they would work their problems out over time; when they would look out for other people. I don't remember the good ole' days quite as pristine as that but I do see their point. They would like it to be simpler and easier than it is today.

We try as a society to fix blame on everything. We try to label one person bad so we can assume that he/she is attempting to hurt a good person. We need a victim and a bully; a sinner and a saint. It is never as easy as that.

The media and other situational vultures need to let us provide a standard of care for everyone in our buildings that is matched to the maturity and developmental level of our students. Good behavior should be expected and supported by parents and the community. When a bad thing occurs and someone is accosted or injured, then we need to investigate it thoroughly, gather all the information and when appropriate, share it with those whose job is to publish it for the community.

As we all know, in many cases, arguments, disagreements and skirmishes do not start at school, they begin in the communities and neighborhoods and travel on the bus with the students and make their way into classrooms. Parents need to support safety and fair play on the sidewalk as well as the school. They need to let school officials know when a neighborhood problem is festering and may come into the building. We can be allowed to solve the problem before it becomes a media event.

Part of what students learn in school is how to get along with each other. Sometimes that is taught by teachers, sometimes by peers and sometimes by situations. Church leaders, school leaders, community members and parents need to work together to ensure that all children know what to do when they are mistreated, what their responsibilities are in telling us their problems, and how to work successfully with their peers.

School officials will continue to work on making the schools safe as possible. I wonder if anyone from the media will be there when it happens to give us credit for trying.

Have a great week!

John

Thought for the Week – May 13, 2005

There is Chinese proverb that states: "Do not label something as good luck or bad luck until you wait to see what happens next." In other words, we have to wait to see what the effect of any situation or action is to see whether it was a good thing or not. I know what they are talking about.

Last weekend, I had the honor of speaking at my niece's wedding. She looked tall and lovely in her simple, yet elegant wedding gown and her husband-to-be was equally handsome in his Victorian style tuxedo. This was to be an outdoor wedding amidst the azaleas, poplars and pines that surrounded a large lake near Richmond, Virginia. The view was breathtaking, the birds sang, the crowd gathered and the music played. They had planned on everything being perfect. However, they could not control the weather.

With 150 people looking on and as the father of the bride began to escort his daughter down the aisle, it began to rain! Not hard but any rain outside at that moment could ruin the mood and the bride's countenance. Some members of the congregation even started to move to shelter. The groom calmly looked at the situation and quickly called everyone back to their places. The deserters quickly found their way back to their seats and the procession continued.

As the bride completed her journey and stood side by side with her soon-to-be husband, the rain stopped, the sun appeared in the corner of the sky and a rainbow appeared over the lake, facing the bride and groom and to the back of the minister who was busy officiating.

Everyone started to whisper and gasp and take pictures of this beautiful scene. They were so happy that they stayed; that they had not left; that they had not missed the rainbow. I hope some of the pictures came out. Which bride wouldn't want a rainbow shining in the background of their wedding?

You cannot get rainbows unless a little rain falls. Sometimes you have to wait and see what may happen and not just make quick judgments or decisions. Sometimes we have to allow other things to be in control. If we don't, we miss the rainbows that be shining right behind us.

Have a great weekend!

John

Thought for the Week – May 27, 2005

Caps and gowns; processionals and pictures; smiles and tears; these are all signs of accomplishments, achievements and the fulfillment of dreams.

These students come in all sizes and march in every venue imaginable. They are walking quickly down cafeteria aisles to find their places on the stage steps. They are walking slowing across the stage to receive their diplomas already thinking about leaving home to attend college. They are proudly walking across well-manicured lawns thinking about making a difference with kids, science, mathematics, engineering or philosophy.

All of these success stories were easy. They just needed a little guidance and some suggestions. They were fun to have in class and we knew they would do well. Some took the more scenic and circuitous route to success. They had to be taught in a different manner, we had to work with them individually or in small groups. They needed us to coach their parents in what needed to be done. They needed us to tell them they could succeed and we were not going to give up on them. Some we thought would never make it and we prayed and cried over them. However, here they are and how they smile!

As you sit once again and listen to songs and speeches and hear various versions of Pomp and Circumstance, watch the faces of the graduates and share some of their pride and some of their joy. Without you they wouldn't be there.

You have quietly, efficiently and tirelessly given them their future.

Have a great summer!

John

Thought for the Week – August 5, 2005

The term "building capacity" has become a commonly used educational term in articles, books and lectures. It conjures up two different definitions – the amount of space you have in a school and your plan on how to utilize that space; the knowledge and expertise of your staff and how to improve or increase their proficiency. One is a management issue; the other is a human issue. One deals with desks, chairs and books; the other with mind, heart and hand. One manipulates space; the other promotes change. Both are focused on helping students succeed.

On Tuesday, our buildings will once again be filled with individuals who believe in their profession and want to do the best they can to help their students do well. They will be worried about the capacity of their classroom and capacity of the building. Our jobs will be to build the capacity of what they know and what they need to know. We need to help them reach their goal, by giving them more knowledge, more strategies and more materials. We need to build up their minds, and their souls.

Teachers are on the front line in the war against ignorance, intolerance and mediocrity. We must help them to find new ways and perfect old ways that will help their students be the best they can be. If we can help build their minds to match their hearts, we cannot and will not fail.

Have a great week.

John

Thought for the Week – August 12, 2005

My grandchildren stayed with us for three weeks this summer. It reminded me that child-rearing is for the young, but we had a great time. The youngest, Andrew, loves music and he would repeatedly sing: "In the jungle, the quiet jungle the lion sleeps tonight...etc" Pretty good for a three-year old to sing the Wemaweh song. Of course after hearing it twenty times the novelty was quickly wearing thin.

On one car trip, (thankfully short), Andrew took the melody of the song and sang the ABC's to it! He was very proud of his accomplishment. He should have been. I tried to sing it and kept messing it up.

On Monday, our hallways and classrooms will be filled with students who have hidden talents. They will love music, math, reading, gymnastics, art, baseball, dance, NASCAR, and science. They would love to share with us what their talents are if we just ask and watch; validate and respect; nurture and encourage. All we have to do is watch, listen and learn.

Children learn in many different ways and our first job is to learn how they learn before we can teach them anything.

The destination is success; the journey can be as various and diverse as the children in our classroom. Let's enjoy the ride!

Have a great week.

John

Thought for the Week – August 19, 2005

Football teams are preparing for the new season. Everywhere fans are reading and discussing how their favorite teams will perform this year. Everyone from coaches to trainers; managers to the water boy, are being asked their opinion of how well the team is going to do and how much better they are going to be this year.

The question to ask is: "What are you going to do differently this year?" and "Are you changing anything this year or are you just working harder at what you did last year?"

If teams do not do anything different from one year to another, they cannot expect to do any better than they did the year before. If all they do is work harder at the wrong thing, they cannot expect to succeed, win and be a champion.

Schools have started their season and like football teams, they have reviewed what they did last year, had discussions on how to improve and have dedicated themselves to being better.

Just like football teams, we need to ask ourselves, "What are we doing differently?" and "Are we doing anything differently than last year?" If we just work harder at things that have not proven to work in the past, aren't we going to end up exhausted with the same results?"

Great teams are great because they never stop adjusting and changing to the world and situations around them. Good teams do what they do very well. Great teams embrace change and remake themselves constantly.

Great schools must do the same thing. We can never stop looking for something different that can help us improve. We can never be afraid of change or think it is a dirty word.

We cannot ask students to take risks and not do so ourselves. It's something to think about.

Have a great week!

John

Thought for the Week – August 25, 2005

I was speaking to a group of fifth graders this week about the importance of learning about the history of this country. In an era of reality TV, Harry Potter, and Spongebob Square pants, (I like that one too), it is easy for young students to lose interest in Western Expansion, the Industrial Revolution, and World War II. It is the fight between the philosophies of now with the review of the past; the High-definition 21st century versus the daguerreotypes of the Civil War; the hard work daily struggle to survive in the new west against the microwave society where things can be warm in thirty seconds. It is a competition that is hard to win.

One fifth grade student told me, "Of course YOU like history, there was less of it to learn when you were in school!" I had to laugh because that was true. In a way, there is so much more to learn because just like the times we live in, history is being made at break-neck speed. Society is moving so fast that it will be amazing to see what those fifth graders' children will have to learn.

So what's the answer? Do we give in to a society that finds itself more interesting than previous generations? I hope not. I do think we need to find different ways to present history and make it more alive and meaningful. These are kids who use IPODS, DSL, electronic encyclopedias and cell phones to take pictures and tell time. We cannot wonder why a two-dimensional book is found boring or uninteresting.

History is so important and we need to ensure that it is taught and it is learned. We need to tell children why this country is great; what democracy is; what mistakes were made; what successes we've had; what challenges we face.

Our students do have more to learn than we did. However we are the best equipped to teach them. We, our grandparents, and parents lived through a great deal of it.

Have a great week!

John

Thought for the Week – September 12, 2005

My parents live 10 miles from Washington D.C. in what is the megalopolis known as Northern Virginia. Years ago it was a quiet suburb with quaint houses, tree lined roads and more stop signs than stop lights. Thirty years later it is a bustling urbanized area with traffic lights every 50 yards and traffic that never slows down. If you live in their neighborhood and work in the District of Columbia, it still takes you over an hour to go ten miles. Most of my parents' neighbors were not born in this country. They work hard to pay a very high mortgage or rent for the privilege of living so close to the Nation's Capital. It is virtually the melting pot that epitomizes the United States of America as the "Land-of-Opportunity".

Things surprise you in a neighborhood like this one. The smells from the kitchens and the languages spoken are as diverse as the backgrounds. People find a way to communicate with each other: Sometimes in English; sometimes in sign language; sometimes with a kind face or a smile. In one instance, two women met at they were taking a walk with their children and the two kept trying languages until they realized that they both knew enough French to have a conversation. Even one of the neighbors has a rooster that crows all day long and there is a Spanish gentleman down the street who is trying very hard to master the Scottish bagpipes.

The sights, sounds, traffic and pace of the area makes you feel you are always running on fast forward. However, my parents don't want to leave the area. It is their home. They have grown old around it and have made changes with it. It is as part of them and they are part of it. Just like the plethora of families that have moved to that area, my parents have made adjustments too. They are as much part of the area as the people around them. They respect the challenges that their neighbors have faced in an effort to help their families.

In recent days, we have had the opportunity to register children of families who lost everything to hurricane Katrina. They are experiencing what it is like to start over in a new place with only a verbal history of their lives intact. We need to understand the challenges they face and help them and understand what they are going through. It should also make the minor inconveniences of our lives seem trivial and mundane.

If my 77 year old parents can accept and respect the people around them, how can we not do the same? All of us can trace our lineage back to a different country and time. However, we are all Americans now and we all benefit from that privilege. Let's help our new neighbors through the challenges that they face. We are educators. Nobody cares better than we do.

Have a great week! *John*

Thought for the Week – September 19, 2005

A person's worth is measured by the number of visitors at his home or work place upon hearing of his passing. It is an acknowledgement of the sudden void created by the loss. It is a demonstration of respect due to a person who has lived a good life; ran a good race; fought the good fight. It is a way to hold on to the person for just a little while longer.

We can list many words to describe Major Benjamin: Leader; principal; father-figure; veteran; patriot; man-of-faith; educator; father; friend. Any of these words would still not fully describe this man's heart, soul, life's work and legacy.

Anyone who met Major Benjamin knew they were in the presence of a man who cared deeply about his work and prayed hard for the children and people around him. Anyone who met Major Benjamin knew that he believed in the power of education, he believed in his country, and he believed in his staff.

Many times in our careers we experience the passing of someone who makes us stop for a second and pause to reflect on a great life. We grieve more deeply, we pray harder, we cry longer and we are changed forever. It is these times that we appreciate the friends we have and the colleagues we work with.

By the numbers of people mourning and visiting Hubert Middle School, the number of candles burned and the number of tears cried, it is obvious that Major Benjamin was a great man and a great principal. He was loved, admired, respected and revered. His legacy is carried on in each teacher, administrator and student that met him and knew him.

Another angel has joined God's choir. He will be missed; but his work will live on forever.

John

Thought for the Week – September 30th, 2005

   My grandson William had to talk to me yesterday. It seems he was trying to convince his father that 8 + 4 = 10. He was sure that his kindergarten and first grade teacher had told him so. He would rather believe in that memory than admit that his father was right and correct his homework paper. His father, a chief financial officer, wanted some help before he went nuts.

   I spoke with William. We talked about soccer and what book he was reading and then I asked him about his homework. He said, "I know that they told me that 8 +4 = 10, but Dad is telling me something different. I asked him if he had ever heard the term seeing is believing? He said somewhat sheepishly that he had not. So I told him to hold two fingers up in the air and put the number 8 in his head. After telling me that I couldn't see the two fingers over the phone, he did what I asked him to do. I then asked William to start with the 8 in his head and count the two fingers he was holding up. He quietly and reluctantly said, (he is stubborn like his father), "9, 10". Next, I asked him to hold up four fingers and repeat the exercise. He counted, "9, 10, 11,...Okay Dad was right! I'll change it. Bye." (It wasn't the greatest of strategies but it worked and William didn't really want his math teaching grandmother to get on the phone.)

   Hearing the same thing from different people is a way of differentiating. Finding ways for students to resolve their confusion and understand even the simplest concept is better than just arguing that they are wrong and we are right. We don't need winners and losers, we need all students to master concepts and work through the confusion.

   "Seeing is believing" is a concept that all learners can understand no matter whether they are 7 or 77. We just need to help them see it and teach them to believe enough in themselves to correct mistakes, delight in learning new things and to not be afraid to say they were wrong. True confidence comes from taking charge of your own learning.

   See it and believe it.

   Have a great week!

   John

Thought of the Week – October 7, 2005

My neighbor came over the other day to inform me that a red-tailed hawk had taken up residence in the oak tree located in my back yard. This particular hawk has been seen by other neighbors and described as huge and hungry. My neighbor, not knows for hyperbole, said that witnesses claimed to have seen the hawk swoop down, capture and carry off a neighbor's tabby cat! He also said he had found fur, feathers and other remnants of previous victims caught by this predator.

Now I have seen the bird. I have heard its powerful "scree" verbal calling card occasionally and I know that my oak tree is a great place to watch the entire neighborhood waiting for your lunch to walk by. To be honest, I really wasn't' that upset about it being in my tree. It may keep the vermin population down. (The fact I don't own a cat and my two dogs would give it a hernia may have helped calm my fears.)

The simple truth is: The hawk is doing what it is supposed to do. It wasn't reading the paper and talking. It was doing what hawks do. Yet, it was building itself a reputation for being more than a regular soaring bird of prey. By doing what it is supposed to do extremely well, it had become the talk of the neighborhood.

Schools can become the talk of the neighborhoods too. They can work extremely hard at doing what they are supposed to do and become extremely efficient educational systems. They can build a reputation by ensuring that every child is known, loved and believed in. A reputation that is built by teaching every child at such a level that failure is not an option and success is inevitable.

Without hawks, there would be more rats, mice and other vermin. (And probably more cats.) Without good schools, there is more ignorance, intolerance, and poverty. The hawk is doing what it is supposed to do. Let's do what we're supposed to do too!

Have a great week!

John

Thought for the Week – October 14, 2005

My seven year old grandson called the other day to inform me that something wonderful had happened in his life. He was extremely proud of this moment and he wanted to share it with as many people as possible.

Now my first thought was that he had been the victorious hero in a recent soccer game. (He plays goalie; I have pictures.) My next thought was that he received an exemplary grade on a paper or project that he had been working on. However, I was amazed when he could calm down enough to tell me that he just received his first library card!

For a child who has had difficulties in learning to read and at one point had stated that he would never learn to read, this was a big day indeed. It easily eclipsed the other possibilities that had first popped into my head. This was a reason to celebrate; a reason to phone relatives and share; a reason to feel proud.

How often do we celebrate academic accomplishments the way we celebrate athletic or competitive victories? How often have we looked at a child who has worked hard at something and given him the pat on the back that the effort deserves? How often do we notice the little victories and acknowledge them as something special?

We teach children through our celebrations what is important to us. We can increase the respect and honor that academics hold by celebrating what is learned and mastered just like we celebrate a competitive victory.

Tonight, I will call my grandson and hear about what books he checked out on his own library card. Maybe he will read some to me and we will have something else to celebrate!

Have a great week!

John

Thought for the Week – October 21, 2005

Last June, I received a lovely e-mail from a parent I had not heard from for a long time. I was principal at the school where her kids had attended from kindergarten through fifth grade. One child was now in college; one was in high school; one was in middle school. The pictures I received were of the older daughter signing a letter of intent to play volleyball for a small college in Virginia. She planned to be an elementary school teacher. She loved kids and loved her family. Her name was Katie.

Last Friday, I received another e-mail. It quietly stated that this same lovely girl had shot herself and had died. For some reason the stress of breaking up from her boyfriend, her move to college and perhaps other reasons we will never know, forced her to do the unthinkable; forced her to remove herself from everything she really wanted. It was not rational; it was not fair; it is very devastating.

As human beings, we try to find reasons for why things like this happen. We try to make sense out of senseless things. We try to put closure on things that have a permanent effect on us. When something tragic like this happens we are changed forever because the family that we knew so well has changed. The happiness and closeness that they were known for would never be the same. Their world had been changed forever and there was no way to change it back.

Every day is precious and once a day has passed you can never bring it back. Families are important and each of us has the blessing of having an extended family that we work with everyday. We need to appreciate them and help them in their daily efforts. We must support all of our students even the ones who are the least loveable. We must reduce each other's stress, not add to it. We must verbally support and physically support each other. We must make sure that none of us ever feels that they are fighting a battle alone.

Every day is precious and everyone you work with a gift. Someone can leave us all too soon and make us feel a little more vulnerable and reminds us of our weakness and mortality.

Let's be there for each other and know that we are not alone. Let's pray that Katie and her family will someday find peace. Unfortunately, that is all we can do now.

John

Thought for the Week – November 4, 2005

Nobody goes trick-or-treating anymore. It is not the way I remember it. (What is?) I know there are still some neighborhoods that have an abundance of young people and they try to make Halloween the candy-hoarding, goblin-promoting event that it used to be but it is not what it once was.

There are some very good reasons for this: There are scary people out there and they don't need another reason to prey on the most vulnerable. We are more interested in eating healthy than ever before. We are too busy to add another event to our schedule that is focused on dressing in costumes and asking strangers to give us things to eat.

I remember Halloween as a reminder that the calendar year was quickly approaching its end. It was a time to compartmentalize the last 9 weeks into what special events were going to happen. You had Halloween, Thanksgiving, and Christmas. Halloween was the beginning of the busiest and most enjoyable time of year.

With the tidal waves, hurricanes, and earthquakes maybe we have been scared enough for one year. When our hearts and minds are concerned about young men and women serving their country on the other side of the world, maybe we have enough ghosts and goblins in real life. Maybe we needed to skip it this year.

Many neighborhoods have started to have parties and hayrides to celebrate Halloween in a controlled, family-oriented way. It is a safe, fun way to make new traditions out of old ones. It is a way to combine the old with the new in an attempt to keep Halloween from being just another way for the candy companies to make money.

On November 1st, I turned on the radio and I heard Christmas music! Maybe Halloween has been squeezed out. I hope we have Thanksgiving; I like having the family around, I like football and I like to eat.

Have a great week!

John

Thought for the Week – December 16, 2005

It has been many weeks since I have put fingers to keyboard to share a thought. Hopefully, many months from now I will be looking through the file of my writings for 2004 – 2005 and wonder what happened to my thoughts dated from November4[th] through today. I have always believed in using my writings to lift the spirit and lighten the load of principals and educators. I have great respect for what you do and who you are. However, the past few weeks have been stressful and unnerving and if you do not mind I would like to share them with you.

During the time frame listed above, my wife Patricia has been battling for her life. What started out as a blood clot in her leg moved to her lungs (luckily not to her heart or brain which would have been fatal). Unfortunately, the clots kept developing and she was in danger of losing her legs. We spent the next few weeks trying to find the cause, medicating with intense blood thinners and pain killers and praying that Patricia would continue to battle and win against incredible odds.

The lowest point was when a doctor came in late one evening and stated that, "If she made it through the next few days and if we can save her legs, we will start to look at what is causing the clots and the pain."

After some tears and a pity-party, the prayers continued and fight continued and Patricia has improved greatly and she is now in the Rehabilitation Center at Memorial Health and is starting to use her legs again and get her strength back. She has a long way to go and other battles to wage before we will all give a sigh of relief.

Patricia is the star I sail by and I apologize for being more personal than normal in my writing today. With all the prayers and the tears going on, we have not had the time to decorate for Christmas. We usually have so many lights the airport can use us as a guide. (I have written about that in an earlier thought.) The lack of lights and decorations have not diminished the importance of Christmas to me this year, it has enhanced it; brightened it; deepened it.

The greatest gifts that I have received in my life: My wife, my family and you my friends, have reminded me how truly blessed I am and how truly loved we are. I thank you for being there for us and I thank you for your prayers and support.

Merry Christmas and my God bless you in the coming year.

John

Thought for the Week – January 20, 2006

In an effort to try to be the best person I can be, I recently gathered up all the empty bottles and cans, magazines and newspapers I had and transported them to a nearby parking lot for recycling. (I was also told to move them before the pile fell down and buried someone.)

The combination of old bottles and old newspapers reminded me of the smell of an old print shop I used to visit. I didn't go there to have anything printed; I went there for the conversation and the company of the owner.

You would never know who might be there or how many other people had "just stopped by". It was not really important if anyone had a print job that needed to be done. It would be completed in due time and with care and efficiency. What was important was the discussion. It was a controlled, respectful debate about what was happening that day. Local and national politics, crime, the price of coffee, the last or next election; any of these were up for grabs. However, no one yelled at another person. No one interrupted another adult. No one held a grudge because of someone's opinion about something. It was an opinion; nothing more. It was enjoyable and because it was done so calmly, you actually had an opportunity to listen and learn something. Sometimes we even told a joke or two.

We are losing the art of conversation. We feel that if we talk louder, we know more. If we sing louder; we are more talented. If we interrupt more; our opinion carries more weight. If we disagree on one thing; we disagree on everything.

The opportunities to share individual thoughts and to have diverse opinions are signs of an intelligent, free society. The patience to listen and discuss different points of view is a sign of an advanced culture. Respecting different points of view is the cornerstone of a pluralistic world.

We have to teach students to truly listen and we have to model how to do that properly. Having the freedom to hold different viewpoints is just as important as deciding what soft drink you drink or what newspaper you read.

But, that is only my opinion.

Have a great week.

John

Thought for the Week – January 27, 2006

A friend of mine in an effort to improve his sound system spent a considerable amount of time researching the different types of speakers available for purchase. He found it to be a more challenging task than he originally thought. There are a plethora of types out there that come in different sizes, colors, and availability. Some look like furniture and some are so small they can be hidden anywhere in the house. A few were really expensive and some looked like they came out of a science-fiction television program.

After a great deal of time and effort, he decided on a certain brand, purchased it, connected it to his receiver and tried it out. Unfortunately, he was extremely disappointed in the sound quality of this new investment in his life. He couldn't figure out what he had done wrong. He had done his homework; read Consumer Reports; visited stores; talked to friends; made the best choice. What went wrong?

The problem was not in his speakers. The new speakers were attached to same old, out-of-date, worn out receiver. Putting new speakers on this stereo is like putting new shoes on a dead horse. No matter what you do, the sound may be louder but it won't be any better.

In education we do that a lot. We focus on fixing one thing and expect everything else to come in line like the planets cosmically aligning. We try to fix the output rather than focusing on the input. We spend time and money; we work hard and care deeply. Yet, we end with the same results and we wonder why?

True and long-lasting improvement comes when we look into the entire process of how we educate and nurture our students. We don't justify success by looking only at products. Kids will find success at various speeds and through various pathways. If we can perfect the process that helps all our students, we won't have to worry about the end product. It will all come out as sweet, beautiful music.

Have a great week.

John

A Thought on Valentine's Day

Five years ago when I came here, I had a goal of building a strong school based upon the ideal of a family-centered staff. Any successful school that has the students as its focus must first believe in and care about each other. You cannot be sympathetic until you become empathetic and aware.

During these last few months, I have seen and felt the affection of the Bloomingdale family. I have seen it care for the little ones and our fellow staff members and use "tough love" when necessary. I have been impressed with the depth of caring and expression.

A family sometimes doesn't pick its members. They learn to love and support each other warts and all. They help each other and walk with each other through the bad times and party-hardy during the good times. That is what a family does.

On this 2006 Valentine's Day, after all the little cards and candy hearts are given out, please remember how much I appreciate all of you. You truly are a family; my family; and I appreciate all of you!

Have a great day!

John

Thought for the Week – March 31, 2006

   After some complaints about which teams were selected for the NCAA Men's Basketball Tournament, and some great games with last second shots and overtime heroics, there are only four teams left and none of them were ranked as a number one.

   One of them is from a small school without a football program – GMU. (George Mason University; My alma mater.)

   Even though we have no one left in our brackets, (including mine), and even though they are the underdog; the Cinderella or Cinderfella team, and even though they may not win tomorrow, we know they are winners.

   We like supporting the little guy; the teams we usually do not see. We like to see them succeed against the bigger opponent; the favorites in the press guide. We love to watch this athletic reality show that is the NCAA. This little GMU team does not have to win another game; they have already found success; they have fought the Goliaths of the NCAA.

   Do we have students who have worked hard against the odds? Do we celebrate the students who succeed without parental support and the lack of an educational pedigree?

   Look around at your little ones who are quietly being successful. They are in the academic final four. They are already winners. We just need to find them and recognize them as the winners they are.

   Have a great week!

   John

Thought for the Week – April 7, 2006

In my backyard, there is a pair of red-headed woodpeckers making a nest high up in a live oak tree. They are not shy about it. They are loud, brazen and proud of their daily efforts. They have meticulously drilled a perfectly round hole in to the trunk of the tree. The time that has been taken would make you think that the inside of the trunk has been transformed into a three bedroom, two-bath bird condominium.

I don't mind that they are there. I don't think they are going to kill the tree. Birds and trees have had symbiotic relationship for centuries and when I see the momma bird emphatically spit out new saw dust from her home, I don't think I want to get on her bad side.

The point of nesting is not to remodel the tree. It is to prepare for a new life to begin. It is to create a safe, loving home. Who can say these are dumb animals?

In this Easter season, we need to take the time to remember the connection between wood and new life. We need to remember the little miracles that are all around us that are so easy to miss. We get so into our own issues and agendas that we become blinded to the blessed reminders that are sent to us daily. If we acknowledge them, they will help us calm down. They will bring us closer. They will let us know to forgive and will allow us to be forgiven.

I cannot wait to the new additions to the bird family and watch them grow. It will remind me that life continues, and that we are blessed every day. We need those reminders; they make us whole.

I thank God for all of you!

Happy Easter!

John

Thought for the Week – April 19, 2006

This week's Time magazine's cover story is entitled: Dropout Nation. It states that 30% of high students will drop out before graduating. Last week Oprah dedicated several shows to this topic and raised the percentage of dropouts to 40%. In both the printed and television media, it mentioned a lack of connection between school and home. Students did not see a reason to be there. Students said school was boring; the schools were too large; that very few people cared about them. (Isn't that what authorities said after the tragedy at Columbine?)

In the book The Principal's Challenge, Mark Tucker states that if we do not improve the public school system, the United States will not continue to be a super power. If we have 40% of our work force under educated in a fast-paced technological age, then Tucker is correct. That is a scary and sobering notion.

It is too easy for us to say parents aren't doing enough. Some are and some are not. It is too easy for parents to say that schools need to change. Many say it but they cannot say how to change. Time magazine makes five recommendations: Teach Reading Early, Create Alternative High Schools, Spot Future Dropouts, Support Vocational Education, and Get The Grownups Involved. Four of the five must start in the elementary school and we cannot be afraid to raise our expectations and rigor and expect students to achieve and succeed. As Oprah said, "We have a society not of low expectations; It is of no-expectations."

However, we must also inspire students to see the benefit of education. We must inspire our fellow educators to look at our jobs as a high calling not a punch-the-clock job. We must know all the students and love them as much as we can. (Even the ones that are hard to love.) We must not be afraid to change even when society will not like it when we make school harder, more challenging, more interesting, more technological and more work-related. We must have high expectations for every child even when very few have high expectations for what we can accomplish.

It can be done. We have to help each other and support each other and believe in each other so that neither the students nor the adults who teach and work with them will feel that dropping out is the only option they have.

Have a great week! Believe and succeed!

John

Thought for the Week – April 28, 2006

A friend of mine called me the other day to mourn the loss of his computer that had suddenly and incomprehensibly crashed last weekend. He could not figure out why his electronic sidekick would not do the things it had always done. Whenever he tried to open a file and save it to his flash drive, it would just freeze up and have a quiet technological tantrum.

He took it to a local store that works on electronics and they told him about all the work that would have to be done to his faithful machine. They explained it with that look of, "I know more about computers than you will ever know" look. The total cost to fix it was over 200 dollars.

On his way back home, he spoke to his neighbor who asked how things were going. After listening to a repeat of this sad tale, the neighbor asked, "Have you installed any new software lately? If you did you might uninstall it and see if the computer would work again before spending all that money at the shop."

After retrieving the computer from the store and canceling the work order, my friend did what his neighbor suggested and the computer now is once again working fine.

We often try to fix thing by taking them somewhere or giving them to someone else to fix. In reality sometimes by sharing our concerns or situations with others we open ourselves up for a better variety of solutions and support. We do not have to fight our battles or solve problems on our own. Not everything has to be a private battle.

Co-teaching is a good example. Sometimes one way of presenting a concept will not reach every child. Sometimes hearing the same thing from two different people will reinforce to students the importance of it. The more adults care about each other and are willing to share with each other, the more they will care and share about the students. Children will achieve at a higher level, when more adults work together for them.

It worked for a computer; it will work with us.

Have a great week!

John

Thought for the Week – May 5, 2006

The other night as I was sitting on my back porch with a beverage of choice, my two dogs suddenly came to life and ran toward my back shed. It takes a great deal to move these two out of their sedentary lifestyle. My black lab is old and has cataracts and learned some time ago that if he runs all the way out to the back yard, he has to walk all the way back. My short-haired pointer is just fat and happy and enjoys connecting her rump to the cool cement of my patio. The other night a large cat walked slowly across the yard and neither the old dog, (couldn't see her), nor the fat dog, (didn't feel like it), moved at all. So it takes something special to move these two dogs out of their reverie. I hadn't seen those two move that fast in months.

I had to follow them to see what they found so enthralling.

For the next forty-five minutes (I am not exaggerating), my two dogs ran inside the shed, then outside, they around the shed and then started the routine again. This regimen went on quietly; without a bark or growl. They were having the time of their lives and I couldn't tell what they were smelling or looking at.

I could have stopped them. I could have scolded them for running around in circles. Instead, I just stood there in the middle of yard admiring their tenacity, energy and happiness. They were enjoying their efforts; I was enjoying the show.

They eventually came back to the porch. They were exhausted from the sudden physical and mental exertion. They hadn't caught anything but they seemed proud of themselves for guarding the homestead. They both slept for hours.

This time of year it seems that there are days when we suddenly are running around in circles trying to catch things that we cannot see. We think they are there and we know what we are doing is important but the prize or the goal is not right in front of us.

In the near future, we will have the opportunity to come back to the porch and rest for a while. In the meantime, let's enjoy the pace of the end of the year. Let's revel in the special events and end-of-year celebrations. Let's have the time of our lives without barks or growls.

These times are over way too quickly. There will be time very soon for quiet, restful sleep.

Have a great week!
        John

Thought for the Week – August 4, 2006

I love commercials. I am the guy who looks forward to the super bowl and plans to go to the bathroom during the game so I won't miss them. My wife talks to me during television shows because she knows that I will be concentrating on the commercials when they come on.

Why? In ten to sixty seconds commercials give us a microcosmic look at our present society. While they promote a product, idea or method, they also show us what is in style or what the fad of that time period is. A car commercial from 1956 sounds almost exactly the same as one from 2006 but the hair styles and fashions have changed a great deal.

My current favorite commercial is made by Sharpie. Here is the scenario: A college-aged young man opens the refrigerator, takes out a half-gallon of milk and drinks from the container. He immediately spits it out into the sink (and all over the counter). He takes out a Sharpie permanent marker, writes the word "BAD" on the milk carton and replaces it back into the refrigerator. It is a perfect example of how a young person might think. (It probably wasn't his milk; therefore he didn't take responsibility for it.)

Soon we will greet new students and new co-workers and it will be easy for us to take out our Sharpies and label them and place them back into their rooms or desks. We can place the responsibility on somebody else to help them, nurture them, and improve them. Unfortunately, if no one else takes that responsibility, these individuals will spoil like the milk and no matter how long it sits on the shelf, it will not get better.

I find commercials fun, humorous and thought-provoking. I find labeling people a quick way to remove us from our collective responsibility to help all succeed.

Let's use our Sharpies to label books and charts and backpacks and let's never label things that should be lifted up instead of placed on a shelf and forgotten. Labeling places a permanent mark on a person's heart or soul.

It is much easier to label than to love but love will always come back to one who gives it.

Have a great week!

John

Thought for the Week – August 11, 2006

My dog is getting old. Kingdog, (I didn't name him.), is 15.5 years old. He will be 16 on January 18th. I picked him out of a litter when he was 6 weeks old. He has been a sweet dear friend for a long time now.

He is just now showing signs that he is slowing down. He doesn't go outside to chase squirrels unless he forgets his age. If it is rainy, he back hips hurt and if it is really stormy outside and I want him to go outside to relieve himself, he looks up at me like I am crazy and goes to his favorite corner, lays down and gives a huge sigh. (Dog language for "Leave me alone!")

Even though his coat is gray and thinning, (a lot like me), and he sometimes forgets the reason why he went outside, (when he actually goes outside), he never loses his dignity and never changes his mood.

He is always happy to be alive!

No matter how hard it may be to get up in the morning and no matter how ragged he looks around the edges his tail wags and he actually looks happy every moment of the day. To Kingdog, everyday is a gift and every moment, either awake or asleep, is a happy, enjoyable time.

We are not dogs. Our lives are more complicated and more stressful than our canine family members. But we can learn things from them: We can celebrate each normal day and celebrate the ordinary. We can take the time to stop and revel in the sunshine and covet an afternoon nap. We can learn to smile and enjoy a sunny day, a nice breeze, a flower that just bloomed or friends we take for granted.

Kingdog gives me a great deal of encouragement and love just for being me. He doesn't ask for much in return and I love him for what he is.

Let's enjoy the days and our friends whether four-legged or two-legged for whom they are. Let's enjoy the breezes and the sunshine that comes our way. Let's enjoy each other and our time together. It is the best time of our lives. Let's enjoy it!

Have a great first week!

John

Thought for the Week – August 18, 2006

My sister and her husband took their four-year old granddaughter, Katherine, to the beach a few weeks ago. It was just the three of them on a little vacation. My sister's master plan, (she always has a plan), was to spend some real quality time playing on the beach and swimming in the Atlantic Ocean.

Unfortunately, Katherine could not be coaxed, bribed or cajoled into the ocean. She would only play and swim in the hotel pool because "She was afraid of the whales!" She felt safer in the pool. It wasn't so big and mysterious and noisy. In the ocean, she felt small and whales are so big!

The challenge of beginning a new school year and teaching in new ways can make us feel like a very small child in a huge ocean. We may want to continue to do the things we have always done because we are more comfortable and we feel safer. We may never want to do something bigger and more creative because we are afraid of things we cannot see.

My sister told me that she was going to continue to work with Katherine to overcome the fear of the ocean and she knows it is going to take time.

We need to take the time to confront the fear of change and work with others to do the same. We know it will take time but being the best always does!

Have a great week!

John

Thought for the Week – September 15, 2006

This week we commemorated the fifth anniversary of the 9-11-01 tragedy. Everyone remembers where they were and what they were doing when our nation was attacked.

Every generation has one defining moment that changes them: Armistice Day, Pearl Harbor Day, the Kennedy Assassination, Martin Luther King's Assassination, and 9-11-01. These events reshaped our history and reshaped our nation.

Each of these events created such an impact that it changed our society forever. Armistice Day was an end of an awful war. It led to the isolationist policies of the 1920's. World War I was so hard we wanted to be insulated from any future European conflict. Pearl Harbor brought us out of our isolationism and mobilized us to become a super power. The Camelot, halcyon days were over as quickly as they began on that terrible day in November 1962. The loss of Dr. King in 1968 forced us to face the harsh reality of racism and realize the error of the separate but "unequal" policies that were in effect all over the country. 9-11-01 made us realize how vulnerable we were because free and open societies are easy targets.

9-11-01 has made us more focused on school safety. We are more cautious. We supervise more intently. We travel less and stay in our homes more. We are less likely to let our children out of sight. We are less likely to trust strangers. We feel more uncomfortable in new situations. We are less confident about the future because we have seen our world change in an instant.

So what can we do in our schools to address this 21st century world? We can create the safest and most caring places for our students to attend and our parents to visit. We can believe that building emotional safety nets are just as important as our academic ones. We need to work with our parents so they trust us to take care of their children and work with us to help them improve. We need to teach our students at a high level so that they can be successful in a world where there are individuals out there who do not want us to succeed. We need to teach everyone to be respectful of others but also how to fight terrorism with courage and not in fear.

Every day that our schools are successful we show the world that we are still here and that we are thriving. We tell that world that we will not let ourselves be destroyed.

Every time our nation has had to endure a catastrophe, we have grown stronger. We adjust. We read more. We become more global and international. We become more dedicated and patriotic. We become a little more mature and less innocent. We take on more responsibilities because we know as individuals and as a nation we will succeed.

To commemorate 9-11-01 let's do what we always do. Let's roll up our sleeves and get the job done! Have a great week!

John

Thought for the Week – September 25, 2006

I was at first shocked at the reaction to Steve Irwin's untimely death. Many of my students and former students were grieving. They talked about if for days. They really felt like they had lost a family member.

I had seen Mr. Irwin on television shows and commercials. I had even seen the numerous comedy routines, (mostly bad ones), based on his voice, stage persona and background with animals. For some reason, I didn't expect the world-wide degree of mourning for this frenetic animal lover.

Why had he such an impact on kids?

Steve Irwin was a teacher! He was like Walt Disney, Mr. Wizard, and Bill Nye. He made learning so natural that everyone connected with him and wanted to learn more. He was enthusiastic in his love for animals and his love for life. He never talked down to his audience and knew when to have fun and when to show caution. He knew true learning was hands-on and real.

Kids loved him and admired him because he taught without a textbook, without a script but with love, respect and passion.

Yes, he was part actor and part business man. Aren't the greatest teachers good actors and don't they use their time and money wisely?

Steve Irwin will be remembered because he was a good teacher. He took risks to show his audience how animals live and how they protect themselves and survive in their environment. He taught kids about life.

If there is a greater legacy, I can't think of one right now.

Have a great week!

John

Thought for the Week – October 2, 2006

In the past year, my wife and I have made new friends. These wonderful people have a major thing in common with us – they get chemotherapy every week.

Most of the "patients" are female and they are all strong and positive and their personalities take over the room when they walk in. They have humor and inner strength even when they have to walk slow and wear head scarves to cover their now balding heads. They don't let the appearance of illness get in the way of their life.

Most of these wonderful women are accompanied by a male spouse or significant other. I have a bond with them and them with me. We are the ones who do not feel the least bit awkward as we carry our wife's purse around from room to room. We do this proudly until we come to the chemotherapy room where we will be sitting for the next four to five hours as our wives receive treatment.

During the times that our spouses occasionally nap, the husbands have a chance to talk about politics, cars, sports and other "guy" topics. We share stories, jokes and a few laughs before someone's wife wakes up and chides us for not being as funny as we think. We take it in stride.

Why do we make the trip? Time is one thing you can never get back. The time together taking the journey is time well spent. The time talking to new friends who are taking the same road is never a wasted. It is uplifting and I admire all of them.

Take the time this week to talk to someone you haven't talked to for a while. Make a new friend or talk with someone we see all the time. It is time well spent and time positively used. Remember no matter how you spend your time, once it is gone, you will never get back!

Have a great week!

John

Thought for the Week – October 24, 2006

The televised campaign advertisements have made me fatigued. I do not care about what political party or platform they happen to be promoting. I do not care what they feel about the other person and how they think the other person will destroy our society as we know it. I do care that in an effort to be elected most candidates participate in character assassination, sound bites and quotes that put their opponent in a bad light.

It is a little ironic to me that churches, civic organizations and the same politicians running for office are concerned about the increase in bullying in schools. Many people want to blame the schools for this decline of civility among young people. They want us to take the responsibility for students who don't have the ability to "play well with others". Quite frankly educators try hard to create a classroom, hallway or school that is a safe and respectful place for all students.

Society is missing the point. When our children see a constant parade of adults who treat each other badly, who are rude and nasty, who seem to make a good living at the expense of someone else's feelings why shouldn't they act the same way? When our children watch shows that make an art form out of insulting another, why shouldn't our students to the same to their peers? When our children see their sports heroes pout and complain and get angry at their teammates in front of thousands of people and the next week seem to get their way, why shouldn't our children act the same on the playground and ball field? It is hard for schools to remain on the high road of civility, when people cannot get out of parking lot without getting angry with one another.

The only way to control our own television is to change the channel or turn it off. The only thing we can control is how we treat other people. The only way we can soar above the rancor and dislike that people show for each other is to be more respectful, extra courteous, more patient and more polite (even when we don't think they deserve it).

You teach young people patience by showing patience; tolerance by being tolerant, compassion by being compassionate; respect by being respectful; civility by being civil; love by loving them unconditionally. We may not win the election or be famous, but we will know that we believe in civility and respect for all people young and old and we will do everything we can to teach children to treat each others politely and correctly.

It may never be as loud or as exciting but respect and politeness never goes out of style. I thank you for your time in reading this thought.

Have a great week!   John

Thought for the Week – November 20, 2006

What are you thankful for? If you ask most people, they will give the usual answers which include family, spouse, children, and home. We may also include our job (or jobs that our children have), our health (or health insurance), and friends (a usually overlooked blessing.)

Are you also thankful for your challenges?

Every challenge that we face in life makes us smarter, stronger and more adept. We do not stress at little things and appreciate what we have more. We realize what is important and become the older and wiser person our parents always wanted us to be.

Every challenge gives us more experience and pushes us to use all our intellect, patience and energy to solve problems, fix a mistake, recuperate from an illness, or help others through tough times.

Every challenge gives us a chance to improve and be better at our job; our life; our faith.

It is the time of year to take the time and be with family and say thanks for what we have been given. Let's be thankful for our blessings, our family and our friends. Let's also be thankful for those daily challenges. They give our lives meaning and change our lives in many ways.

Happy Thanksgiving to you all; You are all true blessings to me.

John

Thought for the Week – November 27, 2006

For those of you who believe that when a butterfly flaps his wings in South America, it has an impact somewhere else on the planet, then you will believe that the reason that I cannot sleep late on Saturday morning's is because I had my trees trimmed last March.

Allow me to explain.

I had the trees trimmed because there were limbs hanging over my house. After the hurricane season of 2005, I felt it was a prudent thing to do. (Even though if we had a hurricane hit here, even cutting the trees way back would not help me. However, it made me feel better.) About a month ago, I was awakened at dawn one Saturday by large thumps heard on my roof. It was followed by several other thumps at various volume levels. I knew it couldn't be fallen tree limbs. There was no wind and the trees had been trimmed.

I went outside to see what was making the noise. (And to make sure that the sound was not coming from my attic.) I saw several squirrels jumping from the newly trimmed tree limbs to the roof of my house. They then jumped from the other side of my roof to a tree in the back yard. These very well-fed squirrels had adjusted to the loss of their elevated tree-roadway and were now studying aerodynamics and waking me up at dawn on the weekends. They have not let the trimmed trees interfere with their heavy eating, fat building escapades.

Adjusting to changes in our lives can be challenging. Certainly, they are more complicated than squirrels adjusting to the loss of their transit system. However, we can take a lesson from them. They made the adjustment and they are fat and happy.

So if you trim your trees, you will not be able to sleep late.

Some say that if you see fat squirrels you will have a long cold winter. If that does happen, it was probably caused by a Chilean butterfly sometime last year.

Have a great week!

John

Thought for the Week – December 4, 2006

Many years ago, I worked for an Associate Superintendent named Dr. Marie Canty. She was quiet, intelligent, personable and driven. She knew everyone by name and made a point to ask each person how they were doing. Dr. Canty never seemed to be stressed or at least she never took her stress out on the people she worked with. She was always dignified, calm and polite.

I learned a great deal from her by just watching her.

However, she had a greater gift: Anyone who worked for her wanted to please her. They didn't want to disappoint her in any way. We worked extra hard for this quietly strong individual. We enjoyed the hard work; it seemed worth it; we felt valued and appreciated.

I still strive to inspire people like Dr. Canty. It is not easy to do. We are more apt to fall into a different form of leadership. We may try the "Follow me and love me or else" management style. We may even try the leadership by control philosophy. This is a management by timeline philosophy that revels in calendars and time frames.

Dr. Canty taught me that you cannot be a leader if no on is following you. Just because a group of people are following you don't mean they are followers. They may just want you to get hit first.

Why did we want to follow Dr. Canty? She was knowledgeable, honest, quietly strong, unflappable, hard-working, patient, caring, and seemed to enjoy her profession. She never stopped teaching and she wanted us to be successful. She was the best!

Who can we lead today? How can we lead today? Who can we inspire so that years from now they will think of us as the best teacher, principal, or boss they ever had?

Everyone needs a role model. How about us?

Have a great week!

John

Thought for the Week – December 11, 2006

I recently asked a group of fifth graders, "How many of you have ever seen or heard an LP? You know a record?" No one raised their hands but after I had given it the appropriate wait time, a few stated that they had heard of them.

It was like I had mentioned the Dead Sea Scrolls.

For these ten or eleven year olds, they have never known anything but the digital age. They were born after the compact disc was invented and records are meant to be scratched by rap artists or disc jockeys (trying to be rap artists). They have teethed on computer floppy discs and been weaned on computer lap tops. Most know or own their own flash drives and have MP3 players or IPODS. Most never had to take a long car ride without the joy of a portable DVD player; (We had to count cars or do license plate bingo.) Many spend time writing in My Space and have developed their own web page. Some have more things on their internet favorites list than I know exist.

No wonder they don't know what a record is!

No wonder they want more technology in the classroom!

We cannot allow our students to literally take a history lesson every time they walk into our classrooms. We cannot allow them to leave their technology at the school house door because we don't know how to incorporate it into our lesson plans or understand all the lingo. We can learn; they did. It seems to be part of their DNA.

If we do not use at least a minimum amount of technology in our classrooms, we can expect our students to be bored, act bored, and not achieve at the highest level they can. Our students should not have better technology driving in a car than they do sitting in a classroom. We need to invest in the technology, use the technology and ask our students to be involved in the selection of the technology.

I have a large record collection and I enjoy playing them. But I know that eventually they will go the way of the ice box (with a real ice block in it), rotary phone and black and white television. That is progress and I would rather have the refrigerator, cell phone and television in HD.

We enjoy technology. Let's use it in the classroom and our students will enjoy it and learn more too!

Have a great week!   John

Thought for the Week – December 18, 2006

Years ago, there used to be a radio station that had the wonderful tag line – "The soundtrack of your life!" I thought it was great. It promoted itself as the music everyone needed to have around them all day long. It was a pretty good radio station too. It was positive and eclectic; it was inspiring and nostalgic; it wasn't afraid to play golden oldies and new standards. If you didn't particularly like a song, all you had to do was wait three minutes and new selection would be coming on the air. No one talked over the music or talked down to the audience. The music was the show and it was a great show!

I like music playing all the time. I like music playing in classrooms and hallways; in cars and in malls; in airports and restaurants. I even like the Direct TV music channels.

What is the soundtrack to your life? Do you have something inspirational and positive playing in the background? Do you have something playing that fights the drone of negativity and pessimism away? Do you have it turned up loud enough to drown out boredom and cynicism?

There is some great music out there and it can inspire, renew and rejuvenate your heart, your soul and your mind.

Find the right soundtrack to your life and let it play loud and clear.

During this holiday season, I wish you peace, joy and love. I hope you receive many gifts; you are mine.

Happy 2007!

John

Thought for the Week – January 3, 2007

Yesterday I watched the funeral of President Gerald R. Ford. I was impressed with the solemn yet simple proceedings that paid a respectful "well done" to a former leader of the United States of America. It was dignified; it was bipartisan; it was government at its best.

During the eulogies and the never ending commentary, President Ford was described as polite, mild-mannered, civil and caring. We were reminded that after a day of battling with congress on a bill or an initiative he could leave his work in the oval office and invite his political adversaries to the White House for dinner. He was a gentleman politician before such a term was an oxymoron.

They spoke more about his civility than they talked about his pardoning of Richard Nixon and the subsequent political backlash. Why? I believe it was because we miss the good ol' days when politicians understood they represented not only themselves but their constituency, their state and their country. The office required a code of conduct and ethics that was just as important as the laws they may enact and the speeches they might deliver. Differences of opinions and the sharing of varying viewpoints were celebrated as a representation our coalition government. It was a way to demonstrate why our system works. (It wouldn't go over well on cable television.)

Why do we revere and honor honest, hard-working, civil and polite people once they are gone and find them boring and inconsequential when they are alive? Maybe we realize that one of the really good guys deserves an appropriate and respectful thank you from a grateful nation. The way one treats another does make a difference.

Saying thank you is never a rude or selfish thing to do. Saying thank you to a former president is a very important and meaningful thing to do. It is the American way!

Have a great week!

John

Thought for the Week – January 8, 2007

Our grandchildren, (with their parents), were able to spend a few days with us during the holidays. We were able to be together for Christmas morning. To have a 4 year old and 8 year old around sharing their anticipation and excitement really energized the house. It reminded us of how much fun and family oriented December is supposed to be.

Every time Andrew, the four year old, opened a gift he would yell out, "That's just what I wanted!" He even at one point looked up in the sky while hugging a newly opened gift and whispered, "Thank you Santa!" It didn't matter whether it was toys or books or clothes. Andrew was excited and thankful. Many pictures were taken to document the excitement and happiness that morning.

It is difficult in our daily lives to be as excited as a four year old on Christmas morning. However, are we thankful for the daily gifts we are given? Do we open our classroom or school door with the same anticipation as a child opens a gift? Are we as grateful for our daily blessings and our daily challenges?

Even though the kids were only here for a few days, I feel that this past holiday season will go down in family history as one of the best in my life. The happiness, the laughter, the time together was important, needed and fun.

Time passes so fast and kids grow up even faster. Let's take the time in our busy days to look up and say thank you for all the things we have been given. Let's enjoy each day and each other as the gift it is!

Have a great week!

John

Thought for the Week – January 16, 2007

My dog will be 16 years old on Thursday. I got him when he was only 6 weeks old and he has been a good friend every since. He has never been mean or grumpy. He has never bitten anyone. (He may have attempted to lick someone to death.) He has never needed much to make him happy. He has a big yard to run in, another dog to play with, (When he feels like it.), a cool spot to lay in and daily pats on the head.

Sixteen years is a long life for a Labrador retriever.

Kingdog, (I didn't name him.), is beginning to slow down. He doesn't chase things all the way to the end of the backyard anymore because he knows he has to walk all the way back. His sight is not as good as it used to be and either his hearing is beginning to fade or he just doesn't want to acknowledge me. (I choose B.) His hips are so curve that if he was turned anymore, he be constantly walking in a circle. Sometimes he goes outside and turns around with a look that says he forgot why he went out there. However, all his bodily functions are working well and he always seems happy and content.

We can learn something from an old dog.

No matter how he feels from day to day, Kingdog finds a way to be happy and to enjoy the day. He is thrilled to be with us and excited about the day. He enjoys the simple things like laying his head on your feet or eating popcorn with the rest of the family. He is the best!

Although we do not have a dog's life, we can decide whether to be happy or not each day. Every time I look at my old dog, he makes me smile and feel good about the day. Let's try to do the same for each other every day we are together.

Happy Birthday K-Dog.

Have a great week!

John

There are no Thoughts for the Week during this time period. My wife Patricia died on February 12, 2007 at 7:45 p.m. She died under hospice care in her own home while her brother and mother and I prayed for her as we stood around her bed.

Patricia died of cancer and from that first Thought for the Week in 2005 where I shared with you her battle with blood clots, we had been together fighting for her life. The clots were caused by the lung cancer and the chemotherapy and the lung cancer finally took her life after a year and a half of fighting.

We had just celebrated a nice Christmas season and Patricia seemed to rally for the children and grandchildren who came to visit. Patricia seemed to weaken right after that. As I look back, it is hard to believe less than two months later, she would be gone.

I had gone to see the oncologist in early January. Patricia was too weak to go, so I went by myself. The oncologist said that the cancer had moved to the bones and that they had tried as much as they could. I ask him how much time Patricia had. The doctor said three months. I cried driving home.

I didn't let Patricia know what the doctor said. I decided to see what the good Lord had planned. In a few short weeks, I had a conversation about having hospice come in due to her pain level. She said yes and then we took the time to plan her funeral. She didn't want anything too long because the little ones would be put through too much. Some special songs and some funny stories were what she wanted. We did exactly that.

The days before Patricia died the house was full of family members and friends. The day after she passed, the house was empty and I was alone. I was devastated and numb and I had lost the most important person in my life.

So I began to walk around my neighborhood. I walked and I prayed and I thought and I went through every stage of grief. I wept, I got angry, I drank, I slept and I lost myself in my work. It was hard being the care taker of Patricia when she was sick and I knew she was no longer in pain. I also hated being without her. For the first time in 15 years, I was living alone with just my dogs and my pain and my memories.

That is why I did not write another Thought for the Week until the beginning of the following school year. At that time, I felt like I needed it for my own sanity.

They begin in August 2007.

Thought for the Week – August 6, 2007

I was recently at Oglethorpe Mall to do some clothes shopping, (every five years whether I need it or not), and I stopped at the food court to get some lunch.

While I was eating a group of soldiers from Hunter came in and ordered their food and sat down close by. Two of them were older than the other one and they were having a great time breaking the new guy in. It was good to see the soldiers laugh.

From across the food court, a little boy no older than five walked timidly up to the soldier's table and respectfully excused himself and then thanked the soldiers for their hard work and sacrifice for the country. The soldiers smiled and spoke to him with equal respect, shook his hand and answered his questions about being a soldier. The whole conversation lasted no more than three minutes but the look on the child's face was one of true happiness.

He was happy that he had taken the time to thank the soldiers for their hard work.

Do we take the time to thank the hard workers around us? Do we take the time to see the sacrifices they make for their families, students and friends? Have we experienced the happiness that comes from thanking others? If a five year old knows this joy than shouldn't we?

As we begin another year and we face the everyday challenges and goals that define the education profession, let's remember to say thank you frequently and receive thanks graciously and with appreciation.

I thank you all for being my colleagues and choosing education as a profession. It is a noble profession because you are noble practitioners.

Have a great week!

John

Thought for the Week – August 20, 2007

   Last Saturday amidst the hoard of visitors, vendors and performers, I noticed an action that was common to every school and every principal – There were people hugging all over the place!

   We received and gave out hugs to current students and alumni; to old friends and new acquaintances; to co-workers and community members. We were showing our sincere affection for people we were seeing again. Every child who found someone they recognized hugged them enthusiastically and happily.

   We must be doing a lot right.

   When we see students that we pushed to excel and challenged them to behave and achieve at a high level and they come up and hug us like a dear friend; that is special.

   We must be doing a lot right.

   When we see alumni and they tell us with excitement where they will be attending school in the fall or what classes they will be taking or how much they miss us.

   We must be doing a lot right.

   Let's remember the warmth of these hugs as we begin this new school year. They will give us the strength and support to go on and achieve. Let us remember to give hugs too. It is sometimes the best gift you can give.

   Have a great week!

   John

Thought for the Week – August 28, 2007

Last Saturday between the rain drops, I worked on weeding my yard. I spent several hours on this noble effort and gathered up enough vines, weeds and other flora and fauna to fill in two large trash bags.

As I looked out on what I had accomplished, the yard didn't look any different than when I started. If someone had walked outside, they wouldn't be able to tell me what I had done. A great deal of hard work with little visible sign of improvement!

Sometimes our daily work is that way. We work hard and tirelessly to help our students and each other. We sweat and toil to do things we need to do and help the ones that need the most help. We do everything we can and yet, we don't see much improvement some days.

Sometimes it takes several days or weeks of hard work to see the improvement we want to see. Not all good works show immediate results. Not all instruction brings immediate mastery.

Some journeys are longer than others but the destination is worth reaching.

Keep working toward the prize and believe that you will reach your destination. As for me, next Saturday I'll be back in yard to continue the work.

Have a great week!

John

Thought for the Week – September 4, 2007

On Saturday, at Virginia Tech, the Hokie nation shared tears, hope and love as they remembered the April tragedy and the lives lost on that awful day. All the coaches and administrators kept saying the same thing: "It is just a game; it is the fact we are together as a family and supporting each other that is important."

It was a well organized, sincere and heartfelt memorial celebration.

It wasn't just another game. It was a sign that they would persevere. That college life will continue even as they remember the fallen. That one person would not be allowed to ruin everyone's life. It was just a football game but it was important for what it represented beyond the game.

Today we start another school year. We could look at it as another opening day with the same transportation hassles and the same nervous teachers and students, (and principals). Yet, it is not just another opening. It is the people around us that will make it different. It is how we take care of each and support each other even during the tough times that will make a difference. We know how to teach; we need to know how to care.

Since April 2007, we have heard the repeated mantra: We are Virginia Tech; we will prevail. Let's paraphrase that for us and make a mantra of our own – We will be successful; we will prevail; we are the best!

Have a great week!

John

<u>Thought for the Week – September 10, 2007</u>

We can tell it is September. The morning and evening shadows look different than a month ago. The breeze feels slightly stronger; the humidity lower. We can't help but remember past Septembers.

Autumn is a time to remember. You remember the falling leaves, the football games, the high school dances, the half time shows, and the fall festivals. You remember when you were little and September meant the gateway to the fall holidays. We knew that it was the preamble to Halloween, Thanksgiving and Christmas. We knew that the last four months of the calendar year would be so much faster than the previous eight. We knew that it would be the most exciting part of the year.

How do we feel about September now? Have we become so mature and busy that we cannot remember how it used to feel? Do we feel so stressed that we cannot feel the excitement that this time of year brings?

Each season of the year can bring a chance to start over and feel renewed. It gives us a chance to be excited about meeting each morning and inspired with every sunset. I hope you enjoy every minute of this fall season. Feel the breeze and enjoy each day. Remember in a few short years, you may look back on the fall of 2007 as one of the best of your life!

Have a great week!

John

Thought for the Week – September 17, 2007

I was driving home one day last week and I decided to take a different way home. Sometimes it is good to change a routine and do something to shake things up. Brain research says that it wakes the brain up after a long day. (There are some days that I really need my brain awakened.)

As I was heading east, I noticed in almost a totally clear sky, one lone cloud and below that cloud was a wonderfully colored rainbow surrounded by a beautiful azure blue sky.

It was an unexpected surprise. It was an inspiring sight at the end of an uninspiring day. I was enthralled by it. I even slowed down to look at it longer. The drivers behind me were not as excited. They started to go around me and blow their horns and go around me angrily.

They missed the view. They missed more than that.

It was September 11, 2007.

Sometimes we need a reminder that we can endure through the toughest of times. We can see the beauty around us again. We can remember the painful times while we can also find strength in the good memories. We can find strength in the friends around us even though other dear friends are no longer with us.

Let's keep looking for the rainbows. Let's not be in such a hurry that we would rather speed through life rather than slow down and enjoy the special moments.

Some people would say, "It was just a rainbow!" That's like saying, "September 11th is just another day!"

Have a great week!

John

Thought for the Week – October 8, 2007

I had the pleasure and honor of attending my nephew's wedding last weekend. It had a special mixture of warm weather with fall colors. It was great to see all the extended family together for a happy occasion. There was laughter and smiles; tears of joy and tears of remembrance. It was a great weekend!

At one point during the ceremony, the priest turned and spoke directly to the soon to be married couple. With kindness he urged them to have a "vocation for marriage and vocation to love each other." In other words, marriage and love is hard work.

Something as important as a marriage and a life time of fulfillment takes hard work and effort. It is a labor of love and worth every minute. It shouldn't surprise us that the things that mean the most to us deserve the most effort.

There is happily ever after but not in the fairy tale way. Happily ever after is worked on every day, side by side, hand in hand, heart to heart, and soul to soul. It is the time spent listening and helping when together. It is the time that you miss them when you aren't together. It is the time you call or write a note when you miss them.

Love and marriage is a wonderfully rewarding and fulfilling job!

Whey wouldn't it be; it is the most important thing you do in your life.

Have a great week!

John

Thought for the Week – October 15, 2007

My sister, a veteran teacher of thirty years, recently found out that she had breast cancer and has begun chemotherapy treatments. She has over 200 days of sick leave that she has accrued, (probably due to years of coming to work with a bad cold or flu symptoms). She has worked for the same school system for her entire career and was even teacher of the year for her system several years ago. She is a dedicated, gifted fifth grade teacher.

She called the Human Resource Office in her jurisdiction to get some information on retirement and sick leave.

The people at Human Resources treated her terribly. They questioned whether she was really sick. They spoke to her curtly and with no compassion at all. My very strong sister, who has worked tirelessly for her school system, got off the phone and cried!

Why do educators treat children with great patience and love then treat each other so rudely? We question rather than support; we are condescending rather than inspiring. We are too busy to lend a hand, give a hug, and offer support to the greatest assets we have – our teaching staff.

Are we like that because that is what we see around us? Are we like that because we are so unhappy with our own lives? Shouldn't we be as supportive to each other as we are to the littlest among us?

My sister was looking forward to getting well, (her prognosis is good), coming back to her classroom before the end of the year and helping her fifth graders make AYP again.

She is retiring as soon as possible. She will get better and she will start the next chapter of her life with new challenges and new successes.

She is done working with her school district.

Sometimes you have to take a stand by proudly walking away.
It will be a loss to the school district. I doubt if they will ever realize it.

Have a good week and be nice to each other out there.

John

<u>Thought for the Week – October 23, 2007</u>

This week, a cable news channel presenter mentioned that the presidential candidates of both parties, when meeting in front of a friendly partisan crowd, were making fun of their rivals, calling them names and enjoying every minute of it. This was all the candidates not just a few from one party or the other.

Last week, Chris Matthews of MSNBC's Hardball, had to ask two guests to stop interrupting each other and let the other one finish before speaking.

Last week, I had a parent threaten another one out on my back parking area.

This year I have had grandparents yelling over the phone, slamming the phone down while talking to a staff member. I have had people come into the building and yell at faculty members.

Go to a church parking lot at the end of service and watch how people treat each other after hearing the word of God!

Watch people on the interstate pass someone just because they are not going fast enough or blow their horn or do an obscene gesture thinking that another driver is intentionally ruining their day.

We have lost our civility. We have lost our mutual respect. We have given up the process of true debate where people can share their opinions with dignity.

Disagreeing does not mean you are enemies. It just means that you disagree.

We, as a society, have come to believe that we have to make everyone agree with us.

We feel that we are being disrespected if people don't agree with us. We also believe that if we yell and scream, we will get them to agree with us and then we win.

In a democratic society, we must allow all parties to share their opinions and ideas without threat of being shouted down, drowned out or shut down. It is not wrong for people to have different opinions but it is wrong to prevent others from sharing their own.

We can control public opinion and political decisions in the voting booth. We can control what we watch on television by turning it off or changing the channel. We can control what we read by what we decide to buy. We can control how our children will treat others in the future by how we treat others in front of them.

Civilization means: A group of civil people. It does not mean everyone wearing the same thing or watching the same thing or believing the same things. It is a group of people who believe that everyone should be treated with dignity and respect.

We are having a guest speaker next week. He is going to work with our fifth graders. The subject: Bullying!

Have a great week! Be nice to each other out there.

John

<u>Thought for the Week – November 5, 2007</u>

I had the pleasure of speaking with two lovely young ladies. They were hard working professionals who both worked in retail and both had goals that included advancement, investment and contributing positively to society.

They both had degrees in education. They both decided that they would never work in education.

They had seen their friends working long hours, under extreme pressure to master and teach the standards, dealing with rude or angry parents, under-supported students and high-energy principals.

We couldn't even use the joke about having the summer off. They told me about the classes teachers had to take and the summer job they would need to pay for the classes they were required to take.

It is a sad commentary when retail looks more attractive than a job in education to young people. It is concerning when we have to go outside the country to recruit new teachers. It is also especially concerning when many of our teachers and administrators will be retiring soon.

Who will dedicate themselves to this very important profession? Who will ignore the bad press and be independent enough to take on this noble and necessary profession?

Sometime this week, go up to the younger teachers you work with and thank them for their hard work and dedication. Thank them for their extra work; for their late nights; for their strength and perseverance. If we don't support our new teachers they may become like the two young ladies I met: Hard working, dedicated and working at something other than education.

Have a great week!

John

Thought for the Week – November 13, 2007

The October issue of Smithsonian Magazine had a wonderful article on individuals under the age of 35 that are making a difference. These people were incredibly bright and dedicated to learning more and achieving at higher levels. They were working in the fields of environmental science, energy, health care, small business, pharmaceuticals, etc. Their goal was to help individuals specifically and society in general.

This post baby-boomer generation was very impressive, very knowledgeable and very caring about their world. Most of them also received their education in the USA!

These young professionals are examples of educational successes that we don't normally hear about. We are too busy discussing the negative aspects of American Education.

It is important to focus on the drop-out rate in high school that is too high and restructure the American High School to meet the needs of twenty-first century students. It is important to help our students learn more faster and earlier so they can be successful in a high school program that will ask them to do more and know more than we did.

However, it is also important to celebrate and recognize the successes and notice the achievements of hard working well-educated thirty-something's.

How well do you know the successful young students around you? Have we become so concerned with the challenged students, (and rightly so), that we fail to congratulate the students who work hard, behave and achieve?

Let's take some time this week to thank the ones that are so easily forgotten in the age of testing, assessment, No Child Left Behind and committee meetings. They will be the scholars of their generation and our greatest successes.

Have a great week!

John

Thought for the Week – November 19, 2007

What gives you the strength to get up in the morning and face another day? Who gives you the inspiration to not just hold a job but to work in a profession you care about deeply? Why do you care so much that you are your own worst critic? Why do you work so hard when public education is slammed daily?

I am thankful for the person or the faith that gives you the strength to be an educator.

I am thankful for the family or the individual that gives you the inspiration to be the professional you are and pushes you toward excellence.

I am thankful for the way you percolate over decisions and lose sleep over children in need.

I am thankful for the way you kick yourself when you feel you could have done a little better.

I am thankful that you care enough to ignore public opinion and work in this noble profession.

I am thankful that you persevere.

I am thankful that you give your all.

I am thankful you are here.

I am thankful you are an educator!

Have a great Thanksgiving.

John

Thought for the Week – November 26, 2007

Food, family, football (for most of us), and conversation are the things that holidays are made of! It is the joy of a full house and a full table that makes all the traveling worthwhile.

I have spoken often about how time is the most important gift you can give another. The talks, the laughter, the time spent together are the blessings that we get from our family. This time together lightens our heart and energizes our soul. It gives us strength to meet the challenges of the days to come. It reminds us of what is truly important.

Our school family can do the same thing for us. The time with them and the conversations we have together can lighten our load and re-energize our soul. Our school family can be the greatest support group we have and we can be the greatest support for them.

During the next four weeks, let's use this holiday time to show our appreciation and affection for our school family. Let's remind them how important they are to us. Let's remind them how much they mean to us. Let's remind them of how much support and affection they give us and how much we appreciate their efforts.

During this busy time of the year, let's not take either our school families or our individual families for granted. We need them and they need us. They are the best!

Have a great week!

John

Thought for the Week – December 3, 2007

   My old dog cannot see that well anymore. At least, I don't think he can. This black lab will be 17 in January, (or gray lab to be more accurate), and he has a difficult time focusing or recognizing even familiar things.

   Recently he has had a difficult time discerning whether the back door is open or closed. He cannot see if there is any food left in his food bowl and sometimes he falls over the other dog who likes sleeping in his general vicinity.

   He has found a way to cope with his declining vision: He barks. He has that old guttural bark that sounds like a tired, raspy "woof". He "woofs" to ask a question. (Like is the back door open or not?) He "woofs" to get people and the other dog to move so he won't fall down. He "woofs" when he needs water and he "woofs" if he wants attention. The old dog has made adjustments to his lifestyle.

   How many kids do we know that bark because they don't see or understand what you are teaching them? How many bark because something is blocking their way to learning? (Learning disabilities, family problems, a feeling that no one cares.)

   Just like my old dog, kids bark to say, "Help me be safe! Help me get it! Help me be successful! Help me like myself!"

   Let's listen to our barkers and find out what their "woofs" mean. Let's help them make adjustments to their lives. If we do, they can have a long and happy life too!

   I guess we can learn new tricks from an old dog!

   Have a great week!

   John

Thought for the week – December 10, 2007

Members of my church decorated last week in preparation for the Advent Season. (I donated a 6 foot fiber optic tree and another family brought in a 9 foot tree!)These wonderful volunteers tastefully used lights, decorations, new banners, wreaths and candles to beautify the space. When it was completed, it looked like a totally different church.

When people began arriving yesterday for the service, one child, who was about eight years old stated very excitedly, "The place looks so much bigger. Look at all the stuff in here!"

The room was the same size as before and yet with two trees, numerous wall hangings and ornaments; with candles and extension cords, to this little child the church space seemed to have grown into the season.

Our minds are like that too. The more we add to it, the more open minded and intuitive we become. The more we know, the more we want to know and understanding more things, enable us to comprehend more material, master more curriculum, and demonstrate more standards.

We must not be afraid to give all students various ways to learn and various ways to show what they have mastered. In this way, our students can feel about their minds and their lives the way that little child felt about the decorated church: Look at all the stuff in here and look at how I've grown!

Have a great week!

John

Thought for the Week – January 2, 2008
_____

I have always been amazed at how one digit can change our feelings about numbers. Forty sounds a lot more than thirty-nine. Fifty sounds a lot more than forty-nine. (A great deal more) Stores sell things for $2.99 because it sounds less than $3.00 and then there are the infomercials that sell most things for $19.95. (But wait there's more!)

I remember as a youth figuring out how old I would be in the year 2000. I wondered what I would be doing and where I would be living and how my life would be at that time. I mused about an unseen future with anticipation and excitement.

January 1, 2008 sounded a lot older than December 31, 2007. Maybe it was because 2007 seemed longer than most. The year was over. It was expected, but it seemed still like a surprise...that time still goes on.

As this New Year gets older and we get used to writing 2008 on newsletters and checks, may it bring you happiness and contentment. May your challenges be met with ease and confidence and may your friends be there for you as you are for them.

Happy New Year!

Have a great week!

John

Thought for the Week – January 7, 2008

A friend of mine told me about a new philosophy coming from California, (where else?). It promotes the idea of being happy all the time. That if we are happy, we will live longer, that a positive outlook will help individuals, or families or businesses be successful.

It is an interesting concept and I believe in the power of positive thinking. However, it is just as wrong to be an eternal optimist as it is to be an eternal pessimist. Sometimes we need to look at thing realistically. We need to look at things clearly without bias and make decisions that are in the best interest of our family, our staff, our classroom and our district.

It is actually harder to look at things realistically. It is much easier to take one side or the other: Either be over critical or Polly Anna a situation. To look at all sides and weigh options, and make the best decision at the time is difficult in an age of "blink" decision making.

I understand the purpose of the being happy movement. It is to fight the negativity that hits us every day in the media, in advertising and our presidential candidates. Many are tired of the name calling, bullying banter between guests and audiences alike.

As I have mentioned before in these weekly missives, they aren't asking really for eternal happiness. They want civility; they want a polite society; they want public discussions about differences of opinion and not defamation of character. They want tolerance and respect in an age of impatience. They want optimism in an age of uncertainty. They want ingenuity in an age of stubbornness.

If we can get even one of these things, we will be better people and we will have become a better nation.

That would make me happy!

Have a great week.

John

<u>Thought for the Week – January 21, 2008</u>

We had a great send off for Dr. Shirley McGee-Brown on Friday. It was called a home-going. I loved that term. The singing and music was wonderful, the speeches were from the heart and the prayers were moving and full of joy.

Her daughter said that Shirley didn't understand why her life was ending but she was at peace and happy.

I am reminded on this Martin Luther King's birthday of one of his most famous quotes: "A person is judged by the content of his character." No one who ever knew Shirley McGee-Brown, worked with her and prayed with her could ever question the content of her character. She was a child of God. She lived as a child of God. She fought cancer as a child of God. She passed as a child of God. She went home to God.

I wish for all of us to have the same kind of send off and home-going when it is our time. That of course, will be up to the content of our characters.

Have a great week!

John

Thought for the Week – February 4, 2008

   After the Super Bowl last night, one of the commentators said that the difference between the Giants and the Patriots was "execution". The Giants did what they had to do in the way it was supposed to be done at the time it was supposed to be done.

   In the book, Execution, by Bossidy and Charan it mentions 7 essential behaviors. Among them was, Set Clear Priorities, Follow Through, and Insist on Realism. In education and other walks of life, we set clear priorities but do not look at what we need to do in "real" way and we don't follow through. We have difficulty making the tough decisions and adjusting to the information we receive. When we are asked if we are successful or doing this or that, we answer: "Absolutely, we are right on track." The answer should be: "We have set the following goals and this is how we are working to get there and these are the adjustments we have made as we have gone through this year.

   We praise coaches who adjust as the game goes on, but we don't think of doing the same thing as an educator, administrator or counselor.

   Execution is the key and realism will give us the direction to go and the adjustments to make. There is nothing wrong with making adjustments. Without this kind of follow through our students will never be as successful as we want them to be.

   Let's be real, set viable priorities, follow through with tough decisions, and execute!

   Have a great week!

   John

Thought for the Week – February 11, 2008

You can learn a great deal about yourself in a year's time. You can learn how to deal with loss. You can learn how to do things on your own again. You can learn to become a better cook. You can learn how to pray more, appreciate more, laugh more, and read more.

You can learn in a year's time how to see things differently. You can learn to value the right things and put things in their correct perspective. You can learn to find strength that you didn't know was there.

What have I learned in a year? I have learned that friends and family are more important that the stuff you have in your house. That the school family belongs to that extended group too! I have learned that memories are not bad things. They can make you laugh or cry and both are good things. I have learned that a picture can be the connection between the past, present and future. I have learned to value each day and to see my friends and colleagues as precious gifts. They provide the strength to face another day and the excitement of looking forward to tomorrow.

What will I learn in another year? I will find out. I thank you for supporting me through the last one and I thank God for the opportunity to work with each of you every day!

Have a great week!

John

Thought for the Week – February 19, 2008

Once again, we are stunned to hear about violence at a college campus. More young, innocent lives lost, another tortured soul pushed to hurt people, parents grieving, fellow students wondering why, and pundits questioning whether the college did enough.

What is worse is that as we experience more of these senseless, unexplainable actions, we are becoming numb to them. We shake our head and then go on back to our lives and thank God that it happened in another state and hope that is doesn't happen here.

It is terrible when it happens anywhere! When young people hurt other young people, we have to look around and ask: What did I miss? What should I have seen? Why did we let our students down?

We can add state of the art cameras and metal detectors and add more police officers, but somebody still has to care about the kids who go there. We need to be vigilant to help students who need help, to offer mental health assistance and work to create small supportive communities all over large college campuses.

We need to create a caring, nurturing environment on our college campuses so that all students feel comfortable asking for help, getting help and giving assistance.

We cannot accept this action as another random act of violence. There has been too many to be random and these are too horrific to accept them as isolated incidents. Try telling that to the families at Virginia Tech and now the families at NIU.

Every family that is planning on sending their child away to college needs to know what safety procedures are in place and if they practice lock-downs. They need to know how well the dorms are secure and how many police officers are on campus during the day and night.

I remember the good old days when I sat down and read about the types of degrees universities offered, classes that needed to be taken every semester and the backgrounds of the professors. If my sons were going to college now, I would be interviewing the college on its safety record. We need to ask these questions. If we don't we will be seeing more candles and flowers at impromptu shrines in honor of other lost scholars.

Have a safe week!

John

Thought for the Week – February 25, 2008

On Saturday, I had the pleasure of volunteering for my church at the new Lowe's in Pooler. We hosted seed planting sessions from 10:00 a.m. – 2:00 p.m. We showed children how to start seeds in a plastic cup that they could later plant in larger pots or in the ground.

While I was helping two of my younger students, (they were working quietly and diligently), they looked up in surprise and said, "You're Mr. King! We didn't recognize you in disguise!" (I was wearing jeans and a tee-shirt.)

After laughing, I realized that sometimes we are recognized by what we wear as well as what we do. The shirt and tie is my uniform and when I am not in it, (or if I have dirt all over my hands.), I don't look the same.

Although clothes make the person, it doesn't define the person. The old adage, don't judge a book by its cover, should pertain to people as well. How many times do we judge other people and even children based on how they dress or how they look? How many future leaders and scholars are around us in "disguise"?

Let's spend some time today looking for students and adults that are hiding in plain view. It may be as surprising to you as it was to my two little ones who saw me in a different way, at a different place and at a different time.

Have a great week!

John

Thought for the Week – March 4, 2008

   I visited some friends on Sunday afternoon. There was a younger couple there too with a young son. As I entered the house, all the guys were competing in a contest to see who could make the best paper airplane.

   Not to be left out of this worthwhile science experiment, I tried my hand at it too. I didn't do too well, (it had been a while), but the time was full of laughter and fun even when we scared the dog, knocked over a plant and lost one behind a large piece of furniture. (To be found sometime in the future when we forget how it got there.)

   Some people may look on this as a waste of time; I look at it as time well spent!

   It showed a little boy that it is okay to play. It is okay sometimes to throw paper airplanes in the house. It is okay sometimes to laugh with friends and forget the stresses of the day. It is also okay for older boys to remember how much fun it is to play too!

   Let's take some time this week to play, to laugh and to not feel guilty about it when we do. I know you are going to work hard. It is okay to play hard too!

   Have a great week!

   John

Thought for the Week – March 11, 2008
<u>_____</u>

Recently, I fixed, cleaned up and filled my neglected bird feeders, (or squirrel feeders if you wish). For several days there seemed to be no takers to these spruced up seed machines. Then I noticed yesterday that to be successful with these bird feeders, team work was necessary.

The first thing I noticed was the little red bird feeder, (filled with thistle seed just so you know). It was being shaken vigorously by a fat squirrel so that other fat squirrels could gather up the seeds and run off with them. They took turns in being the shakers and takers and I had to be quite impressed. (I just don't know if their cholesterol will be going up along with their weight.)

The second thing I noticed was large woodpecker beating the heck out of one of the plastic hanging bird feeders. It would beat it until the seed came out the other end and his partner would gather the seed up for their nest. You couldn't miss him, it sounded like a jackhammer. They came back several times until they got the amount of seed they wanted.

We talk and promote team work all the time but these guys do it naturally. They realize they cannot do it alone and are willing to give and accept help and support. In the end, everyone got fed. (Although I have one torn up bird feeder)

None of us can do this job alone. We need to accept help and give help and do it for the good of the children; the class; the community; the school. It is amazing what we can gain when we give freely. It is equally amazing what we can give when we believe in helping each other.

Mother Nature got it right!

Have a great week!

John

Thought for the Week – March 17, 2008

Someone once stated, "Everything in moderation." The weather over the weekend is a perfect example. If the wind blows at a certain speed, it can move the clouds away, clear the sky, and invigorate our souls. If it blows a little harder, it can push dust and pollen into our eyes and on our furniture. If it blows even harder, it can level trees, tear down buildings and be incredibly frightening.

The same is true for believing in a particular way of teaching. If we use this strategy as part of a comprehensive program, then we are meeting the needs of all our students. If we become more inflexible in the use of other strategies, we can feel comfortable about our efforts but the children who do not learn in that way may be left out. If we push our way even harder to the exclusion of other strategies, the total success of the class will be in jeopardy.

As scholars, we must use any and all strategies available that are matched to the students we have on any given day. We cannot push one strategy over another and not expect it to tear down student's confidence or make them afraid of "not succeeding".

Let's be just as prepared to instruct our students in as many ways as possible as we are to protect them when bad weather occurs. Both will ensure their success in the future.

Have a great week!

John

Thought for the Week – March 24, 2008

    I played for our Easter Sunday service. It was outside and beautiful. (It was a little breezy too.) At the end of the service, several members of the congregation came up to talk about the music and wished me a happy Easter. One of the members, a gentleman I have known for a number of years, told me to wait around a minute.

    I noticed that he was wearing a very nice tie. It has music symbols and clef signs. It looked good on him. I didn't say anything to him about the tie. (I have plenty of ties.) He came back after a few minutes and gave me the tie! He said, "Every time I see the tie, I think of you and every time I see you, I think of the tie. It just has to be yours."

    I was overwhelmed. All I could do was accept the tie. I didn't feel that I could turn down such a generous offer on such an important Sunday.

    As you look at your students, or your grade level or your school, how many of you know, by looking, what the children need? Do you see that some need encouragement; some need a hug; some need to be pushed; some need a shoulder to cry on; some just need you to notice them. How often are we generous with our things? How often are we generous with our love? How often are we generous with our time? How often do we notice others being generous with us?

    We teach others how to act by how we act. We can learn or be reminded of the importance of being generous through a kind deed, time spent in conversation or concern, or even by giving someone a simple but elegant gift - like a tie.

    Have a great week!

    John

Thought for the Week – March 31, 2008

Last Friday, several of our staff members participated in the West Chatham Relay for Life. It is an evening of walking in remembrance of loved ones who have died of cancer; in honor of those who are battling this terrible disease; in tribute to those who survived it.

All groups who participated raised money for the American Cancer Society. Our group raised money via a silent auction, pledges and donations. There was exercise, food, laughter and a few tears.

During each lap we saw the names of our loved ones lit up in form of luminaries that guided our way and touched our hearts and tugged at our memories.

It was a wonderful evening with wonderful people doing an incredible job for an important cause.

There were many educators there. Educators are wonderful people, doing an incredible job for an important cause. They do it for their students. They do it for their families. They do it for their communities. They expect nothing in return because they are determined to be successful in everything they do. They believe that helping others is part of their makeup – it is what they do.

A group of wonderful people who each and every day, do an incredible job, for an important cause. They are already talking about how to do better next year.

Sounds like teachers to me.

Have a great week!

John

Thought for the Week – April 14, 2008

My mom turned 80 on the twelfth of April. A few short months ago, many of us didn't think she would make it to this important day. With a new right hip and a new left hip she has more metal in her than the bionic woman. Mom even joked that after all the procedures she was shorter than she used to be. (She wasn't tall to begin with.)

Her voice was full of strength, happiness and stubborn resolve to get up, use her walker, and do what she needed to do to get the job done for the day. She makes lemonade out of lemons and keeps on plugging along.

With my sister now an official cancer survivor, and my mother reaching another birthday, I see two extremely strong women who quietly fight on and show the rest of us how it is done. It doesn't seem right to complain about minor aches and pains or the everyday nuisances of life. Somehow our problems don't seem so bad in comparison.

It is a brighter day!

Have a great week!

John

Thought for the Week – April 21, 2008

There are some large decorative metal fish on the front of my house. They look nice; they really do. I mean I live near the Intracoastal; what else would you put on the front of your house? These metal fish were made to hold candles and look pretty at night. (You realize I didn't buy them or put them up!)

A few days ago, I heard the chirping of birds coming from the fish. A very loud wren family had moved in and the little ones were obviously hungry! So, I have a fish with birds in it!

Actually, the momma bird was very smart. The family is protected from the weather, other birds and the neighborhood cat. (He would have a difficult time working through the metal fish.) The strange part is that if the birds hadn't of moved in, I would not have noticed the fish again in the first place!

We get so used to things being where they are, that we don't see them anymore. We need something to awaken our eyes so that we see them again. Having birds in a fish is really great and it is exciting to see the momma bird flying in and flying out.

How many kids are in our rooms or schools that are here and not seen? How many would need to dye their hair purple or orange to be seen? How many need to be seen by an awakened eye so they know their life is worthwhile and their efforts are important?

Let's look for the unseen this week and listen for the unheard. They may be as exciting as a fish full of birds.

Have a great week!

John

<u>Thought for the Week – April 28, 2008</u>

We had a guest speaker come to school a few weeks ago. She gave a presentation about testing and assessment. Her presentation was comprehensive, informative and well paced.

On her way home, she was pulled over for speeding by one of the local police departments. She apologized to the officer and explained to him that she had just left a school where she completed a presentation about testing and assessment. She also explained that she was reviewing her presentation in her head to make sure that she had covered everything that needed to be covered.

The officer listened intently and asked, "Do you think your presentation will help the children do better on the upcoming tests?" She answered, "I hope it will." The officer handed her his card, wished her a great day and asked her to drive carefully and walked back to his patrol car and drove off!

Just like the presenter, we have reviewed everything we have done this year and we hope that it will lead to academic success. Just like the policeman, our last action will be to hand out the tests, wish everyone a great day and then walk away. We can't do anymore than we already have. We can't pray anymore, work any harder, lose anymore sleep. It is time to let your students show you what they have mastered. It is time for your students to show you what you have done.

Take a deep breath, say a short prayer and believe in what you have done.

You have done well! They will show you!

Have a great week!

John

Thought for the Week – May 5, 2008

Yesterday, as I was getting ready to go to church, I looked out my front window and noticed two squirrels playing tag in my yard. They were both approximately the same size and coloring and they looked like they were having a great time. Until they started to beat the heck out of each other!

This was not the kind of squirrel fight you are picturing in your head right now. No, it was something that I have never seen before. (In many decades of squirrel watching) The two were fighting like small school children. They were rolling on the ground, looking like a small tumbleweed, with their little fists flying at each other's faces. Their fun playful mood had turned into a spiteful, violent, "Whose going to be the top squirrel now?" fiasco. (I would say the squirrels had gone nuts, but that would be going too far.)

This is the time of year when people can lose their tempers and their kind demeanors over the smallest of things. It is what I call, "May feelings". We have worked together in the same classroom or the same school for months. We have prepared for the testing and now we are in the middle of it. The weather has turned warmer and we are just about sick of each other. (Don't deny it; it's true.)

During this Teacher Appreciation Week, let's take the time to thank all of our peers and our colleagues for their hard work and their efforts this year. Nobody else is going to thank them the way we can thank them. We know how hard the job is; we know what dedication it takes to be an educator. Take the time to thank them for all they have done and for all they continue to do. Or at least don't make them nutty like those squirrels. Everyone deserves to celebrate a week dedicated to them!

Have a great week!

John

Thought for the Week – May 12, 2008

The National Aeronautics and Space Administration has invited the public to think of cheaper ways of space travel. They believe there are some young scientists out there that may be able to find a more cost effective way for us to return to the Moon, travel to Mars and go where no one has gone before.

With the current price of gas, I don't think this is a bad idea. There has to be several innovations that we could try or allow independent companies or individuals try them out. It is a way to domestically outsource the resource and development of space travel. It would be a way to connect with our best and brightest.

We could do the same with the development of new teaching and learning strategies. Let's invite our students and our teachers, no matter how experienced or where they happen to work, to give us ideas for making learning and teaching more successful. Let's not only ask them for their thoughts but also try them out. We might discover that a young teacher has found a way for all her students to read on grade level by having them record their reading so they can listen to the story a second time. We might discover that a social studies teacher has found a way for his students to retain historical information for more than week by having impromptu games of Jeopardy. We might discover all kinds of different strategies and success stories.

If we are willing to share; if we are willing to listen; if we are willing try them out.

We are not good at that. We would rather find success on our own.

It might just be easier to find a cheaper way to get to the moon!

Have a great week!

John

Thought for the Week – September 2, 2008

During this past summer, I have had the privilege of meeting a young pastor at my church. His name was Ben. He was spending his summer helping out the church and working with our younger members. As I got to know him better, I found him to be hard-working, positive, spiritual, (duh), kind, and generous with his time and his works.

Ben left yesterday. He has a new job. He is the Chaplain for a circuit of hospitals in the Philadelphia area. He is excited, nervous, anxious to get started, hopeful that he will do a good job, sad about leaving his summer-time friends, and praying for a good year.

How many of our students will be coming to us today with the same hopes and anxiety for the new school year? How many of them will be sad about leaving their summer behind and hopeful that they will do a good job? How many may even be praying for a better year than the previous one?

The beginning of a new career, going to a new town, or even starting a new school year can be exciting and scary at the same time. A positive attitude can be contagious. A kind word can be a day-changing experience. An actively supportive team can make those day-changing experiences, life-changing ones.

Let's start today. Let's start right now! Ben is. We should too!

Have a great week and welcome back!

John

Thought for the Week – September 8, 2008

I recently learned that many colleges and universities not only have co-ed dorms but have multi-generational dorms. They are creating partnerships with assisted living organizations to house senior citizens in the same dorm as their younger counterparts.

These senior citizens take courses, participate in campus activities and discuss course work, politics and anything else their fellow students might bring up.

It is not the idea of multi-generational dorms that is surprising. It is surprising to know that it is appreciated by the younger and the older students.

The older students are energized by the younger ones and the younger ones receive a different point of view from someone other than their parents. It creates a place for intellectual conversation that will lead to more understanding across the decades.

It would fun to watch a young, multi-pierced, tattooed, co-ed having a discussion about World War II with a member of the Greatest Generation (with a crew-cut hair style).

What these colleges have created is a Learning Community that provides an intense learning opportunity. We are not just talking about increasing their academic knowledge but it will also increase their social knowledge and realize that no matter how old someone is, they think deeply and feel intensely.

They will learn from each other and teach each other many things.

Learning is not a one-way street; it is a two-lane highway. We can all continue to learn and continue to teach no matter how old we get.

Have a great week!

John

Thought for the Week – September 15, 2008

A week ago, I had some dead trees cut down so that a hurricane wouldn't do it for me. Of course after the tree service had "finished" the job, I had some other cutting to do so I could move and stack the lumber. That meant I needed to use a chain saw.

I am very respectful of tools that can hurt you and give you nicknames you don't want. I am also very aware that you use these tools in a safe manner and with the right safety equipment because I would like to keep the toes and fingers I was born with.

At one point I had to adjust the chain and I touched the muffler. It was so hot that it burned my finger even through my leather glove! I knew that the muffler was hot and I knew that I shouldn't touch it but I was distracted from the obvious by having to do something no less important. The chain had to be tight to work right but it can be tightened without burning a digit.

How many times in the course of our busy days do we overlook the obvious while we complete something else? Do we miss a child's frustration because we are teaching a lesson? Do we miss a co-worker's sadness while we finish paperwork that was due yesterday? Do we forget to hug or help because we are trying to meet a deadline?

Deadlines are important and good lessons need to be taught. We also need to give a hug to those who need it and help those in need. We don't need to get so busy with our chains that need adjusting that we forget something else and get burned as a result.

We are in this profession because we want to help everyone that comes to us, (big people and little people), and we are capable of changing their lives.

Have a safe and fun week and don't get burned!

John

Thought for the Week – September 22, 2008

As I was driving to church yesterday going down I-16, I saw lying on the pavement near Chatham Parkway, a three to four feet length of bright yellow rope. It was the kind you see tying down boats or other heavy objects. It had knots on either end and was frayed on both ends.

As I continued to drive, I noticed another length of yellow rope two miles down the road. As I drove further along, I noticed another, then another and then another. All in all, I noticed five pieces of this thick rope, all looking the same from the Parkway to I-95!

It was a mystery to be sure. I also found myself looking around to see if I could find a boat on its side or another large object lying askew on the road because the rope that was supposed to be holding it was now spread out over the last ten miles.

Obviously it was used for something and obviously it was now not where it was supposed to be but, what did it mean?

Metaphors like the "tie that binds", and "tying one on", may be humorous but they do not really solve the mystery. Some mysteries may not be solved, that is why they are called mysteries. We may have to just study them and wonder about them and then move on.

I did wonder how many students come to us who are a mystery. We teach them and help them as much as we can but they still have difficulties. They seem as frayed on the edges as the rope seen lying on the road. They seem knotted up as tight as well and we may not know how to solve the mystery that is them.

As in the rope, we must study them, think about them, change with them and try new things. For unlike the rope, they are living, breathing, wonderfully mysterious things and we are in charge of unknotting them and helping them grow into the person they are meant to be.

May your mysteries be few and the knots you encounter easy to untie!

Have a great week!

John

Thought for the Week – September 29, 2008

I recently read in an educational magazine, (what else?), that students who attend high schools and colleges were being allowed or even encouraged to make up facts to support their written opinions!

Their teachers and professors were telling them it was okay to make up quotes and details in an effort for them to learn how to write persuasively.

Has the internet, You Tube, My Space and chat rooms created a need and an ethic that says it is okay for people to make up things and put them in writing to support their opinions? Where has checking your sources and the use of primary and secondary resources gone to? What has happened to the truth?

I guess it is a sign of the times. A news program had to apologize recently for pushing the idea that China was drilling of the coast of Cuba. It was later found to be a very well written but wrong bit of information. It was a way to incite people rather than inform; a way of pushing an agenda rather than having a discussion.

Have we become so technologically savvy and such information junkies that we will write anything so others will read it and believe anything others have written?

There is still a beauty of the written word and the thought that goes with it. There is still the beauty of the truth as we find it in historical documents and intelligent research. There is still a beauty in reading differences of opinion from caring, respectable, fair-minded, truthful writers.

Let's continue to teach our students in the proper way of writing non-fiction and the time that it takes to ensure that real facts support a really well-thought opinion. Let's not adopt the idea that we can make things up and say anything as long as we win an argument or get a good grade.

It may be a good grade but it is not and never will be good writing!
Have a great week!

John

Thought for the Week – October 6, 2008

I was sitting on my back porch the other evening and I heard a strange bird call. I am not an expert on birds but I do know most of the sounds that come from the normal winged creatures that visit my trees. This one was loud and strident and unusual.

I went out into the yard to try to find the origin of this new sound.

I looked around and looked around and didn't find any bird at all. It must have either been on a tight schedule or passing through within earshot. I was disappointed.

It was exciting to hear something new in the yard. I found myself listening for it to reappear and instead I heard the calls of mocking birds, woodpeckers, flickers, cardinals, wood thrushes and cat birds. These are sounds I guess that I am so used to, I didn't hear them anymore. It took a new sound to help me hear them again.

It is important in our schools and classrooms that we change things up every now and then. Our students need to hear a new sound occasionally to wake up their hearing. It is important for them to hear the usual in an unusual way. We need to play different kinds of music in our classroom. We need to use different material, use a different teaching style, bring in a guest presenter, change the schedule around and not be so predictable.

It was exciting for me to try to find what creature created that sound. It should be exciting for our students to hear what they are going to learn on any given day.

Have a great week!

John

Thought for the Week – October 13, 2008

Yesterday since it was raining, I decided to clean out a closet. (What fun!) It was an effort to get rid of things that haven't been used and clothes that haven't been worn and paper work that should have been recycled a long time ago.

Instead I found photographs.

It took longer to go through the hundreds of photographs than it took to pile the stuff going to the thrift store. Some of the photographs were of recent history some went back several generations. Some were in glossy color accompanied by a CD that saved them digitally. Some were the old black and white kind with yellowed edges and faded corners. They all recorded important events from the last several decades.

A few photos made me laugh and a few brought tears to my eyes.

Photographs are an important visual history of your life and the lives around you. It is a moment frozen forever and it remains there to remind us of a time long ago or of people who are no longer with us.

Photographs remind our minds and our souls of the important things around us.

As you look at your own life, what do you wish to have a photograph of? What things or people would you want to have a permanent picture of? What would you want it to commemorate, celebrate or just record?

Time continues to pass and our individual journeys continue as well. It is up to us to remember to take those important photographs so that years from now we can find them, remember them and thank God for every one of them.

Have a great week and take some photographs.

John

Thought for the Week – October 20, 2008

I recently read an article in the Smithsonian Magazine discussing the year 1908. It had many things in common with 2008. It was an election year. It was a year of technological marvels like the Wright Brothers plane or Ford's Model T. It was a year where many made predictions about what the world would be like a hundred years later.

One magazine of that era predicted that people would be walking around with specially made hats with an antenna so they could have a portable telephone. Another magazine predicted that huge buildings would be built and they would be connected to other huge buildings via elevated walkways. Another predicted that individuals would be able to fly their own planes anywhere they wanted to go.

They were pretty close. We have the cell phone now and huge skyscrapers and many people do fly their own planes. Not bad for a group of people who would become the parents of the Greatest Generation.

Let's take a gamble and make some predictions of what the world will be like in 2108. What technology will we see? How will we learn and how will we teach? Will our challenges concerning energy, health care, and retirement be different or just called something different.

In 1908 many people still didn't have electricity, cars were available only to the wealthy, we hadn't been in a major war since 1865 and many still used their feet to go from place to place.

In 2008, we don't know what to do when the electricity goes off, we can't live without our cars, our feet our supposed to be wearing designer shoes, and we have lived through many wars.

In 2108, what will we be wearing? How will we get from place to place? How will new technology look and be used? More importantly, how will we be treating each other?

Some things to think about….

Have a great week.

John

Thought for the Week – October 27, 2008

I don't know about you, but I have seen a lot of stressed out people lately. They are stressed about their job, their family, their co-worker, what deadlines they have to make and things they have to do. I have seen it on television. I have seen it at the grocery store. I have even seen some of these stressed out people take it out on other stressed out people.

What has happened to us? Why is it more stressful now than before? Didn't we have stress last year? Didn't the deadlines come and new responsibilities come with them? We all feel that there is more stress than last year. I have felt it too!

We must remember that the sun did come up today and this day has no more hours than yesterday. We must accomplish what we can accomplish and then we must take a break, take a breath and rest.

We must remember to read, to sing, to dance, to take a walk, to call a friend, tell a loved one that you love them, write a letter, (okay an e-mail but not a business related one.) We must remember to take a nap, write a poem, laugh, watch something stupid on television, listen to music, go shopping, eat someplace other than home and be served.

We must also remember to pray!

We can't work so hard and be stressed out so much that we forget to live. That can make anyone miserable.

This week take time for yourself as well as for the important work you do. Maybe if we all do this, we will see more smiles and less sneers; hear more laughter and fewer sighs.

Have a great week!

John

Thought for the Week – November 3, 2008

My parents celebrated their 62nd wedding anniversary last weekend! It was a quiet occasion; not like the 60th or even the 61st. It was a blessing this year that they were together at home. My dad's dementia is getting worse and my mom had to be in the hospital and nursing home several times during the last year because of a bad heart, a bad hip, another bad hip, the first hip going bad again and just being 81 years old.

But....They were and are together!

During the last two years as you have read my weekly missives, I have shared how these little celebrations and milestones have intertwined with the passing of others, major changes in our lives and how it has affected how we look upon life and death.

I celebrate all of it!

My parents have taught me to persevere, to hope, to dream, to be surprised, to live through deep disappointment and grief and to expect the unexpected.

We have kids in our rooms that have gone through as much in their short lives and yes, they may not be the sharpest knives in the drawer but they will survive, and they will persevere and they will succeed. They just need us to notice and have a little celebration for them as well every time they have the strength to get up and meet another day!

It is what teachers and other caring people do!

Have a great week!

John

Thought for the Week – November 10, 2008

My pastor at church this week cited CNN.com and their Heroes campaign. It is a list of ten ordinary people who do extraordinary things.

On the website you can read about Tad Agoglia who founded The First Response. It is a group of four men who have taken the responsibility of being the first responders after a natural disaster. They want to be there to help the survivors. You can read about David Puckett from Savannah Georgia. He is helping amputees receive prosthetic limbs. You can read about Maria Ruiz who travels to Mexico to help impoverished children. They really are extraordinary people who do extraordinary things.

I had not heard of them until today. I am glad I did.

Who is your hero? Who has made your life better? Who is the person you think of when we say hero? Were they an ordinary person to everyone else but to you they were the best person you have ever known?

More importantly, are you a hero to someone else?

As educators, parents, and employers, we have the opportunity to be a hero to someone else. We have the ability to be a positive force in someone else's life. We have the power to help them become the best they can be. We can be more than a disciplinarian, authority figure or grader-in-chief.

We can quietly encourage, help, support, cajole, and praise. We can show them that we believe in them and that we will do anything and everything to help them. We will be there for them no matter what.

Just like the CNN heroes, no one may hear about you but you will be doing extraordinary things.

You are all my heroes!

Have a great week!

John

Thought for the Week – November 17, 2008

The other day as I arrived home, I went to the back door to let the dogs in from the back porch. This is a normal event usually greeted with happy dogs that now can finally come in and lay in their favorite and more comfortable spots. However, they weren't in a hurry to come in. They had found something better to do.

A wren had found its way into the back porch and couldn't find the way back out. Now you would think my dogs would be barking and carrying on like the mighty hunters they profess to be….they were not….they were just calmly watching this poor bird fly from one part of the back porch to the other. The dogs were not even agitated, they were just happy to be entertained by something new on their back porch. They were so interested and happy they didn't want to come inside!

(The bird did finally find its way back out and then the dogs scampered into their abode.)

Do you ever do something in your school or your classroom that wakes everyone up for the normal or mundane? Do you ever shake things up so that the students don't know what will happen next? Now you may be saying to yourself, "John, I cannot do that to my students, they will tear the room up!" I am not saying put on a rock concert; but change things up or try some new technology or switch the day around and make the students get excited about being at school and in your room.

Just like my dogs, they may not jump up and down and bark at something new but they just might pay deep attention to what you do and not want to leave.

Isn't being an educator part actor, part scholar and part entertainer?

Have a great week!

John

Thought for the Week – November 24, 2008

What are you thankful for? It may seem like a strange question during these tough economic times with many people struggling to make ends meet. It may seem like a ridiculous time to ask but, I ask it anyway: What are you thankful for?

I am thankful for friends and co-workers who accept me and care for me because of who I am not in spite of who I am.

I am thankful for great memories of loved ones who are no longer on this earth. Memories are a great thing!

I am thankful for new friends, new goals, new memories and even new challenges.
I am thankful for each day that a child improves just a little bit.
I am thankful for each day that I improve just a little bit too!
I am thankful for the right to make mistakes and then fix them.
I am thankful that people forgive me for the mistakes I make.
I am thankful for my family and for their love.
I am thankful for my sons who amaze me every day and make me proud.
I am thankful for those that mean the most to me; that I love dearly; that help me daily.

And, I am thankful for all of you who have dedicated your life to helping and loving and teaching kids. Yes you have to help them and love them before you can teach them.

I wish you the best and most blessed Thanksgiving ever and know that I thank God for each and every one of you.

Happy Thanksgiving!

John

Thought for the Week – December 1, 2008

During the Thanksgiving holiday, I called my sister to see how she was doing, (retired teacher, cancer survivor, yeah Sis!) She told me that she had a group of teacher friends over to play cards and every one of them sounded so depressed. They were saddened by the economy, by the stresses put on them by the school system, by the negative way the local papers wrote about them. Most of them said they were considering retirement. Most of them were excellent, caring teachers.

Sound familiar?

In one way it was comforting to know that low morale is not limited to one geographic location. It is also scary for the same reason. The job has gotten harder the rewards seem smaller and the stress is almost unacceptable. What can we do?

We need to take a minute to catch our breaths and make a plan. We need to prioritize what is important and filter out what is not. We need to remember what we are here for and why we became educators.

Education has been through budget cuts before and will again. There are always fat years and lean years. There are always critics and magpies that make a career out of criticizing anything related to or about public education. Most of them, if not all of them, never worked a week in a school in their lives. We have always had deadlines and paper work and grades and the next "great" thing.

We need to remember one thing: It is about the kids!

As we begin the last month of 2008 and begin the holiday season, let us remember that to most of us, this season is about specifically one special child born on the 25th. Let us also remember the many children come to us everyday looking for help and hope and love and understanding and even a hug. No matter how bad the economy is, love and hope and understanding and hugs are FREE!

I also know that when you give love and hope and understanding and hugs to a child or even a co-worker, it comes back to you even stronger! Nothing boosts morale more than giving and believing and helping.

Have a great week!

John

Thought for the Week – December 8, 2008

Every week at my church we spend a great deal of time praying together for whatever the congregation brings up. In the past, we have prayed for those that were sick, those that had just passed and those that had been sent to Afghanistan or Iraq. Lately, our prayers have changed.

Now our prayers are about finding jobs and keeping jobs; for help during these tough economic times; for families that are feeling the pressure of paying their bills including their mortgage; about caring for those less fortunate during this holiday season.

What's amazing about these prayer petitions? They are coming from the mouths of the youngest members of the congregation! Not only are they aware of what is going on in the world around them, they are willing to offer support in prayer and in works.

Many of our young members are involved in service projects. They are visiting local nursing homes, tutoring each other in math and reading, collecting non-perishable food items for the local food banks and recycling paper, aluminum and glass.

So not only are they praying for others, they are trying to help others. These are kids from the age of four to sixteen!!!

During this month of preparation for Christmas, when we usually think of young people as greedy requesters of anything they see on television, let us remember these little ones as well as the little ones that attend churches all over the area. They do care about others and they do pray for others and they do work to help others.

As we get closer to celebrating the birth of an amazing child, let's learn something from these amazing little ones. They get it!

Have a great week!

John

Thought for the Week – January 5, 2009

During the holidays, I saw an interesting news item about how some zoos were asking for donations of used live Christmas trees. It seems that elephants love pine trees! They get as happy as a kid in a candy store when they get one as a treat. As the news anchor stated, "It tastes good to the elephant and it probably whitens their teeth and freshens their breath!"

I for one had never put elephants and pine trees together. It was out of the ordinary to think of the combination of pachyderms and conifers. It was great to see the huge animal so happy.

In many ways, public education is like the elephant in the room that is rarely connected (by the press) to positive terms. We rarely hear it combined with outstanding, successful, over-achieving, distinguished, compassionate, caring, loving or excellent. Yet, most public schools work hard to be all those things listed above.

However, many people have the wrong idea because they haven't visited a public school in a long time or get their information from one source. They think putting superlatives and the words public school together, would be like seeing an elephant eat a Christmas tree.

I have seen both and I know both have happened! In 2009 I hope to hear more about your successes and the positive results of your hard work. It, like the pine tree for the pachyderm, would take a bad taste out of our mouths.

Have a great week and a great year!

John

Thought for the Week – January 12, 2009

As I was driving to church yesterday morning, it began to rain. Like most of us, I decided to turn on my windshield wipers so I could safely see where I was going. As the wipers continued to move in their rhythmical way up and down my windshield, the left wiper kept moving up. That is, as it continued to work, it would stop farther up my windshield and move out way past the outer edge of my car! In about 10 minutes, the left wiper was only touching a fraction of the windshield but it was doing a great job of signaling a left turn.

Now this was an easily fixed problem and once I reached my destination, I was able to ensure that the next time I drove in rain it would not be so exciting. The strange thing about it was – it was so unexpected! The wipers had always worked well and efficiently. I had never noticed any change in the motion of the wipers or the way they were supposed to work. I couldn't even find a reason why one of them would suddenly start moving and do something radically different and new.

In our own day to day work life, we may see a co-worker or a student suddenly act differently. It may be an action totally out of the norm for the person. It may also be unexpected and we may not see what the cause or causes are. Unlike the wipers, the solution or support may take longer. However, the people we work with and the children we teach are more important and more complicated than a simple machine.

In these difficult times, let's continue to help others and support others so they can see their way through the bad visibility of doubt, and stress. It will not only help them but it will help us feel better too!

Have a great week.

John

Thought for the Week – January 18, 2009

My black Labrador retriever, Kingdog, (I didn't name him), is 18 years old today! To tell you the truth, he looks it. He has cataracts in both eyes, he does not hear too well and he back hips do not work as well as they used to. Why should they? He is 126 years old!

I have had him since he was a puppy and I picked him out of a litter. To tell you the truth, he actually picked me. I went to this guy who looked like Grizzly Adams and he placed the box of puppies on the ground and Kingdog crawled out of the box and ran toward me and jumped into my lap. He was six weeks old and I was 33.

The importance of Kingdog in my life is that he has been with me for more than one-third of it. He has been a faithful friend during the good times and the bad times; the sweet and the bitter; the painful and the celebratory. He has been the best! He never complains. He is always affectionate. He has been there with me throughout the years I have been a principal.

It may take him a long time to get moving, but he still eats well and drinks a lot of water and still barks a graveling low "woof" when he thinks there is something going on. He is a marvel since most Labradors don't live past a decade and he has been the only constant thing that has been with me throughout the last 18 years.

Look at your life and see if there has been any friend (four or two legged), who has been with you through the challenging times. Remember them. They have given you the most support and love throughout your life. If you can, call them and thank them. You will find very few friends in your life that will walk the walk with you, help you and love you unconditionally.

As for me, I am going to buy some soft chewy gifts for the best four-legged friend I have ever had. Who knows, maybe he'll be around for another eighteen years.

Have a great week!

John

Thought for the Week – January 25, 2009

•

Recently, with the colder, frigid weather, I have had to do some doctoring to my outside plants. Even with covering and prayers, some of them received a lot of damage and some parts were brown and not looking very good.

However, as I started to prune away the damaged foliage, I noticed in many plants some new growth. It was green, healthy and slowly rising from the dirt. If I hadn't looked through the damage, I wouldn't have seen the healthy part of the plant.

It is the same way with people. We are all damaged at times...hurt by others, situations, wrong decisions, illnesses, petty quarrels, a lack of forgiveness or an act of forgetfulness. No matter what the cause, we have either been damaged or have damaged others.

Let's take a little time this week to look past the damaged parts of others and see what has grown and flourished within. Survival and perseverance creates a strong root system. We just have to take the time to look for it.

I hope they see the strength in you as you see the strength in them. We need each other's strength to grow, survive and flourish!

Have a great week!

John

Thought for the Week – February 1, 2009

This week we will commemorate the first anniversary of the sugar refinery accident. That terrible day made the national news, touched many families and effected many lives. Many workers gave the ultimate sacrifice or are still slowly, painfully recuperating from the explosion and the fire.

Port Wentworth Elementary is located not far from the refinery. During the most stressful of hours, it was used as base for media and support personnel. We commend the job the firefighters, emergency medical technicians and police officers did that day.

It is not a surprise that a school building was used as a safe haven or headquarters in a time of crisis. It can be an important part of any community and especially important during tough times. It can provide shelter during a storm or support during troubling economic times. It can be a safe haven for children when a parent is deployed, when a grandparent is ill, or when they are just scared. It can be the first place a family turns to when a spouse loses a job, has to move or is diagnosed with a terrible illness.

Schools are not just places where people learn; they are places that support the whole family. Schools are full of people who lose sleep over kids and make supportive phone calls to parents. Schools are full of people who give a hug when it is needed, say a pray when nothing else works and endeavor to make a difference in other people's lives.

Let's take time this week to remember those people who lost their lives in the sugar refinery accident. Let's also be ready to help others when they need us the most. It's what schools do!

Have a great week!

John

Thought for the Week – February 8, 2009

I lost a dear friend of mine this week. In fact, I wrote about him just a little while ago. He had just turned 18 and I had made such a big deal out of it. (I guess he heard and finally figured out how old he was.)

My dear friend was my dog King. (I didn't name him.)

As I mentioned here during a previous thought, I got him as a puppy and he had been a constant companion since I first became a school administrator. He was a kind, gentle soul who in his younger days would look regal and respectful at all times. A friend of mine even made a daily schedule for him: 8:00 a.m. – Look regal; 9:00 a.m. – Cross your paws and gaze at your domain; 10:00 a.m. walk the perimeter of the yard; 11:00 a.m. drink water in a graceful way; Noon – repeat morning schedule.

As I sit here and remember him, I think of how good a companion he was to me. When I was sick with the flu, he would lie next to me on my bed and wouldn't leave my side. When I took him to school with me, he let all the little kids pet him and walk him without a bit of annoyance. (He would just sigh heavily during the drive home to let me know he was exhausted.) As with most retrievers, he never wanted to displease or show pain or hurt a soul.

Late last week, I could see that his race was about over and he was in some pain. I could see that it was time to let the old boy go home. I could see finally, what I didn't want see or face – a world without my dog – a world without King.

I try in most of these messages to connect the happenings in my life to your lives as educators and hard working people. This week I cannot. If you have a pet that you love, give him or her a hug for me and a hug for yourself. Never forget what a wonderful perfect love they give you. They love you when you are brilliant and they love you when you are a buffoon. When everyone thinks you have lost your mind, your pet will lay his head on your lap and make you feel like you can make it through the day. They love you no matter what and that is the greatest love you will ever receive! God Bless all the Kingdogs of the world!

Have a great week!

John

Thought for the Week – February 16, 2009

As we celebrate Presidents Day 2009 which president do you think of? Do you think of Washington, Jefferson, Lincoln, Teddy Roosevelt, FDR, or Reagan? Do you remember your favorites with their faults along with their talents or have you elevated them to just under God status?

Do we balance out the bravery of Washington and the brilliance of Jefferson with the fact that they both owned slaves? Do we respect the fortitude of Lincoln and remember that he was faulted for being too bipartisan. Do we thank T.R. for preserving our first national forests but also see him capturing islands to expand our strength in the world? Do we revere FDR for his work during World War II without remembering that we were isolationists until December 1941? Do we remember Reagan for his role in defeating Communism without remembering his role in Iran-Contra?

Our greatest patriots were not perfect and that is what helped them to do great things. Sometimes as we look to our heroes, we remember the positive and forget the flaws. But it is the flaws that can help us see the ways ordinary people can do extraordinary things. Self-educated men can become heroes; former actors can tell despots to tear down walls; wheel-chair bound workaholics can help a nation out of depression.

They were imperfect people who did wonderful things. So are the many people around us who work with us and try their best. They may even drive us crazy at times. However, when you look past the flaws and faults, you might see ordinary people doing some extraordinary things.

I hope you look past my flaws and faults and occasionally see something there too! As for me, my favorite president was James K. Polk. He said that if he could accomplish everything in his first term, he would not run for a second term. He did want he wanted to do in four years and went home! He is my hero!

Have a great week.

John

Thought for the Week – February 22, 2009

After several chilly nights and freezing temperatures in the last few weeks, I was surprised yesterday to see the blooms of daffodils in my back yard! It was like a miracle that occurred over night. One evening I didn't notice a thing and the next morning five daffodils were proudly displaying their yellow petals and bright red centers.

Those beautiful flowers brought color to an otherwise barren landscape. They were and are surrounded by leaves, brown grass and non-descript dirt. They stand out even more than if it was a spring day with things growing all around and birds flying all around.

Their existence made me look at them; I couldn't help it; I couldn't miss them. They hit the senses and they made me stop and stare and slow down and watch.

It is important at times to just stop and look around and notice that even in the coldest of days or the bleakest of times, there is something beautiful waiting to be seen. There is something out there that can make us slow down our existence and notice them. It may be something or someone, new or old, but it is there – we just have to find it.

Let's take some time this week to slow down, look around and find the beautiful things that are around us. Maybe we haven't noticed it because we haven't taken the time to look.

Have a great week!

John

Thought for the Week – March 1, 2009

Several teachers came up to me on Friday excited about the possibility of snow in Savannah this weekend. I quite frankly couldn't share in their euphoria. I left northern climates to get away from the snow.

In the winter of 2001, my last winter in Northern Virginia, we had so much snow that school year the teachers didn't complete the numbers of days required in their contract until the July 4th weekend! On the radio they were announcing that the summer was half over. I had teachers in tears.

I knew it was time to look for warmer latitudes.

People always are looking for something different than where they live. People up north go on island vacations during their long winters; people down south dream of snow days and building snowmen. Others wish they could go to the left coast because it never rains in California (yeah right).

Wherever you live, there are good points and bad points. In the south, we have warmer weather for a longer period of time but we have to contend with hurricanes. Up north, you have cooler weather but you have longer winters and some zip codes are located right along tornado alley. In California, you have everything from beaches to mountains but you have the possibility of earthquakes and brush fires. In the northwest, you have lush and green gardens and lawns due to the extra amount of rain you receive annually.

Good points and bad points.

We can say the same for people. We all have talents and we all have faults; we all have successes and failures; we all do great things and we all make mistakes. We can count on that like the weather changing from day to day.

I hope during the coming week, we can all accept each other with the excitement of southerners hoping for a snow day or northerners hoping for an early spring.
Have a great week!

John

Thought for the Week – March 8, 2009

This week our pre-kindergarten held their fourth annual Pet Parade. This is a wonderful Kodak moment (are there Kodak cameras anymore?) where each student would come up and share some information about their pet. Some pets were the normal dogs and cats and some were rarer like gerbils, turtles and an occasional snake. (Last year we even had a skunk.)

One student came up and said that his dog was "free" years old and said it was a "Mutt" Another one came up and said his dog was "two" and just shrugged his shoulders when asked what kind of dog it was. The parade continued with a cat that was as big as a puma and rabbit that just wanted to be left alone.

Some students even shared their stuffed animals with the audience. They told them the name and held them as tight as the students who had animals with pulses. You could feel how much the kids loved their animals and how happy they were to see them at school.

If your students were asked to describe you how would they respond? Would they speak of you in terms of endearment, affection, respect or even love? Would they answer easily or just shrug their shoulders?

If you were asked to describe your students would you describe them in loving and understanding terms? Would you see them, warts and all, as very important to you? Would you reaffirm your desire and efforts to have each and every one of them find success in everything they did?

Let's think about that this week. How would you want to be described and how should you describe others? Sometimes when you stop and watch you can learn a lot from a four year old.

Have a great week!

John

<u>Thought for the Week – March 22, 2009</u>

A recent Time Magazine article, (so it must be true), cited a study completed in California, (where else?), that looked at leadership styles or the leadership characteristics in people. It concluded that, to most people, a leader looked like a leader when they were loud! It didn't mean they knew much. In fact, it probably was masking the fact that they didn't know that much. However, if you wanted to look the part and fake it until you make it you needed to lead by loud!

That really bothered me. I don't like people who try to lead by increasing the volume or use the "Believe in me because I am a bully" philosophy. However the study also stated that a group of people who have to work together usually will think a quieter person wouldn't make a good leader either!

There are times, although rare, when the voice should be raised. I certainly do not become smarter because I say things louder. However, there are times when a point has to be raised for the safety or benefit of ones who cannot speak for themselves.

Most of the time I believe that leadership can best be shown by example. You cannot tell people loudly to care about others and expect them to do so. You have to show them that you care and that it is a worthwhile thing to do. You cannot tell people to work hard or else – you need to show them. If we both work hard and care about each other great things can happen.

Finally I think some decisions need to be made after a great deal of thought and discussion and input and prayer. I know people have more respect for the quick and rapid response but I sometimes need some quiet thought time before opening my mouth.

Let's take some time this week to quietly think about how we lead and are there ways to quietly make it better. If you are a Type-A personality, you have already deleted this thought. ☺

Either way, have a great week!
John

Thought for the Week – March 30, 2009

Yesterday evening as I was watching television an emergency warning in black shot on the screen notifying the viewing public of a tornado warning....wanting more information, I changed the station to the Weather Channel. I was just in time to see the local radar and see exactly where the bad weather was located and where it was moving to.

What fascinated me the most about the Weather Channel yesterday was that I noticed for the first time that even when their prediction includes dire or dangerous things like thunderstorms, lightning, hurricanes and tornadoes the background music is upbeat light-hearted jazz. It is like the "Don't Worry Be Happy" television station. Think of hearing an electronic voice stating: "A tornado warning has been issued for your area; take cover now..." while listening to Luther Vandross or Acoustic Alchemy! It is the greatest example of paradox I have ever seen and heard.

Maybe they have a point. It would be worse if as the weather changed the music would be adjusted appropriately. Start with happy music when sunny and move all the way to organ music when you see the sky beginning to darken. It would be atrocious, but funny, to have music that fit the weather...Sinatra's <u>Come Fly With Me</u> during a hurricane or B.J. Thomas' <u>Raindrops Are Falling On My Head</u> during a shower or John Denver's <u>Sunshine On My Shoulder</u> during a clear day or even John Sebastian's <u>Summer In The City</u> during the dog days of summer. Oh well, it is just a thought.

The mix of music to the information did make me take notice and listen and read and watch more carefully. Maybe we need to shake things up like that occasionally to make others pay attention to what we are teaching and saying and believing. Maybe the soundtrack of our world should be changed every now and then. I think it would benefit us and those around us.

I hope your week is filled with good weather and whatever music you wish to hear in your head! I hope it makes you smile and makes your load a little lighter.

Have a great week!

John

<u>Thought for the Week – April 12, 2009</u>

I was blessed this week to have a visit from my eldest son Matthew and his lovely wife Jennifer. They helped me with numerous things around the house: cleaning up this and storing and packing that...we talked a great deal, (shocking I know!), and we did something else a great deal...we laughed!

My son has a very quick wit and I just have a wit so together we would banter back and forth and make puns and other play on words and continue until it got stupid, (often), or we got tired, (rarely).

At one point, my son stated that he missed having the verbal battles with me. He didn't have anyone at his work or watering holes that he could have that much fun with while having a conversation.

I hadn't noticed it before the visit, but I too had missed talking and laughing and exchanging puns with my son and daughter in law too! I hadn't noticed its absence until its return; I hadn't felt what it meant to me until I recognized it again.

Tomorrow we will return to a job and to co-workers that we have not seen in a short while. I hope that as you re-connect with your teammates and school mates and students that you can look at them with rested eyes. I pray that you can notice how important they are and how they were missed. You didn't notice it until you returned; you didn't feel it until you saw them.

I hope as we begin this fourth and final quarter that our students, when they see us can feel the way we feel about reunions: thankful, blessed and joyous with laughter, appreciation and excitement.

Have a great week!

John

<u>Thought for the Week – April 20, 2009</u>

As I was driving home from the airport last week, (Yes I am getting two thoughts from the same event.), I saw a Met Life blimp. It looked strange tied down by its nose; its large gas-filled body sticking up in the air moving slowly from side to side. I couldn't help but stare at it. I hadn't expected it to be there and it was so colorful against the backdrop of green grass and azure blue sky.

It was music for the eyes.

Sometimes the brain needs something different to shake it up; sometimes it needs something unexpected. We all need a jump start sometimes.

How about the people around you? Maybe they need a brain surge too? How about doing something unexpected for them? You may find that they know more than you thought they did.

They just needed something to feed the brain and stretch the mind.

Don't we all?

Have a great week!

John

Thought for the Week – April 27, 2009

Two interesting things happened yesterday that at first may not seem related but you know I will make a connection.

First: During church services, a middle-school student asked for prayers because the CRCT was coming soon. I could hear the nervousness and worry in her voice and the pastor even included all teachers, students and administrators in his prayer. (I will take whatever help I can get.)

Secondly: My mother called me yesterday to see how my packing was going. (I am downsizing and moving on Wednesday.) I told her I would be sending her the new address in a card soon. She told me to: "Just e-mail it to me tomorrow so I will have it!" I could hear the excitement and anticipation in her voice.

So in these two conversations I saw polarized emotions. I saw a teenager worried about how she will demonstrate her knowledge and mastery of a curriculum. I also heard the excitement from an 81 year old woman who wanted me to use technology to get information to her as fast as possible.

We need to capture the excitement from the 81 year old and transfer it to the 16 year old. We need to help them see how much they have learned and not lose sleep over a minimum competency test. We need to hear confidence in their voices and not fear. If an 81 year old woman can learn how to work a computer, than our kids should be able to show mastery at a passing level.

Just like my mother is excited for the next stage in my life, I want the fifth graders and eighth graders excited about the next stage in their lives.

I learned a lot yesterday from a 16 and an 81 year old! They are both amazing people!

Have a great week!

John

Thought for the Week – May 5, 2009

I moved last week. I sold my old house, bought a new house, packed-up stuff, gave other stuff away, threw some other stuff out and unpacked what was left. It had been planned for months, worked on for weeks and came to fruition in days.

It was a change that was needed and prepared for but still a life-altering event.

I am glad of it and I am happy I did it. It is a new start with a new view; it is the next phase of life, work and family. It was meant to be. It was not done in a quick or arbitrary way; it was thought out, planned out and prayed over. It was, in the end, the right thing to do after the right amount of time.

Today we begin administrating a test that will show how our students have done this year. This too has taken much preparation, time, and hard work. Similarly, there has been a lot of packing and unpacking, throwing out and putting in, review, thought and excitement.

The only difference is, the test will not be a life-altering event. You have them ready and you have them confident about what they know. You have worked your hardest and planned and prepared and prayed.

They will do fine. They have you!

Have a great week!

John

<u>Thought for the Week – May 11, 2009</u>

Sometimes dates hit me and then I think about how much time has passed or how much time remains. It occurred to me yesterday, that in a month, the school year for students will be over.   The year has seemed to fly by and even with its share of challenges, budget cuts and individual and collective crises, it has been good.

I am strange in the fact that I like school when kids are in it. I do not look forward to the time of the year when furniture is stacked in hallways, the yearly cleaning frenzy has begun and I am in the office doing the yearly paperwork that defines the ending of one school term and the beginning of another. It is not as exciting as when the kids are here; it is not as fulfilling.

Yet after the next four busy weeks have passed, I will be saying goodbye to another group of fifth graders. A group that is talented, funny, smart and challenging. They have been that way since kindergarten and I will miss them.

I have written many times in my thoughts about the concept of beginnings and endings and have shared many with you. However it is what we do between the two that makes the difference and has the impact! It is not how many beginnings and endings will live through, it is who we help and support and love during the months or years in between.

I hope the next month is a joyful one as we complete another school year and look forward to the beginning of another.

Have a great week!

John

Thought for the Week – May 18, 2009

The other day as I was walking between the cafeteria and the gym heading toward the music room a voice called to me from above....at first I came to the realization that God spoke with a southern accent, but then I realized that I needed to look up....a roofer was up on a breezeway patching a roof.

After getting over the near coronary, I asked him to repeat his question that had eluded me as I saw my life pass before my eyes. He asked, "Have you heard anything about getting a new roof put on this school because it is becoming way too hard to keep patching it?" I told him that yes they were going to start patching it this summer and next and hopefully that will take care of it for the next ten years. The gentleman seemed elated by my news and happily went back to tarring the sieve I call a roof.

What was amazing was that he thought it was normal to just call out to someone from his rooftop location and he assumed that I would be totally aware of everything around me. (I am not. However I am looking up at the roof line a little more often now.)

Do we assume sometimes that others are as aware of things as we are? Do we sometimes assume that they understand what we understand in the way we understand them? Do we put our own slant or view on things and expect others to see it our way?

Maybe we all need to get a birds-eye view sometimes, look around and see what needs to be patched up?

Have a great week!

John

Thought for the Week – May 24, 2009

Since I have moved, my dog, (Roxie), has had some separation anxiety and has torn up some things in my house, (like my entire bathroom), so I took her to the veterinarian so that I could spend money and hopefully make her and me feel better. (Make her feel better emotionally and make me feel better financially.)

So, Roxie was put on medication. (I felt left out.)

Now that Roxie is on medication, she has to urinate more, a great deal more. So I am letting her out and walking her more so she can feel better and not be so anxious. (I thought if you were anxious it may make you want to urinate more?)

Anyway, on Sunday she awakens me at 6:00 in the morning to go for a walk. Letting her outside was not going to do it. I needed to take her outside. Feeling half-asleep and not very happy, I got dressed, put on my shoes and took her outside. To add to the overall joyous occasion, it was lightly raining for the 5th day in a row.

After a few minutes she pulled me around and I looked back to see a beautiful rainbow! It was like it had been placed there for us at that moment and it made the early morning walk not only easier but wonderful.

It was an unexpected gift given when doing a mundane chore.

With the few weeks left in the school year, let's make sure that we thank the ones in our daily life that make our mundane chores fun and our burdens lighter. Let's make sure we thank them for being a rainbow on our cloudy days. Hopefully, we were somebody else's rainbow as well.

Everyone needs one; even if they have to get up early to see it!

Have a great week!

John

Thought for the Week – June 1, 2009

As I have been reviewing the test results from this year's CRCT, I have to say that I am not happy with the math results. I am even somewhat embarrassed by them. We are usually close to the top of the system; we are usually the school that knows how to teach our students to be successful.

I take full responsibility for the scores.

We can blame a lack of alignment or the test or wish our kids were smarter or wish some parents were more helpful. However, we are scholars and that is a cop out. We need now to find out what to do and how to change it.

In the short term, we need to put every available person in third and fifth grade to assist students in basic reading skills and math skills. We need to try to reduce the number of students who did not pass by spending every second of the next week helping them with basic reading skills and basic math facts and number sense and area and perimeter.

We also need to pray that the retest is like the first test.

In the long term, I want everyone to think about what they will do differently in math next year and let me know what that is. I do <u>not </u>want to hear about what you already do fine, or that your test scores were fine so you don't have to do anything. This is a grade 1 – 5 issue with an emphasis on grades 3 – 5. Many of our kids in grades 3 – 5 did not pass the math portion.

We need to do something different. We need to be scholarly and truthful and take the time and fix it.

When you average all the math scores in grades 3 – 5 you get 66% passage rate. As you know, that is a bell curve. We are not a bell curve school.

I take full responsibility for what we have accomplished. We all need to take action to improve it.

Have a good week!

John

Thought for the Week – June 8, 2009

I was walking the dog in the early morning hours the other day. It was still dark and dank from the wet weather. There was no moon light and only the street lamps let any illumination on anything. It was just me and the dog and the wet and the mosquitoes.

Or so I thought.

As we rounded one corner close to our house, there in the parking area, near two cars was a deer! It wasn't that big. It was not worthy of Marlin Perkins and the Wild Kingdom crew or an ESPN hunting show. However, you don't expect to see a white-tailed deer in the middle of a parking area near your house. I suspected it was a juvenile deer trying to break into the cars; a deer gone bad; a runaway from the herd; a sad day for all law-abiding venison.

As quickly as we saw it, it saw us and ran into the woods. My dog wanted to go after it. Luckily, I convinced her that it was not a good idea. She didn't know where the deer had been and certainly didn't know where it was going.

It was a surprise to see nature so close and in a place you didn't expect it – a parking lot.

Now every early morning as I make that turn with my dog, I look ahead, expecting to see the deer again. Alas, I have not. It makes the walks exciting with expectation. The first time was a surprise; now I hope it happens again.

As we complete another year together, I hope you have enjoyed my thoughts for the week. They are meant to help and support the people of this school system and my friends who are kind enough to read them. As I have told you many times, writing is my therapy and it helps me prepare for another week. By reading them you help me greet each day with the same anticipation and excitement that I get when I round the corner looking for something new and different; something awe inspiring and soul strengthening.

I wish the best summer you could ever have. Know that you are the best this noble profession has to offer. It has been my pleasure to write to you once again.

Have a great week!

John

Thought for the Week – June 14, 2009

I was planning to wait few months to begin again the Thoughts for the Week, but this one hit me on the head yesterday. So here it goes:

I was shopping at the Piggly-Wiggly Supermarket yesterday and as I was quietly trying to find everything I might need for this week's attempt at healthy eating, my searching was interrupted not once, not twice, but three times by people who loudly lost their tempers.

The first one was heard loudly cussing about the fact that she couldn't find the soft drink aisle. (She was by herself.)

The second one was heard criticizing an assistant manager who was trying to help him find something. (Nothing was good enough.)

The third one was heard from outside the store. He was shouting at his wife about something and was walking back to his car. He kept turning and yelling and turning and yelling.

It was awkward, embarrassing and ridiculous.

How many of you agree with these adjectives?

How many of us in the last 10 months have acted the same? Have we lost our temper over little things? Have we yelled at others for the most insignificant of reasons? Have we hurt someone else's feelings when they were trying to lead, help, sacrifice, or support?

I would suggest that we look as awkward, embarrassing and ridiculous as the unhappy group of people that all came to the store at the same time yesterday.
Just so you know, I didn't get angry at them; I just found myself shaking my head and wondering if life had gotten so bad for them that they needed to take it out on everybody else. It wasn't funny; it was very, very, sad.

Think about it.....

John

Thought for the Week – September 2, 2009

My youngest son just finished spending a week with me. It was wonderful to see him. I realized as we were talking and catching up that it had been over a year since we had seen each other. We talk all the time on the phone and send each other e-mails, but it is not the same as when you see your child face to face.

During one of our conversations, he reminded me that he had come a long way from the time he was a little kid. He is twenty-six years old now and very quiet, reserved, mature and introspective. (Nothing like me)

When he was young, he was sometimes a challenge but we worked our way through it. Young kids are supposed to make mistakes; they are supposed to forget things; they are supposed to see how far their parents will go. If you can't do it when you are a kid when are you supposed to do it?

As you look at your students, do not expect them to be where they are going to be twenty years from now? Do not expect them to be as mature and reserved as my wonderful son. It took time. It takes time. It supposed to.

Our job is to make our students the best they can be at the age they are. We cannot make a five year old into a ten year old or a twenty year old. It cannot happen.

Just like me and my son, time helps to make us better. Let's give our little ones the support and time they need to become impressive, wonderful adults.

Have a great week!

John

Thought for the Week – September 8, 2009

During my son's visit in August, we went to the beach. During this particular morning, the waves seemed to be a bit rough and the wind blew a little harder than normal. However, it was a sunny day and we had a chance to sit and talk and share opinions and ideas.

After a while, my son said that he was getting too hot and it was time to check out the waves. As we put our feet in the water, I thought the water was a little colder than normal but my son said that it was like standing in a bath tub! I guess his years in New York City had changed his point of view on what was a cold water temperature and what was a warm water temperature.

In a few short minutes, I was back in my chair and he was body surfing to his heart's content.

Do our student's come in with different perceptions than we do? Do we think our instruction is working but later we don't see the understanding? Do we think what we are doing is hot but is hitting our students cold?

Perception is reality. If they believe they can do it, they will; if they believe they cannot, they won't. We must not expect children to understand what we perceive but we must strive to understand what they perceive. If we don't, they will feel like strangers in a new land, trying to learn things that are much more challenging than we thought they were. They will feel like they are from another country or even – New York City!

Have a great week!

John

Thought for the Week – September 14, 2009

In a recent edition of Edutopia the magazine, (okay it is from a year ago but I am catching up), students were asked what they would change about school if they had the power. The students stated that they wished their teachers would talk less and have them do more. They were finding it hard to concentrate on the subject matter when it was given one way – orally.

They weren't being mean about it; just honest. Having a teacher constantly talking or lecturing was driving them crazy and not making them excited about learning.

It shouldn't be that surprising. Our kids are used to text-messaging someone across the street or across the room. They can listen to their IPOD; watch something on television while doing their homework. They might seem mentally over stimulated but it works for them even if it doesn't work for us.

The question is: What does this mean for us? We can't ignore it because the goal is for students to master the curriculum and to be successful. We can't just dig our heels in and expect young people to adjust to us. We can't expect 21st century students to be excited about us teaching in a 20th century way.

We need to use more technology, more hands-on learning and more small group discussion and activities. That is what colleges are doing and that is what businesses are looking for. If we don't, we will continue to see 40% of our students fail to graduate from high school.
It is not what we are teaching; it is how we are teaching it.

Something to think about?!

Have a great week!

John

Thought for the Week – October 4, 2009

As I was coming in from morning duty one day last week, I spotted two really young students sitting at one of the picnic tables located in the front of the building. They were quietly eating breakfast as other students passed them heading toward their respective classrooms. After a short while, one of my staff members asked them what they were doing sitting outside at the table? They replied, "It is just such a nice day, we thought we'd have breakfast out here!"

For two young people to know enough on a beautiful autumn day to stop and smell the roses (or the breakfast), makes me want to stop and do the same. As it was, I allowed the two young men to finish their breakfast and get to class without messing up their reverie. It was a nice morning and most people hadn't noticed.

It is important to take the time and slow down and notice a nice morning; a delicious breakfast; a good friend; a blessed breeze; a good time. It is important not to be so busy trying to complete things that we let other things completely miss us. There are times we need to be reminded that: "This is the day the Lord has made; let us rejoice and be glad in it."

We might find that, like those little teachers having breakfast, we smile with ease and our step is light and we might just learn something if just slow down and look!

Have a great week!

John

Thought for the Week – October 12, 2009

I read with sadness about the passing of Mary Travers, the Mary of Peter, Paul and Mary. I had always enjoyed their music and the voice she gave as the one female in the trio.

Her voice was a simple one but in that simplicity you could hear every word and understand every ballad. It was the music of the Civil Rights Era. They sang songs from the Civil War, songs by Woody Guthrie and songs collected by Alan Lomax. The words were the most important thing because the message was too important to be covered up by the instruments.

It was because of groups like Peter, Paul and Mary, that I learned how to play guitar and learn the songs they sang. They weren't difficult but they were important.

I have two copies of the record, (the big flat things with the hole in the middle that plays by placing a needle on it....you know its analog...never mind!),anyway I have two copies of See What Tomorrow Brings. The first one I played a lot and still do. The second one I found brand new in a church sale with plastic still on the cover and it is still unopened. (I hope there is really a record in there.) I am not keeping it unopened because it is worth a great deal of money. I am keeping it that way because it means something to me. These are songs of a time when singers could push for reform or make us aware of the injustice in the world without being reviled by talking heads on 24/7/365 television shows and called names. They were making a statement with their songs and you could agree or not agree. They were going to sing anyway.

Mary Travers died at the age of 72. She was only 10 years younger than my parents and she was proud of being a singer. She was even more proud that she was a mother and grandmother.

To me she was a singer of simple, sing-able, important songs in an era when the singer and songs taught us one thing: To stop and listen to the words.

Have a great week!

John

Thought for the Week – October 25, 2009

This morning I received an e-mail from a friend who lives in Virginia. I have known her for seventeen years and she was my former PTA President and a great lady. Mrs. Beach has also lived through the loss of two daughters: One committed suicide at the age of 18 (Katie); the other died in a car accident a few years later at the age of 19 (Alyssa). A double tragedy like this can tear you apart and make you want to curl up and die yourself.

In the e-mail was a letter from a friend of Alyssa's who wanted everyone to know how good and kind she was. This friend, Nicole, said that it was Alyssa who saved her life. When she was so down and depressed in her junior year, Alyssa came up to her out the blue one day and hugged her and gave her a necklace with a dove pendant. Alyssa told her to wear it and find peace. Alyssa hugged her once again and walked away. The following day Alyssa would die on an icy patch of road in a one car accident!

There is somebody in your life, somewhere, needing a hug. There is somebody in your life, somewhere, needing a friend. We can do that for them. We can help them find peace. We can be an angel for them as Alyssa was to Nicole shortly before she became a real angel.

We can't put it off; we shouldn't put it off.

Let's go hug a few friends!

Have a great week!

John

Thought for the Week – November 2, 2009

I have always enjoyed Halloween. I enjoy putting out some silly animated "ghosts and goblins", playing scary music and waiting for kids to show up in their costumes. I bought several bags of candy appropriate for school-age children, (Dum-Dums and Smarties).
I sat outside from 6:00 p.m. – 8:30 p.m.

Only one person showed up! (That was a single, lone child who came by way of a van driven by her father. They weren't even neighbors.)

Needless to say I was disappointed. (No I didn't drown my sorrow by eating the candy. I have been called a dum-dum before.)

There are times every week where we prepare for a great lesson, or activity or assessment or production and it doesn't turn out as we planned. It disappoints us and it makes us feel like we did a great deal of preparation for no success or gain.

That is when the real teaching begins! If every lesson or plan goes perfectly, we wouldn't have to teach or lead at all. We could just phone it in, sit back and watch. However, life and school doesn't work that way. (Even Halloween!) We have to keep trying and planning and working and hoping. There is no alternative.

You know what I am going to do next year: The same thing. I like Halloween. I have the face for it ☺. I enjoy it and hopefully more kids will come next year. I will have more stuff and more music and candy again. We keep trying no matter what!

Have a great week! Happy November!

John

Thought for the Week – November 9, 2009

This weekend, as I was watching a college football game (can you imagine?), I saw a promotional advertisement for a news station in South Carolina. They were asking parents and teachers and students to watch an exclusive on a new invention coming to the Low Country. It was "Bullet-proof Backpacks"! It was going to show how they were made and actually demonstrate how well or poorly the backpacks repelled different caliber bullets.

Am I missing something here? Have we become so dangerous in our schools that we will see four-year olds jumping from their cars in the morning with their bullet-proof back-packs?

Have the solution to meanness and violence become dressing our kids up like Robocop? Maybe so!

For the third time since the beginning of the year, I have had to collect my entire fifth grade and remind them about the need to be civil and respectful of each other. I have had to remind 10 and 11 year olds that it is not alright or acceptable to call each other euphemisms, make fun of each other or even push, kick or hit each other.

It shouldn't be really surprising. As I have said before in these weekly messages, you cannot watch any cable news show without someone being derisive, rude, mean or nasty and they are the commentators. The guests are worse! Even the cartoons they watch are layered in sarcasm, veiled messages of intolerance and even hatred.

So instead of working tirelessly to maintain a respectful and dignified co-existence with each other, we now can just dress everyone up in reinforced fabric designed to repel attacks from wherever they may come. Instead of talking about our differences with real listening and thoughtful discussion, we will become more insular and walk around with our personal set of prison bars keeping our enemies out but also keeping ourselves in.

Do not misunderstand what I am saying. We need to be vigilant to protect ourselves and our students from people who would do them harm. However, they are usually people who come from outside, not ones we attend school with and eat lunch with.

Have we become so intolerant of each other that the word debate needs to be eliminated from the dictionary because it has become an antiquated form of civil conversation?

I don't know about you but today and each day, I will try to understand more, love more and care more. The alternative is trapper keepers made of Kevlar!

Have a great and safe week!

John

Thought for the Week – November 16, 2009

This month Sesame Street is celebrating its 40th birthday! It is hard to remember that it was one of the few shows for educating children on television in 1969 (Captain Kangaroo and cartoons were about it.) When then FCC required all television stations to air three hours of children's programming, new shows were created and honed to where we now see Blue's Clues, Dora the Explorer, and many others.

Sesame Street was the first of its kind. It was created for pre-school students. It didn't talk down to them. It used Muppets and real people to teach math, reading, phonics and how to be nice to each other. Long before Elmo, there was Kermit the Frog, Oscar the Grouch, Big Bird, Super Grover, and Bert and Ernie. They even taught kids to speak Spanish.

It was funny and educational and real and special. My kids watched it growing up and it gave me an excuse for watching it too!

In 1982, the actor who played Mr. Hooper suddenly died. Other shows would have just hired a new actor or just write him out of the show. Sesame Street couldn't and wouldn't do that. They used it as way to talk about loss and the love of friends and how to carry on. It was wonderful and touching to see Big Bird deal and talk about the loss of his dear friend, Mr. Hooper.

Sesame Street is what makes television good!

In its forty years of existence they have kept most of their actors. They have matured with the show and have been great! They have been dedicated and wonderful! They are still producing a great show for kids and helping kids learn.

Happy Birthday Sesame Street! Have a sunny day where everything's a-ok!

Have a great week!

John

Thought for the Week – November 22, 2009

I am thankful for friends who appreciate and love me because of my faults, not in spite of them.

I am thankful for the life that I have been given even though it has sometimes been difficult or painful.

I am thankful for the prayers that I have received that I didn't know about.

I am thankful for a job that I love to do when others are looking to find a job.

I am thankful for blue skies, rain for the plants, wind that moves the leaves and the waves that hit the shore. It shows me that God is still here.

I am thankful for family and friends who read what I write, write me back and make me laugh.

I am thankful that I have someone I can look up to and love dearly.

I am thankful for coworkers who work tirelessly to help the children in every way.

I am thankful for all of you.

What are you thankful for?

Have a wonderful Thanksgiving!

Have a great week!

John

Thought for the Week – November 29, 2009

I have been reading an edition of Educational Leadership from October 2008. (Yes I am still behind.) In it I found an article by Steven Wolk. He writes about "Joyful Learning" and the need to add joy to your school. He even suggested eleven joyful things to do. (Not ten or twelve; that's great!) Some of his suggestions: Find the pleasure in learning; Give students choice; Let students create things; Show off student work; Read good books; Have fun together.

I know some of you may think that in the age of standards and essential questions and testing that we are too busy to try the suggestions above or to find joy in anything.
Isn't that the point?

If we present the goals and standards and lessons with a joy that reveals to our students that they are as important as the content we teach, the result could be deeper learning.

If we take the time to talk with the students instead of at them, we might find out that they know more or persevere through more than we knew.

If we make the effort to support our peers through positive actions, they may work harder, feel better and achieve more.

If all of us tried harder to find the joy in our job, (there is only one letter that separates those words), maybe we can help others who feel stressed and anxious about learning, or teaching or leading.

The holiday season is supposed to be a season for Joyful living and anticipation. I challenge all of us in the three weeks prior to Christmas break to find joy in the children and adults around you, (I know, try anyway!). I ask you to find joy in the daily work that you do and the daily efforts that you make to help everyone achieve more. I ask you to find time for one of the suggestions above.

You may think that you don't have time for experiencing something joyful however we need to take the time to do just that!

Have a great week. Happy December!

John

Thought for the Week – December 7, 2009

This year I decided to put up a Christmas tree. I have not done so for several years. I guess it took a while to get back in the mood to get a tree, go through the decorations and place them on the aforementioned tree. However, it seemed like a good time to begin this tradition again.

This endeavor became a more enjoyable one than I thought it would be. A great friend gave me a tree to use and it fit perfectly in the house. So, I only had to bring in the boxes of decorations (lots of boxes), and go through them.

That is when the fun began. I have a lot of ornaments. I have been given most of them or acquired them through the years and it was enjoyable to remember the student that gave me that one or the handmade one that I kept (even though I couldn't remember why), or the one that was a gift so many years ago. There were more ornaments left in the boxes than used on the tree.

It is similar to the gifts we are given in life. We are given so much and then we store them away in our memories or other mental "boxes" and only remember them during a special event or a holiday. We forget that someone cared about us enough to give us or make us a gift. We forget, because we are so busy, that we have been given much and we should be thankful and happy and joyous.

That is why we have this season! This special season is accompanied with its own music and preparations; its own prayers and remembrances; its own memories and memories to be made.

Let's take time this week to remember the many gifts we have been given: Friendship, love, support, understanding, tolerance and forgiveness.

My tree looks great; I hope yours is wonderful too!

Have a great week!

John

Thought for the Week – December 14, 2009

I have a Christmas cactus. I have had it for years and it has not bloomed in years. I kept it because it is a nice looking plant without flowers and since it is a cactus, it is fairly easy to care for. (I cannot kill it by not watering it.)

When I moved to my new house, I placed it on a back covered porch and basically left it alone.

It is heavy with blooms and will bloom right around Christmas! I guess it is because it has received the right amount of cold weather, moisture and light. I am just glad it is blooming. It is a beautiful plant and it is wonderful to see it live up to its name!

It is supposed to bloom near Christmas and yet it is still a surprise! It is a wonderful, beautiful surprise from a plant called a Christmas cactus!

I wish for all of you many expected surprises this holiday season! I wish for all of you many laughs, fun times and new memories. I wish for all of you the wonderful feeling of being near family and friends. I wish for all of you the joy that comes from singing familiar songs and reading known stories.

I wish for all you the best the holidays can bring.

Merry Christmas!

John

Thought for the Week – January 4, 2010

Someone once said, "The only constant is change." As we look back on the past year and begin a new one, it seems that metaphor rings true once again.

Many of us, in the New Year will be facing changes in school design, program focus, grade levels we offer and attendance zones. Those changes will induce other changes like our demographics, clientele, PTA membership, School Council representation, and overall climate of the building.

We can wish things would stay the same; we can hope that it will be pretty close to what we had or we can prepare and get ready!

When I moved last April into a new house, I took the opportunity (and challenge) of going through everything in the house and I downsized. I kept what I thought would work in the new house. I gave some other things away. I gifted some other things to my kids. I actually threw some things away. I then had to go out and buy a few new things for the new house! I decided that I didn't want to try to make the old stuff fit in the new house.

I believe that is what we have to do to prepare for the changes coming our way. We need to keep some things - the love and dedication for our students – the belief that we can make a difference in their lives. We need to get rid of some things – the wish that things would stay the same. We may even have to get some new things – training in a program – the study of a new attendance zone. We cannot make what we did fit in what we are going to do.

For me, the new house became a catalyst for a new part of my life. The changes coming can be a catalyst for a positive new part of our work life too! It all depends on what we keep, what we give away and what we throw out.

Happy New Year!

Have a great week!

John

Thought for the Week – January 11, 2010

With the unusually long cold weather this winter, many of us have had to look for our winter apparel. We search through out closets for coats, jackets, hats, scarves, gloves, mittens, sweaters, and anything we can grab that might keep us warmer on these frigid days. In many cases, we had forgotten what we had put in cold storage, (pun intended), several years ago. We know that if we wear what we have, we will be protected and warm and we will survive until the weather breaks.

When we are confronted with new challenges or harder material do we do the same thing? Do we go back to look for what we have done in the past that we know worked? Do we use our experiences to help others succeed? Do we use what we know in a way to help or students and our co-workers feel safe and secure and protected?

Just like some winter days, our students can feel like they are left out in the cold on some instructional days. They feel that life is too hard and they need to feel the warmth of someone's care and the comfort that comes from our support.

There are many ways to feel cold and there are many ways to bring warmth.

Let's be the bringer's of warmth in a time of cold.

Have a great week!

John

Thought for the Week – January 17, 2010

Every now and then something so horrific happens that it makes everyone sit up and get quiet and reflect and pray. That is what happened last week as Haiti experienced an earthquake that measured 7.2 on the Richter scale. In a short time, it leveled buildings, tore up roads and destroyed houses and lives.

Then the news crews arrived and they began to give us the twenty-four hour a day coverage that showed us the devastation and need; the tragedy and fear; the loss and the tears.

We unfortunately have felt this way and seen tragedies before: We remember Katrina and New Orleans. We commemorate 9-11 in New York, Pennsylvania and D.C. We remember the 1987 World Series in California and the bridge collapse in Minnesota. Now we see an earthquake in Haiti and we see the bodies and we feel their loss and know their need.

It puts things in perspective doesn't?

When we feel put upon or overburdened. When we feel over-worked or challenged by the day-to-day labor or frustrations. When people have us on our last nerve…..Remember…We have our lives, our families, our homes, our electricity, our luxuries. They have not been taken from us in a brief, horrible instant.

I know we will make it through the week. I pray that the Haitian people make it through as well!

Have a great week!

John

Thought for the Week – January 25, 2010

I was reading in one my science magazines, (where else?), that researchers who have been studying bees have come up with a whole new theory on how the hives work. They believe that every bee works together at different jobs that as a result make the hive act like a single-celled organism. There are bees that work to make the immune system work more efficiently. There are bees that care for the hive. There are bees that care for the queen. There are bees that clean and bees that guard. Each bee in the hive has the same DNA because they all came from the same queen! Each bee works to make the hive the most efficient possible.

Isn't that wonderful? Even though they have different jobs, they work to make the hive successful, healthy, safe and literally – alive! If one group doesn't do their jobs as efficiently, it could mean the end of the hive. Either everyone is successful or everyone will pay the price.

We can do this even better. Rather than just doing our own job to the best of our ability, we can help others when they need it. We can assist students other than our own. We can support our peers and our collective community. We can understand differences and celebrate others accomplishments. We can even forgive others when mistakes are made or when things are left undone.

However we must truly believe in this concept: When one of us succeeds, all of us do. When one of us has problems, all of us do too.

If bees can have it in there DNA, can't we make it part of our work DNA?

Have a great week!

John

Thought for the Week – February 1, 2010

During my church service yesterday, my pastor reminded us that the Gospels were simply, words of hope. They give us hope in this world when the news looks bleak; hope to our hearts in tough times; offer solace when we grieve; and strength when we are weak. These words of hope provide the support we need until we are walking tall again on our two feet.

Do we in our day to day lives offer words of hope? Do we offer solace, and strength, and support and prayer? Do our words pick other up when they are down? Do they provide strength when they are weak? Do our words provide support when they need it the most?

In a time when people talk too much and hear too little, let's select our words wisely and offer the most hope that we can. To our students, our co-workers, members of our family, friends and acquaintances let's offer the most hopeful and helpful words we can. We may find that by giving other hope, we find our hearts filled with hope as well.

Have a great week!

John

Thought for the Week – February 8, 2010

This morning I had conversations with kids about two things: One group wants to raise money for Haitian Relief; the other group complained about bullying in the hallway. The first group was trying to help somebody deal with a bad situation and the second group was telling me how they were dealing with their own bad situation.

It made me sad.

Why is it special for a group of young people to want to be nice to people they don't know and normal for other young people to call each other names and hurt their feelings? Why is it the norm for people to be unkind to each other? Why do we want to have a parade when people are compassionate to each other? Shouldn't we all be treated with kindness and respect and dignity? Shouldn't we treat others the same way? Have we gone so far down the road of incivility that we think a nice person is the second coming of Mother Teresa!

As for me, I am going to congratulate my student leaders who want to do something nice to help the people of Haiti. I hope the others find, in the near future, a way to be nicer, kinder, more understanding and tolerant.

It's the kind of world I want to work and live in!

Have a great week!

Be nice to each other out there.

John

Thought for the Week – February 22, 2010

Last Friday, we experienced our first measurable snow fall in 23 years! Now, people living up north would say, "Big deal!" However, to us it was a big deal….in more ways than one!

For me late last Friday began with taking my dog on a walk and watching her in the snow. She would sniff it, collect it on her body and then shake if off her, (and in the process put more on me.) During our walk we met a couple walking (or trying to) their Dalmatian puppy. This animal was really getting into the snow spirit. She would jump up in the air, contort her body and try to catch every large, wet snow flake. If it was Sesame Street, I would have said the snow was brought to you by the letter "S".

Farther down the street, a couple made a snow person, put a bikini on it and placed a bottle of wine in its lap. Now that is artistry!

Around all this activity were long walks appreciating how the world looks different in the snow. You usually don't see palm tree and snow fall. The world looked lighter and felt lighter too. Everyone wanted to stay as long as they could because they knew, soon it would be gone.

Sometimes we need to shake up our own world too! We need to do something different; something not routine; something to shake us out of our mood; something new or rare. We need to do it in our classroom, school and sometimes our lives. It invigorates us. It gives us more energy and raises our spirits.

Now that the snow has melted, let's try to find other ways to change it up; make it different; help ourselves and others feel renewed when the routine becomes just that – routine.

Have a great week!

John

Thought for the Week – March 1, 2010

I am reading the book, <u>Fearless,</u> by Max Lucado. It talks about how we are anxious or afraid of things from losing money to friends to health to reputation. It also talks about how we have to put our faith in front of our fears to help us make it; help us remain happy and calm and strong amidst a storm that might rage around us.

Be not afraid. It is easier said than done but we must model this if our students or our co-workers are to have courage as well. Unless we truly believe that what we do will make a difference in their lives, they will fear and we will fear. Unless we truly believe in making the harder decisions rather than the easier "give-ups" our students or our schools will never do as well as we want.

In the middle of earthquakes, tsunamis, government squabbles and mean people everywhere; we must be fearless and believe that each day we can help one person be better than the day before. And hopefully, there is a person out there that will help us be better too!

Have a great week.

John

Thought for the Week – March 15, 2010

The other day, as I was putting gas in my car, I noticed a teenager on a skateboard. He was moving smoothly from one end of the parking lot to the other moving around pedestrians and cars with little or no concern about his safety. This would seem to be a normal picture of youthful energy but he was also texting the entire time! He was safely and quickly moving on his skateboard while texting someone who was probably not far off riding his or her own skateboard.

Incredible!

Our students are more technology savvy that we sometimes give them credit for. Technology is what we do after important things like – school. Texting and other ways of communication have been placed in the box marked entertainment rather than a tool for education.

We need to rethink that. The brains of our young people have been trained from an early age to multi-task, multi-hear and multi-comprehend things that come to them from different technologies. They learn better via technology than textbooks. Why shouldn't they? They have never known life without a computer, cell phones, PDA's, IPods, and YOU TUBE.

I realize there are good and bad parts to that. Every type of technology has it. We have had to teach kids about Cyber-bullying and how words in print hurt just as much as words spoken aloud. However, I remember when rock and roll was supposed to be the end of the world and computers were big, loud and slow.

If our kids can ride a skate board and text at the same time maybe they can learn a lot more with technology than we give them credit for.

If we get good at it, we might just end up on YOU TUBE!

Have a great week!

John

Thought for the Week – March 25, 2010

I have come full circle when it comes to the concept of Spring Break!

As a young student, I used to look forward to some time off and hoped that spring has finally begun and that I could spend the week recuperating and enjoying warmer weather.

Later on, I had the same dreams about spring break. I hoped to go to the beach and take a vacation with friends. Usually, I was working and that did not really happen. It would have been nice to tell people, "What happens at Tybee, stays at Tybee." But, that did not happen either. What they show in the movies usually doesn't.

Now in 2010, I am back to anticipating some time to recuperate, some time to enjoy the warmer weather and relaxing and preparing for the last months of the school year. We all need it!

I wish the best for you during this break. If you are traveling be safe and if you celebrate Easter, say a few prayers for the needs and cares of our students, our parents, our fellow teachers and ourselves.

Have a great spring break!

John

Thought for the Week – April 5, 2010

I went to funeral on Saturday. It was for a friend not a relative. It was for a woman who was already old when I first met her. She had endured much and had experienced more than her share of love and loss and pain and redemption.

Many times at a funeral, you will hear things said about the departed that you know is a little (or a lot) inflated from what we knew about the person. Sometimes you even wonder if the minister knew the person at all.
Not this time.

The pastor had known her for years and everything that he stated was true and real and a reminder of who she was and how she lived.

She was always patient and generous; always understanding and forgiving; always prayerful and knowing; never judgmental. If she heard something negative about someone, she would say, "Maybe there is something going on we don't know about." She might say, "That is just the way he is." Or "The Lord knows the whole story." When her pastor would call her a saint, she would say, "No I am NOT a saint, I am just working toward being one someday."

She made it. I have no doubt.

Sometimes we learn things from people just by knowing them. We learn things by observation and by just being in their presence. We learn things by watching their example and seeing what they do.

What are people learning by watching us? What examples are we setting each day? Are we as forgiving? Are we as non-judgmental? Are we as accepting?

None of us are saints, but, we can sure work toward being one someday!

A happy Easter to all of you!

Have a great week!

John

Thought for the Week – April 11, 2010

The other day, as I was sitting on my back porch, I noticed two lizards stalking each other. They were playing a cold-blooded version of tag.

I watched them as they went from one side of the porch to another. (It is not a big porch but when you are three inches long it is an endeavor.) During this gecko ballet, both the lizards turned from brown to green to a brighter green and back to brown! I don't know if they were trying to impress the other, or scare the other, or fool the other into thinking they were something they were not.

After about 20 minutes, they twisted and turned and jumped and eventually slowed down and went on their individual ways.

How many times in our lives, or our schools, or our classrooms, do we meet people who try to be stronger than they actually are? How many try not to show emotion or pretend that everything is all right? How many need help or support but do not ask because they think it is a sign of weakness? How many prefer to strut and pretend?
How many do we miss because we fail to see and ask and look?

As we begin the fourth quarter, we should know which of our students or co-workers or peers need extra support, or assistance. We should know which ones need more time. We should know the ones that need our help. We should be able to look through the camouflage and see what needs to be done.

And as always: We need to help them because that is what we always do!

Have a great fourth quarter!

Have a great week!

John

Thought for the Week – April 19, 2010

Recently, I bought five new ferns. Two were placed on my back porch and three were placed on my front porch. The two on the back porch proceeded to do extremely well. However the three on the front porch proceeded to do terribly. I watered them and fertilized them and worried about them. The ones of the back porch made me look like farmer John and the ones on the front porch made me look like John the plant killer.

I moved the three ferns from the front porch to the back porch. I guess the front porch since it faces west was getting too hot for the ferns and I needed to provide for them a better, more nurturing environment from which to grow. I had to understand that I could water and fertilize and work as hard as I could but it was still not going to help the plants thrive and survive.

It is the same with our work and our school and our students. When something is not working, we need to try something new. If we see someone who is not thriving or growing the way we would like, then we need to change something, be creative, collaborate, consolidate, differentiate........etc. What we cannot do is perseverate on what has already proven to be ineffective.

If we do, our students will be successful and grow and be healthy. We will know it is happening because just like the ferns.....they will show us!

Have a great week!

John

Thought for the Week – April 25, 2010

I was listening to the radio the other day and the commentator described how agents from the National Basketball Association have announced that they have found the next LeBron James, the next great basketball player. They were also several colleges attempting to recruit the young man.

Then I was told that this young man was only 10 years old!

Here is a child of ten being wooed with the idea of fame and fortune and fans and adoration and a life beyond what he could imagine.

I hope it happens for him. I truly do. I hope it begins when he is 18 and a young adult. I hope in the meantime he is not hurt, (physically or emotionally), and that his talent is honed and not just used.

I also hope that for all the 10 year olds out there. They are with us; they have skills and dreams; they have hopes and aspirations; they have gifts. Their talents need to be honed and built upon and nurtured and their weaknesses need to be understood and addressed as well.

Every child that we know can be loved, adored and understood. Not everyone may be born for greatness but everyone can become great! They can become a great father, husband, brother, helper, worker, teacher, administrator, preacher, and friend. They all can be great; it up to us to get them there.

Have a great week!

John

Thought For the Week – May 3, 2010

It is not without a bit of irony that we celebrate both Teacher Appreciation Week and administer the CRCT this week!

It makes sense when you think about it.

Your efforts, dedication, worry and prayers should be appreciated and you should receive appropriate accolades from a grateful community, state and country. You have worked diligently to prepare your students so that they can individually show what you have worked collectively to give them: knowledge, application, understanding and thoughtfulness.

You should receive gifts of food, and cards and certificates and pats on the back because – You deserve them and you deserve so much more.

So during these next few days, we will not only be thanking you for all that you have done since September, we will also be praying that your students have listened, and learned and believe and thus – achieve!

It is why most of us became a teacher – to make a difference in the lives of children. You should be thanked and appreciated and lauded and fed and applauded.

It is the least we can and should do. You are the best of what is a noble profession!

Have a great week!

John

<u>Thought for the Week – June 7, 2010</u>

Once again we hear about the sudden loss of a loved one. We feel sadness; we pray for those left behind; we are reminded of the preciousness of life.

We should also be reminded of how to treat people when they are alive and not just remember them when they are gone.

There is a lack of compassion in the present world. Life has become more of a competition than a place for caring, loving and kindness. It has become a place where everyone is ready to say something mean about someone rather than take the time to understand where they are coming from. We are ready at any given time to compare ourselves to others in an effort to exalt ourselves or make ourselves feel better. Or we want to win an argument or have the last word. We are so much better than everyone else and everyone else should know that.

We have lost our way and we must regain it.

We complain about how mean our students are to each other and yet we have been a lousy role model. We readily slam a colleague and then shake our heads when a young person does the same to a school mate. Isn't that the definition of hypocrisy?

We can all do better. We all need to do better.

Our colleagues deserve it and everyone deserves to experience it before they aren't around to see it or hear it.

Compassion + Dedication = Success ……was it a motto or a discarded antiquated ideal that died a long time ago?

It is up to us.

John

Thought for the Week – August 30, 2010

A recent TIME Magazine cover article discussed summer vacation. It basically supported the view that it was unnecessary; it caused the "summer slide". It stated that it was great for kids who came from families who could afford camps and educational trips but it was disastrous for kids who were stuck at home all day while parents worked and toiled to make money for the necessities in life.

Today, you are going to see both! We will have those that will write numerous paragraphs about "What they did during summer vacation." We will also have those that will answer that question with two words: "I waited."

They are waiting for us to help them, to nurture them, to see them as an important part of their class, grade level and school. They are waiting for us to give them a new start and a new direction. They are waiting us to give them a hug, or a handshake; a pat on the back, or a helping hand; a supportive nod, or a praiseful look.

They have been waiting for us. We need to let them know that we have been waiting for them too!

Welcome back! Have a great week!

John

Thought for the Week – September 7, 2010

Right before the beginning of the school year, we were running around painting walls and doors and poles. We were trying to make the school look as good and inviting as possible. We were putting on a new coat; sprucing it up; improving its look for the coming year.

The histories in the walls and behind the doors were the same. The efforts and successes; the disappointments and tears had still occurred. However, now we could start new. We could do something different. Tackle things in a different way. Find new innovations and technologies to help us. Care more......love more.....work just as hard!
All the history and effort and tears still looked better under a new coat of paint.

Our kids are coming back to us with new shirts and skirts and slacks and belts and shoes. They are breaking in new lunch boxes and backpacks and pencil boxes and notebooks. Even with their own new coats of paint, they come with they own histories and successes and pain and challenges.

In both cases, it looks better, but both need our help, our support, our prayers and our work to make what works inside the best it possibly can be.

Have a great week!

John

Thought for the Week – September 13, 2010

A seasoned principal with 30 years experience was asked what his ten most important rules were. The number one answer on his list was, "Your school must be for all kids 100% of the time!"

In 11 words, he has put everyone on notice as to what our jobs represent and what our efforts must focus on. We must find a way for all the kids who walk in our doors to be safe, secure and successful.

Wow!

Have you asked the question already? Have you looked inward and outward and truthfully responded to that call? Is your school for 100% of the kids all the time? Do you include the disenfranchised, the angry, the hurt, the despondent, the challenged, the gifted, the needy, the average, the silent and the loud? Do you equally care for the most adorable and the most annoying? Do you try and pray as hard for the 5% that take 95% of your time?

If you said yes, do you really mean it? Would it be better to say yes, but I know I can do better? I would!

We do have the power to teach tolerance by being tolerant and love by being loving and stubbornness by being tenacious and forgiveness by being forgiving.

I wish for all our schools to work toward the mantra: "We are for all our kids 100% of the time!" Hopefully that is the reason why we do what we do!

Have a great week!

John

Thought for the Week – September 20, 2010

At the edge of my little garden area, amongst the big lantana bushes and red tips there grew up a little stick. It was no more than 4 inches high when I first became aware of its presence. It wasn't much to look at and I thought for a while a little kid came along and in fun had stuck a twig into the ground.

In time miniscule branches grew off that stick and in a few short weeks that little twig in the ground was covered with beautiful, tiny, yellow chrysanthemum blooms! It was lovely and charming and amazing and surprising.

I have been watering it ever since that day. I want it to be around for a long time. You see, I had forgotten that I had planted a small mum at that spot over a year ago and it slowly pushed its way through the soil and became this lovely flower.

You might have kids like that. Kids that all of sudden show you something you weren't expecting: Kids that are doing well and surprise you with their knowledge and confidence and competence; kids that are success stories.

You too have forgotten the work that has gone into that success: The teachers, who have made every effort to help him, the many years that it may have taken to create this success story.

We can sometimes forget what we have tried to do, but we can never forget to do it. There amongst all the dirt and paper and sweat and tears is something beautiful trying to push its way toward the light.

Have a great week!

John

Thought for the Week – September 27, 2010

In a recent poll, people were asked what things kept them the most organized and calm and happy. A majority stated their faith as number one and technology as number two!

At first blush, we may be slightly taken aback or appalled. We may think that Guitar Hero and Sim City have become almost as important to us as our religion. Some may think with the time people spend on each, it may be the other way around. However, I think they are talking about technology as it is used for communication and information.

Let's face it. We use technology to instantly contact a loved one to make sure they are okay. We use technology to send a birthday card or a kind word. We use technology to check on the weather where our kids go to school or where our parents live. It is immediate and current and alive. As a novelist recently stated, "I cannot use a missed phone call as a way to increase the suspense in a story anymore."

What does technology have to do with us? It is the next frontier in educational equality; the new way to teach; the 21st century solution to a world-wide challenge – educational mastery in a global economy.

We as educators who were born in the last century must use the technology that evolves literally every minute to educate those who were born in this century. Any elementary school-aged child knows how to use a computer, text, e-mail and most even have their own face book account and several I am sure are blogging right now. (I am all a twitter!) (sorry)

We cannot continue to teach 21st century content in a 19th century way. We can reach our students at any age by using the technology that is around us already. We just have to have the courage to use it.

We can make the leap from slate boards and chalk to magic-slates and Smart Boards.

We can; we have to. It is the 21st century after all.

Have a great week!

John

Thought for the Week – October 4, 2010

Earlier this week, our pre-kindergarten students had their annual – "Gingerbread Man" – activity. The teacher leads the students around the school meeting everyone from the School Secretary to the Media Specialist to the Kitchen Manager to the Principal and Assistant Principal to the Counselor to the Head Custodian. This is done while trying to find the Gingerbread Man who has left a mess in the room. All of us were given cards with our version of "Run, run as fast as you can, you can't catch me, I'm the Gingerbread Man....look for me in the Kitchen...etc." It also gave the kids a way to learn about who worked in the building and what they did. The kids were excited and happy and learned a great deal as they walked around the building.

All the adults who were asked to help in this activity, found themselves to also be excited and happy and we learned about our little ones too!

Let's be clear: It was loud and there was laughter and kids were moving all over the place and five or six were talking at the same time. However, we knew they were learning while they were having fun; they were learning amidst the noise.

True learning is not always found in a quiet place, with tacit responses and mood music playing in the background. Sometimes it is found amongst laughter and yelling and manipulatives falling on the floor. It is found as little ones play follow-the-leader looking for a Gingerbread Man. It is found when adults play along and smile and laugh with them.

Learning does not have to be sterile and stern; nor delineated by students sitting in rows or designated areas.

Find time this week to laugh, smile, and play. I guarantee you will learn something about your students and about yourself too!

Have a great week!

John

Thought for the Week – October 13, 2010

On Thursday, October 7, 2010 at 7:30 a.m. one of the most amazing people I have ever known passed away.

My mother never went to high school but was very smart and ran the finances and household of a family with two adults and six children. My mother always stressed two things to her children: Education and hard work. You were expected to get an education so that you could get a decent job. You were expected to work hard and not complain about much. She had been through more and endured more than her children would ever see.

She was proud of that!

She was proud of her children. She was so proud she would remind us of things we should do or things we shouldn't do. She was my momma after all.

Mom was not perfect but neither is her son. She could be demanding and stubborn and inflexible and opinionated and I will miss all of that.

I will miss most of all the weekly Sunday phone call where I would update her on my life and what her grandchildren were doing. We would laugh together and she would always thank me for calling her even though I could hear the tears in her voice.

Years ago, when my father's last uncle died, Dad looked at me and said, "Now we all move up a rung on the ladder!" I now understand what he meant. You are always a son when you have a momma around. You are always reminded of silly things you did and occasionally you still feel like an awkward twelve year-old. (Especially when your brothers and aunts still call you Johnny after all these years…..I didn't mind…I knew momma always called me Johnny unless she was mad at me.) When you are a Johnny you cannot feel too old.

So I guess I have moved up a rung on the ladder too. It is however a well-made, strong, and sturdy ladder. It was made by the hard-working, God-fearing, tiny woman who will always be my momma!

God bless you Vivian. Heaven has good cook in heaven and if given the chance, she will rearrange the place!

John

Thought for the Week – October 18, 2010

On my way back from Virginia last week, I had to drop a family member off at Reagan National Airport. The airport is a stone's throw from the Pentagon and Washington D.C. and at 7:00 a.m. there is a lot of car traffic and pedestrians walking across eight lanes to get to their respective check points.

As I was watching the throng of people heading to and from the airport, I saw one well-dressed gentleman walking confidently toward his destination. He moved comfortably amongst the throng with the air of someone who had made that sojourn many times before. What was also amazing is that he adroitly used his tall white cane to remind him of the curbs, drainage grates and fellow travelers who were not as knowledgeable of the area as he was.

It was a great sight to see. He was comfortable in his own skin and it was not a disability; it was a minor inconvenience.

All of us have them. Some of more noticeable than others; and all of us have been taught to overcome them. We have also been taught to walk confidently and to deal with our own minor inconveniences.

Now it is our turn to help others learn the same.

Have a great week!

John

Thought for the Week – November 1, 2010

I am sure you have heard that several young people have taken their own lives as a result of bullying. This bullying was not the usual punching and name calling. It was brutal cyber bullying. Its aim was total destruction of an individual's character. Its aim was to bring a peer to their knees and to make him or her feel as bad as possible.

They succeeded beyond their wildest dreams. The attack so totally destroyed that the victim felt no course but to leave this earth because they felt the damage could not be undone; it couldn't be fixed; they couldn't survive the assault.

I have asked this question before, but I shall do it again: "Where did we get the idea that we can say whatever we want about whoever we want?" This is not a first amendment issue. I believe in freedom speech and sharing opinions. However, we have lost the ability to debate in a civil way. We have lost the ability to listen to other opinions and learn about and respect different points of view. We have lost the will to write things and state things in a dignified and appropriate way.

We have somehow allowed our peers and our youngsters to believe that they can publish via e-mail or twitter or blogs whatever they want to say. They believe it is their right to slam anyone they wish or send pictures in an effort to be as mean and hurtful as possible. We have promoted this because we watch shows on television that have older adults doing the same to each other every night in prime time.

We only show concern and outrage when defenseless youngsters commit suicide!
It is similar to putting a traffic light up right after a tragic, senseless, deadly crash occurs at an intersection.

Well, we have had the tragic, senseless, crash. It is a head-on collision between civility and rudeness; between understanding and mockery; between compassion and derisiveness....between love and hate.
It is up to all of us.

You may disagree with me and that is your right and privilege. I just hope we can have a respectful, dignified discussion before we lose more young people because they felt there was no way out and no way to continue.

It is sad day for all.

John

Thought for the Week – November 8, 2010

My sister and brother have taken on the unenviable task of cleaning out my parents' house. It has 30 plus years of stuff in it and we are not talking about heirlooms and other things destined for the Antique Road Show. We are talking about of lifetime of aprons and scarves and photographs and knick-knacks. It is like wading through the flotsam and jetsam of people's lives.

Prior to this endeavor my siblings had asked the family to tell them if there was anything in the house they wanted. I asked for two things: A wooden sign that said Mental Ward on it, (another story for another time), and the 48 star American Flag that was draped over my Grandfather's casket when he was buried at Arlington National Cemetery. I received both my requests a few weeks ago.

Then last week, I received something more. In the mail, I found my grandfather's Honorable Discharge Papers. I say papers because he was discharged from the Army in 1918 and from the Navy in 1945! George Raymond King was a doughboy in the war to end all wars and a naval fighter in the war that came after that. The first one stated that he had enlisted at the age of 21 and second one stated he was discharged at the age of 48.

My grandfather was not a perfect human being. In fact, he lived a very colorful and interesting life but he did serve his country and was eventually honored with military honors in 1961 for his service to our country.

As we celebrate Veterans Day this Thursday, let's remember all of our friends and family members who have served their country and given us the opportunity to have the freedoms we enjoy. Some of these fine men and women made the ultimate sacrifice. Some, like my grandfather, were lucky enough to survive two wars and earned the right to be buried at Arlington.

We need to remember those who like my grandfather were born in the late 1800's and those who fought in the wars that came afterwards. They are all heroes and they all deserve our thanks. As for me, I have put the flag in a shadow box and it is hanging in a place of honor in my house as a reminder of his service and his life.

Have a great week!

John

Thought for the Week – November 22, 2010
_____

Webster's defines thankful as – Feeling or expressing thanks. During this very busy week that kicks off the holiday season, I ask you - what are you thankful for? What makes you stop and thank someone for what they do for you or have done for you; for what they have given to you; for what they have brought to your life?

Let me try:

I am thankful for the love in my life. It gives me strength and the awareness of something and someone greater than myself.
I am thankful for friends. We support each other and allow each other to be human and imperfect and they like us anyway.
I am thankful for parents for they are too soon gone and we immediately become older, and are no longer somebody's child.
I am thankful for laughter. It lightens the heart and soul and makes our burdens and responsibilities lighter.
I am thankful for responsibilities and challenges. It reminds us that life is productive, viable, and purposeful.
I am thankful for children. It makes us realize we aren't perfect either.
I am thankful for a God who put me here with you at this point in time.
I am thankful being able to sense the wonderful world around us. Even the tears and fears are worth the sensation.
I am thankful for another holiday season.
I am especially thankful for all of you.

Happy Thanksgiving!

John

Thought for the Week – December 1, 2010

Several school systems across the country are trying to make financial ends meet by agreeing to allow advertising on school property. These ads have taken form on the sides of school buses (local insurance companies), on the walls of the cafeteria (local restaurants), and even on the roof of the building, (so people flying in to the town can see an ad for a rental car business).

I am not concerned with the students seeing ads. They are so bombarded with ads on every piece of technology they use; they have learned to ignore it. They can do 5 things at one time and ignore ads and us at the same time.

My question is: If you were given the opportunity to create an advertisement for your school or department, what would you say? Would five out of seven parents recommend you? Would a recent survey list your accomplishments? Would the kids recommend your class or school to others?

We don't need billboards or moving LCD displays lauding our accomplishments. We have living and breathing advertisements sitting in our rooms every day. They are walking display ads for what we try to do and what we try to accomplish. They are our works-in-progress in some cases and our completed art work in others. They are a reflection of us, our efforts, our trials and our accomplishments.

The over-arching question is: When you are finished are they Cadillacs are they Edsel's?

Have a great week!

John

Thought for the Week – December 6, 2010

I was at a local grocery store picking up the normal stuff for the week. As I went into the check-out lane, there stood an elderly gentleman speaking quietly to the check-out clerk. He didn't have a cart with him and I noticed there were no groceries lying on the belt waiting to be scanned.

The gentleman asked the clerk, "How much is that entire grocery cart over there?" He was pointing at a stuffed cart placed near the check-out lanes used to remind buyers to help the less fortunate during this holiday season. The clerk said, "I am not sure." The gentleman stated, "Well there is only one way to find out." So, the gentleman rolled the cart to the clerk who then pulled every item from one cart, scanned it and then placed it in a different cart. At one point he looked at me kindly and said, "This may take a while. I am sorry for making you wait."

I had all the time in the world. I was glad I hadn't missed it. The gentleman paid for the cart, moved its contents to a box located in the front of the store, and then walked out quietly with a smile on his face. He was the embodiment of the Christmas season; a quiet giving angel; a ghost of Christmas Present.

He reminded me that this is the season of giving, not getting; of selflessness not selfishness; of helping others rather than helping ourselves. I don't know who he was or his name. However, I did know at that moment I had received a great gift – I was reminded of the true Reason for the Season.

Have a great week!

John

Thought For the Week – January 6, 2011
==

During the severely cold nights of December, many of my outside plants took a beating and ending up looking destroyed. It was not a pretty sight.

Finally a short warm spell came and I could actually be outside and feel my toes and finger tips. I decided that I would take the opportunity to cut the plants down, throw them away and think about what plants I would replace them with when the warm weather came back for more than a few days.

As I cut away the damaged, frozen portions, I suddenly noticed underneath, several new shoots growing out of the soil. They were fat and green and healthy and beautiful. The plants weren't totally dead at all; the new growth was just being covered up by the old, used stuff.

New growth hidden under the old; progress hidden in plain sight; hope ready to emerge; things better than they seemed.

Sounds like a pretty good New Year's prayer:

During 2011 I hope you find something new in the everyday. I hope you notice the little successes that happen around you. I hope you see the new growth that is hidden under the old. This new growth is only waiting, patiently waiting for the sun's light to lengthen and strengthen enough to reveal......something.....incredible!

Have a great week!

John

Thought for the Week – January 10, 2011

If you happen to watch any playoff game or bowl game, you will notice fans from both sides wearing the team's colors and screaming their support during every play. They are called the 6th man in basketball and the 12th man in football. They are fanatic in their support and love and loyalty to their team. They are joyous with every win; heartbroken with every loss; ready for the week to pass so the next game may be played. They love everything about the team and overlook the faults and weaknesses.

Can we become the same kind of fan for our classrooms and schools? Can we overlook the faults and flaws and give our kids and co-workers the undying loyalty and support they need? Can we cheer for every little success and every minor gain? Can we be joyous with everything they learn and heartbroken over the ones who have not....yet found success?

Can we be the 12th man for the ones who need us the most?

Have a great week!

John

Thought for the Week – January 19, 2011

During one of the recent freezing early mornings, I bundled up and began walking my dog. I must admit I was grumbling as I left my nice warm abode and began the trek around the neighborhood.

As we made the turn toward the large pond located near the entrance of the sub-division, I noticed that a thin layer of ice had formed on the surface of the water. This ice provided a wonderful way for the moonlight to be reflected and made a beautiful, yellowish glow that hovered over the water.

Near the edge of the pond I also noticed amidst the moon glow a blue heron standing in the water. It stood there stoically, waiting patiently for something to move in the water. It wasn't bothered by the cold. It didn't seem frustrated or impatient. It seemed confident; sure that his patience would be rewarded and unwavering in his watching and waiting. The moonlight created a perfect avian silhouette. (Yes it was alive. I saw it move.) In spite of the cold, I was spellbound...I wanted to stand there and watch. You could almost ignore the traffic and the cold and think you were looking at a photograph of a wilderness located many miles from there.

Eventually, the blue heron's patience was rewarded and then he quietly flew away.
In our daily efforts in our classroom or school, do we have that same confidence? Are we as stoic and patient with an unwavering perseverance? Do we know that we will be successful now matter how challenging our job is? Are we comfortable with the knowledge that no matter what we have to face during our journey we will still be successful in finding the final destination?

It is amazing what you can see and learn during an early morning walk in freezing weather with only moonlight to light the way!

Have a great week!

John

Thought for the Week- January 31, 2011

A little over a week ago, I attended the annual Teacher of the Year Gala. This year's was very special since one of the finalists was from Bloomingdale Elementary. It was an honor to dine with her and her family.

Before the Teacher of the Year was announced, they showed a recording of each of the finalists teaching and sharing their philosophy of education and what their job meant to them. Each of them were humble and were touched by being nominated by their peers. Every one of them also spoke of having a "calling" to teach. Each of their stories were inspiring, touching and I was proud of all of them.

We can learn from them. We can be reminded that teaching is a calling to a challenging but noble profession. We can be inspired to do better; to do more; to relish the small successes; to be less critical and more supportive of each other; to pray more and be thankful for what we have and what we can give.

Like the finalists, we can remember that we were called to something special. I know I am going to try to remember that every time I enter a school and every time I enter a classroom.

Have a great week.

John

Thought for the Week – February 7, 2011

I had the opportunity to help my best friend by assisting in trimming up some trees and moving some others and cleaning up the yard. It was a 61 degree day and I could get my hands dirty and feel the soil in my fingers. I could smell it and see the fruits of our labor. It was a great day! It was great to do some gardening again! I knew that once the growing season started her gardens would look good and her yard would look even better and I was happy that I could have a hand (or both hands) in it.

Every day we should toil and work with our children the same way we toil and work in our gardens. We know we are going to get dirty and we know we are going to make a mess before something grows and blooms and shows us the fruits of our labor.

Every day we should know that hard work is a blessing and that all we do will make a difference. Sometimes it will take nurturing and tender care. Sometimes it will take trying something new. Sometimes it will take some quiet time….thinking about how to get them better and how to improve.

Just like toiling in the soil, it is worth it; they are worth it; you are worth it.

Have a great week

John

<u>Thought for the Week – February 14, 2011</u>

We are changed over time. We hopefully become stronger and more malleable; able to endure more challenges. In time we hope to have sage wisdom to accompany our lighter hair color. In time we hope to foresee the bumps or potholes in the road prior to hitting them head on. In time we hope to be able to use our knowledge to help those less experienced. To give them advice on how to live their lives better than the way we lived ours. In time we hope to be better than we were; to be more compassionate, more mature, more sure of ourselves – smarter.

In time – we are all changed. We cannot remain the same no matter how hard we try. The people we meet change us. The people we work with change us. The people we love change us. The people we lose change us.

In time – we become better due to all those we meet and work with and love and lose. It is in honor of them that we become who we become: Hopefully a person with more faith, more courage, more patience, more wisdom. But it does take time! We are not the same as we were years ago.

As we work this week, let us remember that the ones we work with and teach and care about are being shaped by us! In time, they will also be better than they are and better hopefully due to our efforts, love, care and hard work. In time, they will also be better due to our prayers, love, patience and forgiveness.

In time.

Have a great week.

John

Thought for the Week – February 22, 2011

This past weekend, I had the pleasure of visiting my son and his wife. They live in Blacksburg, Virginia. He is a professor at Virginia Tech (he takes after his mother), and she is a graphic artist. They are happy, hard-working, and comfortable in their life. It was fun to see them again and catch up with what they were doing and learn how they were doing. It was a fun, relaxing, low-key weekend and I enjoyed every second of it.

To get to Blacksburg, you fly into Roanoke Airport. You land in the midst of the Blue Ridge Mountains. You see the blue sky as it touches the Blue Ridge and you are reminded of how pretty western Virginia is. You see the puffy clouds and you see snow falling farther up the mountain. You feel the inevitable wind as it pulled up from the foot hills to Giles Cavern and beyond. It was like being in the middle of nowhere with a whole bunch of people. I felt closer to nature and closer to the sky.

It felt like I was back at Blacksburg some 20 + years ago. I recognized most of the buildings and the surroundings, (although there were more good places to eat now.) I also recognized part of me in a 30 something young man who not only was going to Tech but was teaching there. I felt a mixture of pride, appreciation, gratefulness and excitement. I was reminded that as I try to make an impact on students ranging in age from 4 – 12; my son was trying to do the same to students ranging in age from 18 – 25.

You may not be able to go home again, but you sure can visit, reminisce and be proud of how far your children have come and thankful you were able to see it, share in it and create memories. It is those memories that are more precious than pictures and more valuable than time.

Have a great week!

John

<u>Thought for the Week – February 28, 2011</u>

The other morning, I awoke to find the neighborhood covered in a deep fog. It was so thick you couldn't see across the street and everything was so wet it looked like it had been raining. We were literally lying in the midst of clouds. Everything was opaque, obscured and eerie.

In a few short hours, the sun rose and you could see the clouds quickly disappear revealing a beautiful blue sky, equally intense green grass and several trees in bloom!

It was worth the wait and it was as if a film had been lifted from our eyes to reveal a more beautiful reality than expected. It was amazing and beautiful and it was as if spring decided to start right at that moment.

I am glad I got up early that day.

Sometimes as we go through our day-to-day existence we do not realize the fog that has developed. We don't notice how it has obscured our view and has blocked out the good things around us. This fog is caused by worry and busy-ness and deadlines and concerns. It is compounded by phone calls and e-mails.

We must look forward to the sunshine that burns away our fog and clears our vision to see what successes are around us and what beauty lies ahead. Our sunshine is found in the friends that help us, the prayers that lift us up, the laughter that makes the load lighter and the love that we all need.

This week, may you see the wonderful sky and the beauty that is around you.

Have a great week!

John

Thought for the Week – March 14, 2011

During a recent chilly morning, as I was walking my dog around the subdivision, I walked down toward the pond. (You know my route by now from a recent missive about the blue heron silhouetted in the moonlight.) Anyway, as we made the turn toward the pond, I noticed not one or two birds but several flocks of birds resting near the pond or swimming in it.

There was a family of Canadian geese; at least a dozen teal ducks; several dozen white egrets and a couple of larger birds that I couldn't make out in the early morning fog. (Mine and the ponds) It was beautiful and wonderful and I was amazed to see so many birds in such a small area.

Also sitting on the edge of the pond watching in silent reverie was a small black cat. It moved its head back and forth as if it was observing a tennis match. It had a look on its face of awe and appreciation; of answered prayers and great responsibility. You could almost read its mind: "So many birds, so little time." "If I get one of the big ones, I will be a legend!" "And people think it is crazy to leave the cat out all night long." "I wish there were witnesses but I don't want it to be another cat." Etc.

It was so overwhelming and such an extreme sensory overload that the animal didn't do anything because it couldn't decide what to do. (And probably didn't want to get pecked to death.) Even my dog was so impressed with the numbers of birds in the pond she didn't even see the cat.

In our day to day efforts to help and teach others, we may get so overwhelmed by our responsibilities and deadlines that we don't see the little things right in front of us. We don't see a child make a small leap of improvement. We don't see a colleague do an act of kindness. We don't see someone wipe a tear from their eye as they grieve in silence. We don't see a child endure a cruel classmate and do the right thing. We don't see the efforts around us because we are too busy trying to make it out of our own individual fog.

There are good things that happen every day. There are good people out there making a difference. There are beautiful things right in front of us ready to be seen. There are good people, little ones and big ones, just waiting to be noticed.

Have a great week!

John

Thought for the Week – March 21, 2011

I have been reading Mark Twain's Authorized Autobiography. I received the tome as a Christmas gift and I am currently half way through. After completing the preface and introduction, the book has become very interesting and Mark Twain's writing has not disappointed. He would not let his autobiography be published until a hundred years after his death. He wanted it to be an honest and unfiltered review of his life and at the same time he did not want to hurt anyone's feelings. He also didn't want to have to be worried about anyone's reaction to the blunt review of his life.

Interestingly enough about 200 pages into the book he writes and I paraphrase, "In this edition of my autobiography there will be no opinions included. Maybe in a hundred years people will be interested in opinions, we will see." That was written in 1906!

He was very prophetic in his remarks and 100 years later all we seem to be bombarded with is each others' opinions. The definition of opinion according to Webster's New World Dictionary is – A belief not based on absolute certainty or positive knowledge but one what seems true and valid or probable to one's own mind; what one thinks; judgment.

There is nothing wrong with having an opinion. It should be respected as one's belief or judgment. However, other opinions need to be respected as well. Then comes the hard part: We must actually spend the time to gather facts and information in order to adjust our opinions.

In this age of social networking, we have the freedom to say what we want and opine on any subject we wish. We also have the responsibility to be open-minded, fair and understanding when we read other opinions. In this way, social networks can be utilized to share ideas and information and be a powerful force in education. Or it can be used as a way to filter information and only show selected opinions.

Mr. Twain had the advantage of making us wait 100 years to hear what he had experienced and felt throughout his life. We have the advantage of checking what we write before we hit the send button.

Of course, this is only my opinion.

Have a great week!

John

Thought for the Week – March 28, 2011

The NCAA Men's Basketball Championship, aka March Madness has lived up to its name this year. We have seen and read about countless victories by lesser known schools with smaller players. We have heard the experts counsel the multitude as they listed the reasons why this lesser seeded team was going to lose. We also heard the same experts explain why they were wrong when their chosen team lost by 16 points in the 3rd round.

It seems that the schools that won didn't really pay any attention to the expert analysis. They believed in themselves. They believed in what they were capable of doing. They understood how to win; how to be successful; how to be their best. Why? Because they were taught to be successful; they were coached in the right things to do; they knew people believed in them and what they could accomplish.

Our kids can be taught that too! Our students can be coached to be the best academically. They can be given the tools needed to win the game we called test taking and how to find the best answer. They can be shown that we care about them and support them and believe in them.

The experts may have been surprised by some of the teams that were victorious in the last few weeks. However, the schools, coaches and players were not surprised. They expected to be there and they expected to win.

In just a few short weeks, there may be some surprised people when our children are victorious with their summative exams. However, the kids and hopefully their teachers won't be surprised. We need to expect them to be there because we did the work to get them there.

Have a great week!

John

Thought for the Week – April 4, 2011

One of my guilty pleasures is to go to a restaurant and eat food that someone else has prepared. It somehow always tastes better than what I could have done; even though I haven't poisoned myself or anyone else (lately).

I am also willing to drive any distance to eat at a particularly excellent place. It is worth it to me. It is a more than an even exchange. I will drive, 30 minutes, 45 minutes, even 60 minutes if I can get something there that I either cannot make myself or where the combination of the food and the atmosphere makes for a special dining experience. It creates a special occasion; it creates a wonderful memory. It is not a burden but a treasure. It is not something to avoid but something to look forward to – to anticipate with excitement.

Do our students look forward to coming to school with the same anticipation and excitement? Do they make memories because they know they are loved and cared for as well as educated? Do they find being here a treasure and not a burden? Is everyday something to look forward to? Would they be willing to take a longer car or bus ride just to be with us?

We may not be able to make our daily work be as enjoyable as a wonderful meal. But we can make it where our students will look forward to being with us. We can be supportive, understanding, loving, prepared and excited about helping all of our students and our co-workers.

Just like a chef, we know what we can combine to make every day the best for them and the best for us. Our students will look forward to their daily work and our daily efforts. It will make their job and our job more enjoyable and fulfilling.

If you are hungry for that kind of work!

Have a great week!

John

Thought for the Week – April 13, 2011

A new student came to us a few days ago. He has been in several schools this year. He is currently in foster care and he will receive extra services to help him be successful.

We are blessed to have him! Yes….we are blessed to have him! He is happy to be in school. He is happy to know that he is loved. He is happy to not be where he was. He is a strong little survivor who has conquered much in his short life. With all that he has survived, he is still full of smiles, love, understanding, empathy, kindness and compassion.

I have never seen a child so happy to be in school. On his first day, he couldn't contain his happiness for being back in school. He went up to every child and said hello. He already loves his teacher and she already loves him back!

He is a walking, talking, learning miracle. He is also an injured, little person who needs us as much as we need him. He is a constant, daily reminder of why we are here and what we can miss when we look more at books than at children, more at timelines instead of tenderness, more inwardly than outwardly.

We are blessed to have him! You are blessed too. You have little miracles walking around your building too. They are survivors. Look at them and watch them and know that you can learn as much from them as they learn from us!

Have a great week and a great break!

John

Thought for the Week – April 28, 2011

As I get older, I find that my prayer list gets longer. This year alone I have added my mother who passed last October and a new granddaughter for my brother. I tend to mention the newly born and the ones who have passed during my daily prayers. I believe it is a way to provide support for the little ones who cannot take care of themselves and keep the ones who have passed in my memory.

The lists for both have lengthened over the years. It shows that the circle of life is alive and well. My brother's new granddaughter, Emily, was born on my mother's birthday, April 12th. That will be another way to keep her in our memories as the years pass and the little ones grow up strong and healthy.

That is how some prayers are answered. Quietly and it may seem like a coincidence; something serendipitous; a happenstance. I think there truly is much more to it than that. Maybe, the practice of praying for others actually helps us just as much as the ones we are remembering Maybe being part of the circle of life provides more comfort and strength than we know.

We can't see it and maybe we can't prove it, but, I will remember it every time little Emily celebrates a birthday.

Have a great week!

John

Thought for the Week – May 6, 2011

I passed a church the other day. On the message board were two words: Call Mom. I loved it. It was simple, to the point and a reasonable command with Mother's Day coming soon.

Having lost my mother earlier this school year, I realized it will be the first Mother's Day that I will not be able to call her. Every year it was a requirement. She would wait by the phone and when we called, we would be informed of who had already called and who she was still waiting to hear from. She was also easy to buy for. She loved cut flowers or potted flowers or bouquets. One year all of the kids sent her flowers. She said her house looked like a shrine.

But, more importantly we called.

Spending time in a conversation is the best gift you can give any loved one. It is the most precious gift because you cannot get it back. It shows how you feel about the person because you sat down, called and took the time to talk.

Since I don't have a mom to call this year, let me wish all you mothers out there a great month of May and a great Mother's Day. May you receive many phone calls, flowers, gifts and cards. May you also get the best gift of all – Time talking to people you love and with people who love you!

Have a great weekend.

John

Thought for the Week – May 18, 2011

Ten years ago, I began my tenure at Bloomingdale and in this system. I had moved from Virginia and was in the middle of completing the three most stressful things a person can do, (according to Time Magazine), move to a new town, get a new job and buy a new house.

Through the past decade there have been many changes. Some of the changes we had no control over. Some others were a result of people moving away, matriculating to other schools, or changing their names due to marriage. Instructional changes have been made by changes in curriculum (QCC's to Standards), personnel changes at various grade levels and textbook adoptions or additions.

Through the past decade there have been cosmetic changes as well. The school has been painted red and white (school colors) and had one minor renovation (2002) and one major renovation (2010). The 47 year old building looks pretty good and the magnolias, boxwoods, live oaks and river birches have grown to create shady areas that keep the grounds cooler during hot Savannah days.

There have been a lot of changes over the last ten years. However, the kids never change. They come in ready to see if we care; ready to see if we can help them; ready to see how the community comes together to help families; ready to see how much they can learn from us and how much they can teach us.

That is the point. No matter who stays and who goes and what year it is, the kids come to us and we are the ones who have to do the work, take the time, show the love, and make them better.

Thanks for the last ten years. Bring on the next!

Have a great week!

John

Thought for the Week – May 31, 2011

My best friend and significant other gave me some cuttings of a plant she has had on her deck for a long time. She said that all I had to do was replant it in good soil and it would do fine. It would take root and grow and it would do just as well for me as it had for her.

Even though she had done all the work and had fed it and taken care of it during the growing season and had covered it during the colder weather, I was now the beneficiary of her efforts; her care; her dedication.

We are now getting ready to do the same thing with the students in our classroom or building. We have worked hard and we have dedicated our time to help them grow; to nurture them; to build their root system to prepare them for the next grade level. In many cases, we don't see the fruits of our labor. Our efforts sometime need to ferment and marinade for a while before some of our students reach the level that we want. We know that they are improving but some of them may not fully germinate until the following school year.

Just as I can be confident that the cuttings I was given will germinate and grow and thrive with me, we can be assured that the work we have done has not been done in vain and the children we send on to the next grade level will grow, be successful and achieve great things.

Just as every gardener knows: You have to get your hands dirty to do it right but after a while you can step back and look at the great things that have grown around you.

Have a great week and be proud of who you are sending on. They are the cuttings that will take root, grow and thrive!

John

Thought for the Week – June 6, 2011

A baseball fan once stated that with 162 games to be played, every team would win 54 games and every team would lose 54 games, it what they did with the other 54 games that would determine whether they were a championship team or a team with fans saying, "wait 'till next year."

Every school year begins with about 180 school days. These are separated in to 90 day semesters and then 45 day quarters. Unlike baseball we cannot afford to lose 45 days and hope that the other 135 will make up for it. We have to make every day count from day one to day one hundred eighty. Unlike baseball, we cannot sit there and say "wait 'till next year." In short, what we do is not a game and we cannot relegate what we do to simple numerology. Every day and every class and every child and every teacher and every principal, counts.

During those days we have ensured that our students have breakfast and lunch. We have given them backpacks and uniforms; we have supported them during Thanksgiving and Christmas; we have connected them to social agencies to help them during tough times; we have called the Department of Family and Children Services when we needed to; we have provided school counselors to help our kids get over the loss of a family member or their parents divorcing or a parent's deployment.

We have done all that in preparing the kids for what they need to learn and they cannot learn when they are hungry, scared, nervous, grieving, lonely or sad. We have done this because that is the hidden curriculum that we teach. We teach caring by caring and love by loving and tolerance by being tolerant and understanding by showing that we understand.

What you do is not a game. It is important and impactful and noble and necessary. I congratulate all of you on another great year! I wish for you a great summer break and if you have time relax and take in a few baseball games!

Have a great week!

John

Thought for the Week – August 15, 2011

My significant other and I love plants. If we have an extra centimeter our respective gardens, we go out and purchase something new to put in that spot. Our goal is for something to be blooming all throughout the growing season. We are doing our part to turn the world green.

We have added all sorts of plants from ornamental grasses to lantana to mums to Shasta daisies to day lilies. Some needed light and some shade and some needed something between the two.

Some plants also needed more care and attention to thrive. They needed more fertilizer. They needed more water. They needed more weeding. They needed more work. However, after a short time most of our plantings have taken root and done well.

In a week, our students will be coming back to us. Some will need more work. Some will need more attention and care. Some will need more nurturing. Some will need a great deal of effort. Some will even need prayer. In the end, after all our work, they will have taken root and they too will have done well.

What makes gardens special? People walk by and see the beauty but they don't see the hard work and the dirty hands.

What makes classrooms and schools special? People see the end result but don't see the hard work and sweat and prayers.

Both end up beautiful things.

Welcome back! Have a great week!

John

Thought For the Week – September 19, 2011

Last Thursday as we cleaned up from Back-to-School Night and our PTA meeting, I was locking up the main wings of the building and waiting for the PTA to finish up in the cafeteria. I waited.......and waited and waited.....but, they weren't coming to the front of the building to tell me they were done. I didn't want to seem like I was rushing them but I wanted to know if they needed my help now that everything else was locked up.

As I opened the door to the cafeteria, I suddenly realized why they had not come up to the front. There was a bat flying around the cafeteria! It apparently had come in through the open doors which had been propped open during the cleanup. It was a pretty good size one and it was frantically flying around from one side to the other. They were afraid that I would be angry or that I would upset with them. I wasn't; I couldn't be; I laughed.

This is not the first time I have had to deal with a bat flying inside a school building. I have had them in the gym and my goal was to not harm it or hurt it in any way. However, I still needed to get the thing out of the cafeteria because it would be slightly distracting during breakfast tomorrow.

We re-opened the doors and then using brooms we tried to move it toward the doors on the left side. We almost got it out the door several times when it would make a bat appropriate u-turn and be right back where it started. Finally, the bat flew to the left and exited the building the same way it came in.

It was now 9:00 p.m. But, we were bat free.

The longer a person is in education the more they can say, they have seen and dealt with nearly everything. They deal with all kinds of animals, all kinds of people and all kinds of students. You learned to go with the flow, find a solution to whatever problem you face and calmly move on to the next thing. You don't dwell on it because you have to get back to teaching and learning and helping.

Thus you learn how to deal with the strange, the obscure and the unusual .....like a bat in the cafeteria.

Have a great week!

John

Thought for the Week – September 26, 2011

The Savannah Morning News printed a very informative and sobering article focusing on the increase in the number of local families presently living in poverty. It gave a great deal of statistics and added quotes from parents and comments from local politicians and service deliverers. You could sense their frustration: They wished that it was better; they wished they could do more; they wished it didn't hurt children as much as it does.

We have all seen the stress in a parent's eyes as they try to find a new job. We have seen the stress level increase in children because they worry about their parents when they are at school. We have seen the number of homeless families increase. We have seen an increase in the number of students receiving free lunch.

What we can't see is what hitches a ride with poverty: pain, embarrassment, nervousness, anxiety, under-nourishment, illness and absenteeism. There is the feeling of loss and feeling like a failure.

We can help. We can not only connect our neediest students with services and agencies, we also continue to help with moral support, encouragement, understanding and empathy. We can reassure them that we know that it is hard to learn new things when we are hungry and worried and stressed. We can let them know that we will work with them and not give up on them.

We have to. We may be the only ones left who care and who can make a difference.

Have a great week.

John

Thought for the Week – October 5, 2011

As I was opening my pantry door the other evening, I heard an unfamiliar sound followed by a ceiling light blowing out. It was the fallout from the ceiling light blowing out and landing on the back end of my dog that was waiting patiently for a treat from the aforementioned pantry. Once the fallout had landed, my dog ran to the other end of the house afraid that she had caused the minor disaster. (For a change, she had not.)

My pantry door has a spring-loaded ball bearing that sits on the top of the door. The ball bearing is supposed to sit in a metal depression located in the door frame. This wonderful scientific invention keeps the pantry door firmly closed when it is working properly. For some reason the ball bearing had come loose and became a projectile when I opened the door. It flew and landed perfectly in the middle of the nearest ceiling spotlight. The remains of the light bulb then complied with the law of gravity and fell on the rear end of my already valium-laden dog.

It didn't take long to clean up the glass, find the ball bearing and put it back in the door and replace the light bulb. It took slightly longer to calm the dog down with some hugs and more snacks.

An ordinary action became an extraordinary series of events that led to some clean up, fix up and calm down.

Sounds like an ordinary school day. We find our ordinary schedule interrupted with family struggles, childhood challenges, and sometime medical emergencies. This is followed by some clean ups, some fix ups and definitely some calm downs.

So, I took the minor devastation in stride and cleaned it up and moved on, just like we do on a daily basis. We have been trained and we can take care of most anything that comes our way.

Now my dog is a different story.

Have a great week!

John

Thought for the Week – October 10, 2011

In a recent Education Week article, Howard Gardner shared parts of his new book entitled: Truth, Beauty and Goodness Reframed: Educating for the Virtues in the 21st Century. He writes, "Truth is about statements and propositions….either something is true, false or indeterminate…Beauty is about our expression…one person's idea of beauty need not clash with another……Good and bad …the ethics of roles…what does it mean to be a good worker or good citizen." Gardner goes on to suggest that schools should discuss ethical issues to try to reach some consensual agreement.

Wow!

Schools should be a place where you can find truth, beauty and goodness. The truth that is found in math, the beauty that is found in the arts and literature, and the goodness that is found in the hearts of caring teachers, staff members and students.

Schools should also be a place where discussions should take place and where students can feel comfortable to share their opinions without fear. Students and adults would be required to support their opinions and not just rely on Wikipedia or Op-ed pieces in the newspaper. It would be the best place for students to learn how to be good citizens and good co-workers.

Some will think that schools don't have enough time to do that; we have testing and training and pacing guides and deadlines. But we discuss ethics every time there is an altercation on the playground; every time there is a discussion in history class. We look for beauty every time we observe an art class, visit a music lesson, or sit in on an English Literature class. We look for truth every time we try to find the best way to help children succeed academically or socially.

The 21st century is busier and more complicated but we can still find truth, beauty and goodness while we do our best to make the best citizens we can.

Have a great week!

John

Thought for the Week – October 18, 2011

    As I was walking down the main hall of the building, I walked past our Freedom Shrine. This is where copies of famous historical documents are framed and mounted on the wall for all to see. We have the Declaration of Independence, the Constitution, the Emancipation Proclamation and other important documents. As I was walking past a kindergartner walked toward me, pointed at the Freedom Shrine and said, "Nice writin' Mr. King!"

    I didn't know whether to be honored because he thought I wrote some of the most important documents in history, or appalled because he thought I was old enough to write them.

    More importantly, I was reminded that the Freedom Shrine was there. It is easy for things to be hidden in plain sight when you pass them every day. Just because they are there, doesn't mean people read them.

    One of the pillars of Character Counts is Citizenship. One of the ways for us to be good citizens is to remember what these famous documents say, what they mean and the courage it took for it to be written. One of the ways we can teach children to be good citizens is to remind them why we have a Freedom Shrine.

    Sometimes our little ones help us to remember what we need to do.

    Have a great week!

    John

Thought for the Week – October 26, 2011

My dog is now on more expensive medications than I am. At eleven years old, (77 in dog years), she gets very nervous and uncomfortable when I leave her alone. As sweet as the dog is to anyone and everyone when she is with them, she is as destructive as she can be when she is alone. She is quiet and happy when you are with her and you wouldn't believe what she can do when you are not around. She is the Dr. Jekyll/Ms Rawhide of the dog world.

She didn't use to be this way. Roxie was originally my late wife's dog. She used to stay outside all day and chase squirrels and guard the perimeter and probably sleep. She didn't mind being left alone especially when Kingdog was alive. But, in a year's time, Roxie lost her owner and her brother and that had a great impact on her life.

Now without medication she can remodel a kitchen or bathroom in no time at all. I have learned a great deal about cabinetry, plumbing, carpets and pharmaceuticals. It seems she needs them to help her stay calm when I am away and she is by herself. So, I either spend money on medication or on fixing the house. I choose the former.

There are kids who come to us everyday who may be scared and nervous and apprehensive when they are with us or when they are not with the ones they love. We have to be aware that just like Roxie, they need understanding and patience and support and help. Like Roxie, they need love and understanding. Sometimes we may even have to learn new ways to help make their lives a little more palatable and bearable.

I hope Roxie is around for a long time and I will continue to try to find ways to help her. I hope we continue to do the same for our two-legged friends.

Have a great week!

John

Thought for the Week – November 8, 2011

Last week on Halloween night, I had my house all ready for little costumed visitors. I had a large bowl of candy ready to be distributed. I had a large spider (not real) hanging down near my front door. There was a skull (also not real) sitting on one outdoor table and on the other stood a dancing skeleton (looks real).

The dancing skeleton moves his hips from side to side to the tune of "Super Freak" when a button is pushed. Its jaws move and eyes light up as the music is played. It makes me laugh even though I have seen its act hundreds of times.

Early in the evening, a little girl who looked no more than two came toward the house in great anticipation of her first memorable Halloween. She was dressed as a beautiful princess and I knew she would love to see and hear my dancing skeleton.

She wasn't.

The little princess took one look at it and screamed and ran back toward her mother. I gave her some candy and tried to show her that it was a toy, but she just wanted to go to the next house and be as far away from me as possible. (Mental note, do NOT turn on the skeleton in front of 2 year olds.)

A little later another little princess came up and thought the front of my house was amazing. She came right up to the little skeleton, found the button and began to dance with the music. The second time she pushed the button, she held the skeleton's plastic hand. It looked like they were dancing together. It was cute and it made me feel better after scaring the other little one.

Each day, we present to students the best decorated, practiced and modeled lessons we can deliver. We have to understand that some people may be afraid of it and some people may look like it is the greatest lesson they have ever seen.

They are both right.

Just like a dancing skeleton may not be as fun to some as others, our lessons may not hit every child the same way. We have to know our students so we can adjust our lessons to meet their needs. Otherwise, it might be a little too scary for some of them.

Have a great week!

Thought for the Week – November 14, 2011
<u></u>

   Since I have a bi-polar dog, I walk her twice in the morning prior to leaving for work. We go first at 0-dark-30 before anyone or anything else is up and then again twenty minutes before I leave for work. I would say that I do it for exercise but when your dog stops at every bush, tree, flower and mound of pine straw, this is not what I would call an aerobic exercise. It does make me more patient as I deal with the two-legged animals during the day after dealing with the four-legged variety in the morning.

   This morning was interesting. When I walked Roxie the first time, it was cool but clear and I could see the moon shine reflect off the little pond. About a half-hour after the first walk, it had become very foggy and you couldn't even see across the courtyard or make out cars as they drove by on the main road. By the time I walked Roxie on her next Paw-de-deux, the sun was up, the fog was gone and sky was blue and clear.

   Our kids can be different for us as they go through the day. They may start in a fog and then do their best work in the afternoon. They may start off good and slow down at 2:00 p.m. They may need a break during the day to keep on keeping on so they can learn what they can learn to be successful.

   We have to know them all and be aware of how they are and what we need to do to help them through the fogs and into the bright light of morning. We might as well; we are the ones who are making that walk with them.

   Have a great week!

   John

Thought for the Week – November 28, 2011

I had the opportunity this past week to go into school and do some touch up painting. I touched up the staff bathrooms and around all the door frames of every classroom. It was a way to make the old building look more inviting and cleaner. It is amazing how a coat of paint hides a lot of wear and tear.

I was thankful for the paint and the opportunity to touch things up and in a way to say thank you to the old building that is used for so much on a weekly basis. The paint didn't change the age of the building or the wear and tear it receives. It did cover up the scrapes and scratches it receives daily.

The building deserved it; the people in the rooms deserved it. It didn't take that long to do.

We see kids every day that are dressed well and clean and pressed and they still have problems and stresses and anxiety and concerns. We also have kids who come to us looking like they need a new coat and something to cover up their scratches and scars. They both need our love and help and dedication and understanding.

Like this old building, all our kids need some type of tender loving care and support even when they don't look like they need it. A coat of paint may help the outside; our efforts will help the inside.

Have a great week!

John

Thought for the Week – December 6, 2011

I was shopping over the weekend at the mall, trying to single-handedly improve the economy one purchase at a time, when I noticed an elderly woman waiting patiently for the cashier. She was in a wheel chair and had maneuvered herself through the racks of clothes and shirts and miscellaneous stuff that were strewn all over the counters, floors and aisles.

She waited quietly for her turn and handed her selections and a credit card to the cashier. The cashier said that she would bring a paper copy for her to sign so she didn't have to stand up. The elderly woman stated very quietly but firmly, "I can get up so I can sign on the machine like everyone else." She pulled herself slowly, but confidently, stood and signed her name and then grabbed her bag, sat back down and moved on in her wheel chair.

She was wheel-chair bound, but she was not handicapped.

How many kids do we see on a daily basis that we mistakenly believe are handicapped by their address, their lineage, their parents, or by physical or medical problems? We need to remember that we can help them stand tall and be confident. We can help them feel pride in what they can do and believe that with hard work they can be even better.

We can make sure that no one is restrained by their limitations but open to whatever they put their minds and hearts to. They can learn to maneuver easily through all the stuff that blocks their paths too.

Have a great week!

John

Thought for the Week – December 14, 2011

Think back in your life and picture the best Christmas gift you have ever received. Think about how you felt; how it affected your life; how you were changed.

I personally remember the walkie-talkies my brother and I received one Christmas. We wore those things out. We would go out for hours pretending to be spies, and talk until the batteries went dead. Then there was the time I received my first real wallet. It was a sign of growing up. (Or telling me that I needed to grow up.) Those are the gifts I will always remember and those are the blessings of Christmas' Past.

The other gifts that I have received through the years have been the human kind. Friends that have crossed my path, changed my life, and made me a better person. Significant others who have supported me and helped me up when others have knocked me down and who have loved me unconditionally. Mentors who have taught me how to do my job better without being judgmental or harsh. Co-workers who have quietly shown kindness, perseverance, patience and generosity. Individuals who have given so others may have gifts under their tree. Teachers who wouldn't give up on a child that everyone else had given up on. Administrators who always tried to think of the children first and did the best they could do help them.

Those are the best gifts I have received and many of you have been or are the greatest gifts that I have ever received.

I thank you and I wish all of you the best this Christmas Season. I hope all you receive a gift you will always remember!

John

Thought for the Week – January 3, 2012

I had the pleasure of flying to California to see my youngest son over the holidays. I was looking forward to seeing him but I wasn't looking forward to the long flight. As I boarded the plane from Atlanta to San Francisco I noticed another passenger carrying a dog onto the plane. This was not a tiny dog hiding in a purse. This was a medium sized dog that you couldn't hide from anybody. It looked to be a cross between a poodle and lab (Labradoodle). She was sweet and cute and ended up sitting right next to me. (With her owner of course.)

As I spoke with her owner, I discovered that she was a service dog. She provided comfort to those feeling anxious or nervous. Great, I thought, I hate flying; this is perfect! I heard another passenger state that he was sure happy the dog didn't sit next to him. I told him that the older I got the more I preferred animals.

After takeoff, her owner quickly fell asleep and soon I had a white dog head resting on my knee looking up at me. I felt as if she was tacitly stating, "I am here to help. That what I am here for. Do you need help? I am right here. Look at me!"

I was glad to have the dog with me on the 4 hour flight and it was a pleasant unexpected surprise. It made the flight seem shorter and the dog did make me feel less anxious.

I wish for you in 2012, plenty of wonderful fun surprises that lift your spirits and make your days wonderful. Or you can get a Labradoodle for yourself; it worked for me!

Have a great week and a great year!

John

Thought for the Week – January 10, 2012

In the Haight-Ashbury area in San Francisco, there is a huge record store. I was going to say vinyl store but I was afraid most of you would think that I went crazy about flooring.

This record store is close to the size of a city block. It has huge bins of LP's organized in alphabetical order. If they do not have an obscure Dylan album from 1967, they will find it for you and send it to you. They had albums from bands I have never heard of. They also carried compact discs and various artists were available in a variety of electronic media. The owners were also willing to take your name and send you, via e-mail, updates on newly acquired LP's or special sales. They even invited you to check out their website.

In other words, they were selling vintage vinyl in various ways. They were not limiting themselves to a corner of Haight-Ashbury in a mortar and brick building. They used the technology at their disposal to help promote the products of the past.

We can do the same. We can take the best strategies, materials and methods and meld it with technology, new applications and ideas and help all our students and grade levels succeed. There are some instructional practices that will never go out of style. These practices can be improved with the use of digital technology, flexible groupings, differentiation and even reinforced by YouTube. We can keep the things that work and improve them with the technology available.

Right now, I am going to listen to one of my Duke Ellington albums as it plays on my old turntable with the sound coming out of my digital speakers.   Perfect!

Have a great week!

John

Thought for the Week – January 17, 2012

I promise this is the last story about San Francisco.

My son told me one morning that we were going to take a short drive and take a hike in a nearby park. We drove over the Golden Gate Bridge and in 15 minutes we were walking in the middle of a redwood forest. The trees were not as tall as the sequoias located farther north on the Pacific, but there were still bigger and taller than anything you might see in southern Georgia. The trees were so impressive and gigantic that my son took my picture at 11:00 a.m. and it looks like it was taken in the middle of the night. It was beautiful, awe-inspiring and amazing.

The age and majesty of the forest could make one feel insignificant, tiny, and inconsequential. However, for me it was worth the trip to see something so wonderful and learn something I didn't know. It was one of the highlights of a very enjoyable trip.

Our students can sometimes feel tiny and insignificant amongst all the other children trying to get our attention. Our students can also feel that they are lost amongst the towering responsibilities of their class work, homework, family stresses and responsibilities. Our students can feel like they are trying to get out of a deep, dark, scary place.

We have to be their guides. We have to lead them through and show them that it can be a beautiful thing and not a scary hike in the dark. We have to show them that it can be wonderful and exciting to learn something they didn't know. We could be the highlight of their year.

Have a great week!

John

Thought for the Week – January 25, 2012

   For the past two years, we have had a wonderful group of brothers attend Bloomingdale. They are loving and sweet and kind and funny. They work hard and try to follow the rules and wouldn't hurt another soul. They have also been in foster care and have been through more than most people go through in a lifetime.

   You usually don't see that combination: hardship with a smile; cheerfulness throughout a challenge; love shown even though love wasn't given. They are extraordinary boys.

   We found out this week that they were being placed with a different foster family and would be going to a different school. It was like losing our own children. It was like part of our family was being taken away. There was sadness and tears, (from the teachers). The boys were fine. They were going to be fine. They have always persevered and they would again.

   When you think your day's work is wearing thin and people are on your last nerve and you think life is not going your way, remember four boys who just keep on keeping on. Remember four boys who walked into their new school, Largo – Tibet, with a smile, with excitement and bringing joy with them.

   It is not something we can teach, but it may be something we can learn.

   Have a great and joyful week!

   John

Thought for the Week- January 31, 2012

According to Education Week, colleges and universities are beginning to look at applicants Facebook and Twitter entries. Prior to accepting them to the freshman class, they want to be sure that the students wrote appropriate material, cited correct and accurate information and treated their peers with mutual respect and dignity.

This is a good example of colleges embracing the technology of the 21st century and providing a scholarly intent to social networking. Some may say that social networking has nothing to do with college classes, however, the same students want to use Twitter to discuss classes, communicate with their instructors via e-mail and download their term papers, research, theses, mid-terms and finals.

Colleges and universities have always been slow to use and accept new technology. They wanted to keep the little blue exam books for as long as possible. They wanted students to read manuscripts written on vellum and discuss face to face the intricacies of their subject.

With a poorer economy campuses have begun to embrace distance learning, Moodle, Skype and other technologies to help more students make the grade from home and at all times of day or night. In return, students will have to follow a similar code of conduct and ethics that students have agreed to for decades. They understand that cheating and plagiarizing would not be tolerated. They understand that misconduct and being rude or disrespectful could lead to probation or expulsion. They understand that not completing course requirements would lead to a failing grade. In other words, once they go to college, they understand they have to be ladies and gentlemen and scholars.

I think that it is something to really tweet about!

Have a great week!

John

Thought for the Week – February 15, 2012

Five years = 260 weeks = 1825 days = A lifetime ago!

A great deal has happened in the last five years. I am different; I am changed. I have become older and wider (not wiser). I am more patient about some things and less patient about others. I have learned a lot about myself and had to learn a lot about being myself; about being comfortable in my own skin. I learned to face grief and renewal. I learned to be more faith-filled. I learned to believe in myself and to do what I think is right. I learned that the opinions of others or what is funneled through the rumor mill doesn't define me. What I do, how I work, my prayers, my blessings, my beliefs, and the people I love – define me.

It has been five years since Patricia passed away. Her memory, her love of life and her love of teaching have not diminished. I remember her every day in prayer and every time I see her picture. I was molded by her life and I have been molded by her death. I have learned to love again because I learned how to live from her.

Five years – such a long time and yet, such a short time; I am different, I am changed, I am better, I am happy, I am strong, I am blessed, I am loved. But, I never, ever forget.

Have a great week!

John

Thought for the Week – February 27, 2012

I am a master-worrier. I used to fight it but I now embrace it. (Otherwise, I would worry about it.)

I worry about my significant other, my sons, my Dad, my teachers, my students, things I read in the news and even things I can't do anything about. I have been told that God does not give grace for worry. But then I started worrying about that.

Let's be clear. I am not talking about losing sleep over things or wringing my hands or being incapacitated due to over thinking problems. I am not like that. I just worry about how best to do things, fix things, write things, grade things, help others, be better, take care of those that are dear to me and still keep my blood pressure low (thank you pharmaceuticals).

I am my father's child. I was not raised in a "whatever will be, will be" family. I was raised in an "education is important/money doesn't grow on trees/God helps those who help themselves" family. I don't mind it. I understand it. It is part of me.

I get things done and keep up with my calendar and paper work and birthdays and other important dates because of my worry. I go to the doctor when I am supposed to and take my medication and make sure my dog takes hers because of worry. I can plan and look ahead and know where I want to be five years from now because of worry.

I need the challenges and daily trials that come with any job in education. Without it I don't know what I'd do....except worry about why it wasn't there!

Have a worry-free week!

John

Thought for the Week – March 9, 2012

The nursing home where my father resides has gone into lockdown because of a virus that has made several people sick. In an effort to keep the virus at bay and protect the residents, they have asked them to remain in their rooms, eat their meals in their rooms, and wait for further information. They are dealing with a medical outbreak that could be life threatening to the elderly, so they are keep the residents isolated while checking on them continually.

My father doesn't like it. He does not understand why he can't walk around and talk to people, visit other areas and eat his meals in the cafeteria. He has been caught several times and returned to his room. My brother has even tried to explain to him why he can't do what he wants to do. He is worried that dad's dementia is getting worse.

I am not so sure. I think my father, who started working at 16 years of age and was always a "follow the rules" kind of guy, has discovered that he likes being a rebel. He understands that the world didn't stop just because he snuck out his room. He actually gets more attention and gets to talk to people and he knows that he won't get kicked out if he does it again.

We have students who do the same thing. They will act out or rebel because they know that we will give them attention and we will not abandon them and will continue to work with them. We will try to change their behavior and do what we can but they know we will be there for them and care about them.

My father and challenging kids – rebels with a cause!

Have a great week.

John

Thought for the Week – March 27, 2012

Recently my significant other and I were sitting outside and eating lunch at a restaurant in Thunderbolt. The weather was great and the food was phenomenal. During our meal, a mutual acquaintance stopped by and started the conversation with, "I have dung beetles." Needless to say, I have never heard a dialogue start with that particular phrase so I corrected her by saying, "You mean outside you have dung beetles." She ignored me and went on to explain that they probably came off the boats that come into the harbor and was fascinated that she was now being visited by a bug not indigenous to the area.

Another mutual acquaintance, not to be left out of the conversation, stated, "I once had a Madagascan Hissing Cockroach in my house. (She also lives in Thunderbolt.) I immediately, thought that this would not be a good way to sell property in Thunderbolt. "Buy in Thunderbolt, get a free exotic pet."

Now I lived in Thunderbolt for several years and all I had was dogs, squirrels, chipmunks, woodpeckers and an occasional owl or hawk. If I had dung beetles or a cockroach from any country, I would not be advertising the fact or sharing the information with pride to my friends. I would be quietly calling an exterminator.

Usually stories like this come from our students. They feel comfortable enough with us to share everything and anything. They will tell us stuff that their parents or guardians would not like us to know and sometimes they even share their goals, their yearnings, their hopes and their grief. Their pests and challenges didn't come off a boat from a foreign land. The ones they deal with come from their neighborhood, family situations or home life.

We have to be good listeners and work toward being the exterminator of their fears and worries and dreads. Then they can feel more at home at school because we listen and help and keep them safe and away from things that hiss and hurt.

The world is full of a lot of scary things and not all of them live in Thunderbolt!

Have a great week!

John

Thought for the Week – April 25, 2012

Loss.

Every time I hear of someone's passing it creates a connection with me. I feel for the family because I know what it felt like. I pray for the children because I have looked into the eyes of other children during times like these. I grieve because I know they are grieving. I thank God for what I have because it can so quickly be taken from you.

We all work hard and we all try hard and hopefully we all pray hard. We do it because we believe in what we do and we want our families and significant others to be proud of us. We want to take care of our families and leave a positive mark on the world. It may not be remembered by all but it will be remembered by our own.

I thank Otis Brock III for his dedication and his efforts. I will pray for him and his family. We all will feel the loss because we are all part of something great as we work for something better.

Have a prayerful week.

John

Thought for the Week – May 11, 2009

Sometimes dates hit me and then I think about how much time has passed or how much time remains. It occurred to me yesterday, that in a month, the school year for students will be over. The year has seemed to fly by and even with its share of challenges, budget cuts and individual and collective crises, it has been good.

I am strange in the fact that I like school when kids are in it. I do not look forward to the time of the year when furniture is stacked in hallways, the yearly cleaning frenzy has begun and I am in the office doing the yearly paperwork that defines the ending of one school term and the beginning of another. It is not as exciting as when the kids are here; it is not as fulfilling.

Yet after the next four busy weeks have passed, I will be saying goodbye to another group of fifth graders. A group that is talented, funny, smart and challenging. They have been that way since kindergarten and I will miss them.

I have written many times in my thoughts about the concept of beginnings and endings and have shared many with you. However it is what we do between the two that makes the difference and has the impact! It is not how many beginnings and endings will live through, it is who we help and support and love during the months or years in between.

I hope the next month is a joyful one as we complete another school year and look forward to the beginning of another.

Have a great week!

John

Thought for the Week – June 1, 2012

Years ago I had the opportunity to visit Arlington National Cemetery. I did so to find the site of my grandfather's grave. He fought in both World War I, (He lied about his age.) and World War II. He earned his spot in the hallowed ground of Arlington.

It is an awesome and sobering sight to see hill after hill of small white crosses and stars of David. It is an awesome and sobering thing to remember and appreciate all the ones that gave their full measure. They are all heroes and patriots.

On Monday, as I walked my dog around the development I noticed more American Flags hoisted than during most weeks. It is a good thing to see. It is one of the ways we can acknowledge some of the greatest people we have known and never known. It is a tacit way to say thank you and we remember. It is a simple way to show respect for them, for our armed forces, and our country.

As this Memorial Day week concludes let's take the time to remember the fallen, acknowledge their sacrifice and pray for those who fought and who are fighting for us now – lest we forget!

Have a great week!

John

Thought for the Week – August 1, 2012

During my summer break, I decided that I wanted to place a couple of humming bird feeders on my front porch. I have seen a few flying around the neighborhood and I was hoping to attract one or two. (I find them beautifully fascinating.) So I got two humming bird feeders, filled them with sugar water four times sweeter than sweet tea and I waited.

In less than a day, I observed two humming birds flying around the front porch, landing on one of the feeders, drinking from them and flying off in a dash to someplace only known to them and other hummingbirds. In a few days, the word must have gotten to other humming birds, because now I seem to have five or six at any one time. They seem to enjoy the man-made nectar while attempting to chase off other hummingbirds. (They seem to be quite territorial.)(They're tiny with an attitude!)

After a few days, it was time for me to change the water in the feeders and I made my way calmly out to the front porch. As I was taking them down, my head was dive-bombed by at least two of my new feathered friends. They were taking great umbrage to my removal of their feeders even if it was temporary. I found myself telling them, "Hey, I will be right back! Keep your feathers on!" I looked around hoping that no one could hear me. Oh well, it least I have an excuse to talk to myself. In a few minutes, the feeders were back in their places and all was happy in hummingbird-land.

In just a few weeks, our doors will open and we will be welcoming our students back for another challenging and satisfying year. On some days, you may feel many things flying around your heads apparently trying to get our attention. We may hear ourselves say, "Hey. I am here. It's going to be fine." You may also feel that there are more than five or six flying at you at one time. Take a deep breath and remember that you do know what you are doing and you will be able to handle what flies your way. You can give them what they need to survive and what they need to be successful. You can deal with anyone who comes your way. Even if they are tiny with an attitude!

Have a great week! Welcome Back!

John

Thought for the Week – August 17, 2012

The other day while I was walking Roxie the wonder dog, a four or five year old boy passed us on his scooter at a high rate of speed, (fast for a five or six year old boy on a scooter.) He stopped at the corner and looked at us, smiled and said, "I got a new pair of shoes. They are great!" I said, "Yes they are." He continued, "My momma said that they are special shoes, they will make me go fast!" I said, "Momma's always right!" He smiled again and raced down the sidewalk. It seemed like the wheels weren't even hitting the ground.

He was happy and confident all because his momma said his new shoes were special and therefore he could do something special.

We can do the same thing. We can greet the students in about a week and tell them that we are going to give them something special and when we do, they will be able to do things better than they have ever done before. We can tell them that they will know more, do more and accomplish more than they have in the past. We can tell them that they can succeed at a higher level than ever before.

What do they have that they haven't had before? No not shoes, or magic pencils, or new book bags or new uniforms. What do they have now that they didn't have before?

They have you!

Have a great week!

John

Thought for the Week – August 27, 2012

A few Fridays ago, I had the pleasure of going home to a very hot house. It seems my air conditioning went out on a Friday night! My dog looked at me with the look of, "You are an idiot! Why is it so hot in here?" Miraculously, I found an air conditioning company that would come and at least officially pronounce the unit dead and give me a plan of how to replace it. (Still had to wait until Monday)

When the gentleman arrived, he took the time to meet my dog and pat her on the head and talked to her kindly as he checked out the unit. Soon Roxie was following him wherever he went. I told him, "You must have a dog." He said, "Actually, I have fourteen dogs. My wife and I provide foster dog care to dogs that have been abused or abandoned. They just need love and understanding.

No wonder Roxie loved him. She knew he was loving, caring, understanding and patient. She knew it automatically.

When the days get tough and someone or something turns up the heat, will our students and our peers know how much we care and worry and love them? Can they rely on us to help them through anything no matter what? Will our students just feel and know it automatically because it is in our blood and it is part of us?

The house has a new air conditioner, Roxie still thinks I am an idiot, and she looks occasionally out the window to see if the gentleman she knows is a dog lover will ever come back.

Have a great week!

John

Thought for the Week – September 5, 2012

A few weekends ago, I had the privilege of being the best man at the wedding of a dear friend. I have known Vince for 40 years! We have been friends since we met in high school as sophomores. (We acted sophomoric on many of occasions too!)

It was wonderful and touching for many reasons. First, this was Vince's first wedding at 54 years of age! He had waited all his life to find Kelly and he could finally say I do. Second, many people made the statement, "If a person finds a friendship that lasts like you guys have you are a lucky and blessed man!"

They were right on both counts. To have a friend whom you can trust and talk about anything with and to have someone whom you can cry with, pray with and laugh with is a rare and wonderful thing. To see that friend find the one thing he was lacking and look as happy as I have ever seen him, (as the commercial says: "Priceless!"). It was a once in a lifetime event for a once in a lifetime friend.

We met so many years ago and yet, when we see each other, it is like old times and it feels like an old comfortable pair of shoes.

I hope all of you have that kind of friend in your life and all of your children have a least one in theirs. They are truly a blessing from God and it lasts a lifetime.

Have a great week!

John

Thought for the Week – September 14, 2012

My watch stopped working the other week, (actually I think it is a dead battery). I don't have the special tool you need to take the back off. Since, I don't think using a lock wrench will help; I need to take it to the store where it was purchased so they can do it neatly.

The problem is: I am so used to a watch that I keep looking at my wrist and it is not helping me. I have tried using my cell phone like all the youngsters do. (They don't own watches and I don't remember to put the cell phone on my hip.) I have tried to use my IPAD clock. (I don't remember that either.) So the lack of a watch combined with the onset of senility has become a daily challenge.

I wonder why the switching from a watch to another mode of time keeping is so difficult. I wonder why my arm feels weird without a watchband tightly bound around my wrist. I guess my watch was something I could rely on – it always worked; always did what is was supposed to do; gave the information efficiently and quickly – at a glance. It was part of my comfort zone.

It is a simple problem with a simple solution and soon I will have my watch back and I will feel whole again. Until then, I will continue to work on using other, more modern technologies to help me know what to do next in the day. That is, if I can find the time!

Have a great week!

John

Thought for the Week – September 26, 2012

A few days ago, I was walking Roxie the Wonder Dog in the early morning darkness around the neighborhood. I walk her twice before leaving for work in an effort to keep the house and furniture in one piece.

As we were walking around, Roxie walked by a small rabbit sitting in the grass, no more than two feet away. She just went right on by. A little farther down the block, she walked right by a tiny black cat sitting on a front porch watching me watching her. Finally, we went around the corner and near the pond and there in the middle of the sidewalk was a snake coiled up right in the middle of it!

She actually saw that one!

Not only did Roxie see the snake, she wanted to get over there and investigate it, smell it and figure out what it was. I instead pulled her the opposite way. I don't want to deal with a snake in the middle of the day let alone at dawn. Roxie had totally missed two less formidable creatures so she could complete a food chain. She ignored the cute little rabbit and delicate looking cat but went straight for the curled up viper.

We sometimes do the same thing. We concentrate or perseverate on the worst part of the day or the hardest thing we have to do and we forget to appreciate the calm things; the good things; the things that keep us going. We can overlook the kind words, the funny situations, or the smile of a child. Those are the little things we can miss as we confront the snakes lying in our path.

Let's try to see more of the good things as we try to maneuver through our own daily walks. I am going to do the same. As for Roxie...we are going to start walking a different route early in the morning!

Have a great week!

John

Thought for the Week – October 3, 2012

In four days it will be the second anniversary of my mother's death. My siblings and I have spent a great deal of time thinking about her and how much she gave to the family during her lifetime. She has reminded us of the adage, "You don't miss it until it is gone."

I am not just talking about missing her presence. I am talking about realizing how much she quietly brought to the family table. She was the big decision maker, not my father. She was the one whom kept the family orderly and on track. She was one whom helped my father focus on what he had to do and not worry about a family of 6 kids.

Mom was also the one who remembered all the important events in the entire family. Even as we got older and the family expanded she knew what should happen next. I remember her calling me one October afternoon to ask me, "Have you gotten anything for Matthew's birthday?" She was calling me to remind me of my own son's birthday. (I had not forgotten; I do have some of her genes.) She wasn't asking in a nasty way. Mom's world was an orderly and punctual one. Everything was right in the world if the budget was is in the black, the house was clean, the calendar was up to date and she knew where Dad had gone off to. (That was the hardest.)

You really don't see what your Mom does until you don't get to see her anymore. I still miss her every Sunday when I used to call her. But she does still talk to me all the time. Mom's have a way of doing that.

So if your Mom is still on the earth, take some time to call her and just talk and listen, even though they drive you crazy. Remember, if you are a parent, you drive your children crazy too. It is traditional; we have to do it.

Have a great week!

John

Thought for the Week – October 11, 2012

This week I have been reminded once again of the bumper sticker that was popular a few decades ago: MEAN PEOPLE SUCK!

I realize that I could have softened the language by saying mean people stink, mean people are annoying, mean people are ridiculous...etc. However, MEAN PEOPLE SUCK really says it all.

There seems to be a plethora of people who get upset at the word hello. Their coping skills are non-existent. Their main way of handling minor difficulties such as a stop sign, standing in line waiting their turn, or exact change required is to go ballistic, yell and stomp. Their response to being asked to follow the same rules as everyone else, complete standard forms and follow all standard legal operating procedures is to look at us like we are crazy and they are being treated like inmates at Guantanamo Bay.

Their faces turn red and their teeth grind and I think I may have to perform CPR at any time because they are asked not to park next to the sign that says, "No Parking". They feel picked on and abused because we ask them to complete the correct forms to allow their child to take the medication they want them to take. (Read that one again.) They act like the world is about to end because their child got a bad grade on an assignment that the child never turned in.

Instead of losing whatever sanity I have left, I say a short prayer and refuse to let them take my joy away. I, as many of you, have gone through much worse things than listed above. There are much harder things to live through than a protocol, a rule or a clock. I look at my time in line as a time to think, reflect and renew. I look at my time in traffic as my quiet time with no one else around. (The radio is off.) I will not have apoplexy because of a minor inconvenience. I want to be ready and strong enough for the real tragedies that come along.

So let's smile and take a deep breath and move on. We cannot change the attitude we get but we can control that attitude we give. Happiness is the greatest revenge.

Have a great week!

John

Thought for the Week – October 19, 2012

Yesterday as I opened my front door to the dark early morning October sky, there standing in the grass in front of my house were two deer. They were standing there looking at me and my dog looking at them. They looked like they were dropping off the morning paper: The Doe See Doe Digest; the Buck Stops Here Bugle; the Carnidae Chronicle; the Ruminant Register...etc. They quietly and slowly walked off toward the nearby woods. They weren't really afraid of us and the dog was too dumbfounded to chase them.

It not that we haven't seen deer before; it's just we didn't expect it with traffic zooming by at that time of the morning. We expect it off the beaten path and away from the maddening crowd. They seemed to be as surprised to see us as we were to see them. They went on with their routine (foraging), we went on with our routine (waking up).

The change of pace was a welcome change to the daily regimen. It shook things up and energized me for the day. It was different, out of the ordinary and memory worthy.
We need to do that every now and then. We need to shake up the schedule or have the class do a different type of activity or invite a guest to come in to help the students learn something new or reinforce something known. The students would be more energized (in a good way) and more excited about school because they may not know what is coming next.

The deer thought we had better tasting grass and I wasn't expecting them to be close enough to ring the doorbell. The kids need to know that sometimes we might just shake it up a little. Not too often though.....then it would become routine!

Have a great week!

John

Thought for the Week – October 26, 2012

A few Saturdays ago, I came to school to catch up on a few things. (You know how that is.) As I was parking my car, I noticed one of my students coming up on his bicycle. He came right up to me with a look of total surprise and asked, "Mr. King, do you live here?"

Several things went through my head as a possible response: "It sure feels that way!"; "I do live here. I have a secret elevator that goes down to my secret principal lair...it is kind of like the bat cave without the electronics."; "I just can't get enough of the cafeteria food."; etc. I finally decided to just tell the truth and say, "I am catching up on a few things this morning, so I came in to school today."

I could have told him something different but, he is in a CRCT grade so I figured I needed to help him succeed and not confuse the devil of out him. He went back to riding his bike and I went inside to find the top of my desk.

The truth is we DO live at our school. We may not be there physically 24-7 but we take it home with us every day. We worry about kids and pray for families. We hope that we know enough. We hope that we can learn enough to help those who need the most support. We try to make the right decisions and we pour over data continually to make sure no one is left out and all are successful. We lose sleep over challenges faced or problems unresolved. We try to keep up with all the timelines. We strive to be the best so that our co-workers, class or faculty can be the best they can be. We beat ourselves up when we make the mistakes human make. We don't sweat the small stuff because it is all big stuff! We wake up in the middle of the night reliving the day before or rehearsing a tough meeting coming up. We worry about everything, everyone, every situation all the time. It is who we are; it is what we do.

So the next time I am asked by a child at school, "Do you live here?" I will have to say, "Yes I do and I wouldn't have it any other way!"

Have a great week!

John

Thought for the Week – November 1, 2012

I had a tune in my head a few days ago that would not go away. It was from a classical piece of music and it kept playing again and again in my head. I finally decided I had to look through my collection of LP's. (You know those things with a hole in the center of them but they are not CD's...never mind if you don't know.) I knew in my head the color of the album and where it was supposed to be on the shelf. I found it with relative ease and played it on my stereo's record player. (I am not even going to explain what that is. Just read on.)

As I listened to the full recording, I was reminded of the entire beauty of the piece. There was more to it than the little part of it that kept rolling around in my head. It was a known surprise; a forgotten joy; a rekindled memory. I enjoyed every part of it.

You have to do that every now and then. Good literature can be read many times. Good music (all kinds, not just classical), can be listened to again and again. A good recipe can be enjoyed more than once. They all bring back good memories, warm feelings and connect you back to past events. We need it for our own mental and emotional health. It really does reduce stress and increase smiles.

Do something like that for yourself this week. As for me, I have a lot of vinyl to re-listen to!

Have a great week!

John

Thought for the Week – November 7, 2012

As I was observing a first grade class earlier this week, the teacher asked the kids to show "thumbs up" for every word that had a short u sound in it. As I was busily scripting the lesson a child turned around and looked at me and said with a thumb pointing up, "Don't you know what a short u sound is?" He kept pointing a thumb up and looking at me like I was a Neanderthal. I told him, "Okay, okay." and pointed my thumb up for the rest of the correct responses. The child smiled turned back around and shook his head.

The good part about that is that he was obviously comfortable with me visiting the room and he had expectations that I should and would participate in any activity the kids were doing. If it was important enough for him to do it, it should be important enough for me to do it.

He's right.

We shouldn't be so busy writing or listening or watching that we cannot sing with the students, move with them, talk with them, write with them, read with them and give an occasional thumb up sign with them. If we do maybe they won't look at us like we are complete idiots. (Maybe)

Have a great week!

John

Thought for the Week – November 29, 2012

I received a catalog recently that was selling "vintage items". That is a euphemism for stuff we don't really use or need anymore. There was an old rolodex file to keep your telephone numbers in. (They are all in my phone now.) There were wooden toys that were popular sometime last century. (They would not be popular today because they don't explode or cause something else to explode.) There were playing cards. (We play on line now.) Alarm clocks, (again on my phone.) and label makers (I can do the same stuff on my computer.)

See the pattern? Our technological advancement has created a need for a catalog to store all the data dinosaurs we don't need any more. Ironically, they were not cheap either. Seems the more of a dinosaur you are, the rarer you are and the more expensive you become.

Do we really need to keep antiquated stuff that is just there because it is a connection to an earlier time? Do we need to revel in it just because it has become an antique in our lifetime?

We can do the same thing in our schools, offices and classrooms. If we are trying to find items to replace our stuff that is worn out and antiquated and the only place we can find them is in an overpriced catalog, then maybe we need to move on to the next generation of instructional tools. Maybe it is time to truly go digital and embrace BYOT. Maybe it is time to catch up by downloading; become more individually successful by interconnecting; join our students in the 21st century.

I am going to try really, really hard. If nothing else, I can take all this old stuff and put it in a catalog – I might make a killer profit!

Have a great week!
John

Thought for the Week – December 6, 2012

I asked a young student the other day what he wanted for Christmas. He answered me with the normal answers: Several toys I had never heard of...video games that he will never get since they are rated M (at least I hope he doesn't), and then he said..."time".

I asked him what he meant about time. He said he looked forward to spending time with his family and his dad and other relatives he hadn't seen in a while. So I asked him, "Of all the gifts you want, time will be the best gift?" He smiled and said, "Absolutely!"

I hope he gets age appropriate games and toys I don't recognize and I hope he gets all the time he wants and needs.

Time is the greatest gift you can give anybody. It is precious and you can't get it back. Years from now that is what he will remember. It won't be the toys or the games. It will be the time that was spent with the most important people in his world. It is a memory; it is precious.

Let's plan to spending time with the most important people in our world. It will be a precious memory for us too!

Have a great week!

John

Thought for the Week – December 15, 2012

   Throughout this week, we have been looking at the wish lists of fifty families who needed our help to make Christmas a great day for their children. This has been largely due to a very generous staff, local businesses with giving attitudes, anonymous benefactors who leave envelopes filled with money on the office desk and wonderful parents who believe they have been blessed in their own lives and want to give back.

   Superimpose that with twenty children who will not be opening presents this Christmas and parents grieving the hardest loss imaginable. Think of the adults who were educators and staff members just like us and so quickly they became a memory. Think of an individual so unstable that he would go to an elementary school and kill the most vulnerable before killing himself.

   The random acts of kindness are fighting against the random acts of violence.

   I had noticed this year, that in many neighborhoods Christmas lights and trees were put up and turned on much earlier than usual. In fact, I was not the first one in my neighborhood to celebrate the holiday season. Maybe now I know why. We need the reason for the season to ensure that the evil in this world does not blind us from seeing the good. We need the lights around our houses to remind us that kindness and caring and generosity and understanding has to win over hatred, fear and brutality.

   There will be many families in this area that will be grateful for the help they were given in making Christmas a happy time for their children. There will be a whole school community who will be grieving and mourning and Christmases to come will be a heart breaking reminder. Let's pray for them and remember them during the holidays. They were and are just like us and that is the most sobering part about it.

   Have a blessed and safe holiday season and let's pray for Sandy Hook Elementary School.

John

<u>Thought for the Week – January 14, 2013</u>

Last week, when I met with my grade level teams, a theme kept coming up with each grade level that I spoke with. As we reviewed our tier 2 and tier 3 kids, several teachers stated that their students were showing more confidence and were achieving at a higher level. It was important to discuss this qualitative data as well as the quantitative kind.

It is hard to discern whether their confidence grew because they are finding more success or they are finding more success because of their growing confidence. Either way, it is a good thing and I was glad to hear that the teachers were seeing an increased confidence in the mannerisms and work of these students.

In the midst of all the data that is coming to us in every subject while using every letter of the alphabet, it is important to remember that all of us can be confidence makers or confidence shakers. We can encourage and build up or we can ridicule and bring down. We must not only look at the numerical values of these students, we must also look in the eyes of these students. We must make sure that they understand they are capable of being better and we can coach them and help them and support them make them more confident.

Teachers realize the importance of building confidence, the necessity of recognizing it when they see it and the importance of celebrating it as loudly as any numerical score. It is a quality we would like to see in every child while we are improving them quantitatively.

Have a great week!

John

Thought for the Week – January 28, 2013

A couple of weeks ago, as I was visiting one of my classrooms, a student who was working on an individual project, looked up at me and said, "When I grow up, I want to be a leader."

His teacher and I asked him, "Do you know what a leader does?" "Do you know what a leader doesn't do?" He told us that a leader was in charge and had to make good decisions. We went to discuss what future leaders had to learn and that it was not just telling people what to do. I reminded him that it is a leader's responsibility to filter out things that will not be helpful to the group and to communicate a larger, positive vision for whatever the group or company is doing. I finally told him that a leader also has to keep working and learning and become better every day. Leaders have homework just like students.

The student looked at the both of us and went back to his work on the computer. He did still have a smile on his face. We didn't scare him away from his dream.

With the new lessons on career and college readiness, we are going to have to have those conversations. We want all students to have dreams and aspirations, but, they also have to know what skills they need and what training and education is required. We then must help them create a plan that they can follow that will lead them toward fulfilling their dreams.

This past week we commemorated the birthday of one leader and inaugurated another. We need students who want to be leaders. They will be in charge someday. We have to help them be ready and lead them so they can lead others in the future. We just need to help them. That is what leaders do.

Have a great week!

John

Thought for the Week – February 7, 2013

On a recent walk with Roxie the wonder dog, she spied a friend of hers walking slowly down a wooden ramp leading from her front door to the ground. (Dog lovers will understand.) This was Southern, a two-year old German Shepherd who has had two leg operations in the last year to strengthen the ligaments and align the spine. She has been through a great deal and Roxie was as happy to see her as Southern was to see Roxie. My 12 year old was acting like a puppy again as their tails wagged and they whined in canine gleeful unison.

Southern's owner did not want to overdo it, so, she calmly asked for Southern to climb up the ramp and come back into the house and rest a while after having a wonderful reunion with her friend. Southern looked at her owner for a few seconds and then she leapt gracefully over the ramp that spanned 6 steps from the ground to the porch and landed safely inside her living room! Southern's owner looked at me and said, "I guess she is recuperating better than I thought! I didn't think she could do that!"

We have plenty of students we work with everyday who come to us with all different types of injuries. Some educational, some emotional, some lacking confidence, some lacking a filter. Some with no support except from us and some who have endured more in their short lives than most do in decades.

Just like Southern, they are making progress and they are getting better. We may not see it yet and they may not know it either but it is happening. Why? Because you are the ones doing the work and you ARE that good.

Let's continue to help all our students fly over the things that block their way and that hold them back. If Southern can do it, they can too!

Have a great week!

John

<u>Thought for the Week – February 21, 2013</u>

We recently had a child move away and go out of state to live with another relative. We were not happy to see her leave. She had made such progress with us and was becoming more confident and competent. We were saddened by her move and we already miss her presence.

This child was not loud or boisterous. She was not the life of the party or someone who took over a room when she entered.   She was a fourth grader who had grown up with us and had slowly, incrementally improved and matured and was becoming more comfortable in her own skin.

Isn't that what we are supposed to do? Isn't it our job to help each child feel better about them while they overcome their academic and social shortcomings? Isn't it our job to be so involved and dedicated to each child that we are pained by their absence? Shouldn't we miss having them here and shouldn't we miss helping them succeed?

In our world filled with threshold testing, surveys and educational acronyms that use every letter of the alphabet, we need to remember we affect the whole child when we dedicate ourselves to the whole child. Maybe, just maybe, they will miss us when they are gone too!

Have a great week!

John

Thought for the Week – March 7, 2013

My favorite class in high school, where I had to actually learn something, was bookkeeping. I was responsible for keeping a mythical budget in a brand new ledger. I was taught how to write things down properly, how to debit and credit amounts. The most important thing I had to remember was –If I spent $200.00 on something, I had to show that I gained a $200.00 piece of equipment on the other side. Both sides needed to match; be equal.

In Tom Armstrong's new book, <u>Neurodiversity in the Classroom,</u> (ASCD), he asks educators to look at a child's strengths first. He believes that all children and especially special education students have been given strengths to counterbalance their learning disabilities. He further asks us as educators to help students have a "Positive Niche" in their classroom and school. If we focus on their strengths instead of just focusing on their weaknesses, we can help our students see their whole selves and not just see themselves as children with deficits.

Threshold testing, RtI, remediation and support programs are all valuable parts of 21st century education. However, we need to also remember to look for our students strengths. They are there. It could be artistic. It could be athletic. It could be qualitative. It could be quantitative. They could be role models or a wealth of knowledge about a certain subject or topic. They are there. We just need to take the time and look for their strengths and acknowledge their strengths and nurture their strengths.

If we nurture and work on their strengths as hard as we remediate and support their weaknesses, we will have created a personalized balanced ledger book for every child. We could be the best bookkeepers in the world!

Have a great week!

John

Thought for the Week – March 15, 2013

Last weekend, as I was going a pile of guitar music, I discovered a song by Glenn Campbell (no, it is not the one you are thinking of). The beginning part sounds like this:

Let me be a little kinder
Let me be a little blinder
To the faults of those about me
Let me praise a little more
Let me be when I am weary
Just a little bit more cheery
Think a little more of others
And a little less of me

Let me be a little braver
When temptation bids me waver
Let me strive a little harder
To be all that I should be

Let me be a little meeker
With the brother that is weaker
 Let me think more of my neighbor
And a little less of me

In the last few weeks, I have seen adults and students treat each other with rudeness and attitude. They have been quick to anger and quick to judge. They have been even quicker to blame others for their actions and think it is okay to say whatever they wish to say in whatever way they wish to say it.

I hope that we can just take a few minutes to look at the lyrics of the song typed above. If we take care of what we do, maybe the rest of our world will become a kinder place as well. I pray that is does for all of you. As for me, I am going to be singing this song a little bit more this week.

Have a great week!

John

Thought for the Week – March 22, 2013

The other day as I was driving home, I passed by a house that had their windows open. I assume that it was trying to enjoy the warmer weather and air out the house. On the ledge of one of the windows, I saw a very fat cat hanging halfway out the window. It didn't look very comfortable and was trying to save face with a look of, "I meant to do that." However, it didn't look like it could back up and get back inside. It was definitely in predicament: It was not life threatening but it was definitely stressed out.

Many of us lately have felt like we are hanging halfway out a window except our window may not be on the first floor like the cat next door. Just like the cat, even though what we are going through may not be life threatening, we are still feeling highly stressed, highly vulnerable and like we are fighting our battles alone and unarmed.

Take some time as we prepare for a well-deserved break and the Easter Season to take a deep breath and realize that we all are feeling a bit overwhelmed and fatigued. Let's help each other and hold each other up even after the break. Just like that cat, we need someone to either help us back in or help us land safely on our feet. Let's be that help.

As we help others, we invariably and irreversibly change ourselves!

Have a great week and break!

John

Thought for the Week – April 12, 2013

      In the book <u>Aim High; Achieve More</u> by Jackson & McDermott (ASCD 2012 page 68), the authors write about the Latin word <u>spirare</u> – which means to breathe. It is where we get the word inspire from. So if we inspire people, in other words, we can breathe some life into them. We have the opportunity to excite and invigorate them. As a consequence we may even become more excited and energized ourselves.

      As we get farther along in the fourth quarter, we will need to remember "Spirare". We need to support, help, inspire and encourage one another. It is very easy to let stress and work take the air out of the room and the life and energy out of you.

      So as the weeks progress and as we aim toward a successful end of the school year, let's take a deep breath and make it a goal to inspire others so we don't perspire and certainly don't expire.

      Have a great week!

      John

Thought for the Week – April 19, 2013

This morning, as I was walking Roxie the wonder dog, a car I didn't recognize, came around the corner in front of us. The driver blew his horn, rolled down his window and flipped me off! I stopped for a minute and tried to figure out what I or my dog had done to deserve the one finger salute. We hadn't slowed him down, blocked his way or pooped, (the dog that is), on his shoes or urinated, (usually the dog) on his car. We kept on walking and I kept on thinking.

Since I didn't recognize the car or the driver and since I couldn't remember doing anything in and around the neighborhood, I was hoping it was a matter of mistaken identity. (Really hoping.)

Now Roxie is an escape artist but, I doubt if she has learned to unlock and open doors and escape during the day and return before I arrive in the afternoons. (I really, really hope not.) But the thing that really puzzles me is why should an adult who is on his way to work, do that anyway? Is this individual so unhappy and angry about his life, that he feels that he needs to give an inappropriate gesture to people he sees? Have we gotten to the point where it is acceptable to take our anger, frustrations and defeats out on anyone just walking around?

This week, we have had to deal with students not getting along and even some parents not getting along. My teachers call it "drama". I have been tempted to call it something else. As I have said before, we are in a culture of confrontation. Every conversation can become a battlefield where there has to be a winner and a loser. Compromisers are considered weaklings and pragmatism is as popular as lawyers and used-car salesmen.

We have to continue to strive to make schools a safe haven for students and adults that work there. We need to make it an oasis of kindness amid this desert of self-centeredness. We need to make our schools a place where all students can learn that respect and dignity is the norm instead of anger and harsh words. We need to teach tolerance by being tolerant and fairness by being fair.

As for me, I will pray for angry people and I will definitely drive home with my windows up and eyes looking straight ahead.

Have a great week!

John

Thought for the Week – April 29, 2013

      On Saturday, I went to the grocery store to pick up necessary items for the week. As I was standing in the checkout line, one of my students ran up to me and happily gave me a hug! She was smiling and yelling my name as she ran back to tell her mom.

      It was amazing since I had just seen her the day before but to her it was a welcome surprise and my presence seemed to make her day at the grocery store. (This kind of thing usually doesn't happen at the package store….usually.)

      That is the kind of impact we have on students. We are a constant to them and they can rely on us to care about them and help them and protect them. They get to know us almost as well as their own parents. Our presence is so constant that they get surprised to see us at sites other than school. They figure other people take care of buying our food and cleaning supplies. (Some kids do think we live at school. Some weeks I feel like I do!)

      I am always happy to see my students away from the school. It is a good sign that they recognize us when we are not in our normal professional garb. When they happily recognize us, it shows that we have made a positive impact on their lives and shows their parents that we have established a good relationship with their child.

      It is also good to get a surprise hug every now and then – we all need that!

      Have a great week!

      John

Thought for the Week – May 11, 2013

I received one of those phone calls this week that you hope you never get. I heard that my niece, who was in her thirties, had suffered a severe stroke and later found out that she was pronounced brain dead and had passed.

She was about the same age as my sons. She was also the only child of my youngest brother who died at the age of 21. Rebecca was very young when he died and never knew him.

Rebecca was an educator and a wife and a daughter. She died too young and too early. Young ones and daughters are not supposed to go before their parents. It breaks up the way it is supposed to be. It reminds us once again of the fragility and terminality of life. It also makes you think of your own children. Even if they are adults, you pray a little longer for them and tell them you love them a little louder and worry about them a little harder.

So this week, call your children or if they are close, hold them a little longer and say those things you always feel but may never always say.

It is my belief Rebecca has now met her father and seen my mother again in a great and loving reunion. Another angel joins the chorus.

And the prayers continue….

John

Thought for the Week – May 22, 2013

When I attended the funeral for my niece last week, I noticed something amazing at the gravesite. I was amazed to see so many young people there.

They were Rebecca's students and you could tell, for many of them, it was their first time dealing with the loss of someone they knew and cared about. You could tell by the tears in their eyes and how they shook their heads. You could tell by how overwhelmed they were by the view of this last resting place on the top of a lovely hill in the shade of a maple tree.

They were there because Rebecca's life's work had made an impact on their life's worth! They felt the loss because they knew the value. They were grieving because they understood their blessing.

That is what teachers do. That is what Rebecca did and that is what you do. Remember this when the times get tough and the days get stressful and you don't know if you are making an impact.

You do as Rebecca did.

Let's remind everyone we know of this fact. Then they won't have to wait for a time when quiet prayers on a cool spring day ends in a final, tearful yet grateful goodbye.

Have a great week!

John

Thought for the Week – June 11, 2013

"When the night has come, and the land is dark, and the moon is the only light you see…"

Several years ago at a different school, my music teacher thought it would be a great idea to teach the choir the song Stand By Me for the end of the year performance. They went through the words and the rhythm and even listened to the wonderful Ben E. King version (no relation darn it!). Then my music teacher began to teach a choral version of the song.

"I won't cry, I won't cry, no I won't shed a tear; just as long as you stand by me…."

It started with one child who came into my office with tears running down her face saying, "I just started to think about my grandma and it made me want to cry." I asked, "So your grandma passed away?" She said, "No. She is still alive. It just made we want to cry."

Okay.

Several students followed her….one was crying about her dog..(He actually had passed.)…one about grandfather, another about a cousin and even one about a great grandparent they had never known. Finally I had to go to the stage and tell the music teacher…. "The kids cannot stand….Stand By Me….We are going to have to pick another song."

"Whenever you're in trouble, you can stand by me….stand by me….stand by me….stand by me."

Unlike my choir, you all have done a great job standing by your students and your teachers; your peers and your parents. You have walked with them carrying their load and making their lives successful and their paths straighter.

Thanks for standing together during this very challenging but successful year. Have a great summer and know that we will stand again together next year.

"No I won't be afraid. No I won't be afraid. Just as long as you stand, stand by me."

John

Thought for the Week – August 1, 2013

A mother brought her young child in to register the other day. The child did a pretty good job of waiting and tried to take care of the sibling that accompanied him.

After mom had completed all the paperwork and handed over the necessary documentation to finish the process, she thanked everyone profusely and said that they were looking forward to a great year.

Then the newly registered child had a tantrum. Not because he was going to be starting school and didn't want to. He was crying and screaming because he thought he was going to start school that day! He was excited about it; ready for it; mentally prepared. We messed him all up. He wanted to be in school now!

In a little over a week, he will have his wish of finally starting school. I hope all the other students will be just as happy about starting a new year with new things to learn, new challenges to face, and new accomplishments to achieve!

I hope that all the adults that come back next week, feel the same excitement and anticipation and have the same goals and dreams.

Have a great week!

John

Thought for the Week – August 18, 2013

A weekend before school started, I decided it was a great time to wash the cars and vacuum them out in preparation for the school year. I guess I thought if it might help me get ready....people might think: "He is sometimes a jackass but his car is really clean." or "He can't be that bad since his wheels rock!"

Since I had multiple cars to sterilize, I decided to take them to a local car wash. The plan was to fill them up with gas, have the car wash to the hard part, wipe the cars down, vacuum them out and be clean and done!!!

Halfway through the car wash with the first car, the car wash broke down. It just stopped right in the middle of the suds cycle. (You know how frustrating that can be!) So I had to slowly and carefully back my soapy car out of the currently not working car wash. (How embarrassing.)

I then had the brilliant idea of driving down to another car wash in Pooler. I figured it would be fine since the car was halfway washed already. I went inside the establishment and asked them for a number for the car wash and was told..."It really isn't working properly. I wouldn't use it if I were you."

Since I now had experienced two dysfunctional carwashes, (I felt so abused), I decided to go back to my house and do it the old-fashioned way......by hand and with a hose and a bucket.   Although, I was worried at this point that the hose was going to have a hole in it, the bucket was going to melt in the heat or a main water line would mysteriously shut down just as I turned the tap on. However, everything turned out fine, the cars were shining and the insides looked clean enough for human habitation and my wheels did rock!

There will be times in the next 10 months that something will break down, not work or not create the expected results we really wanted. We will have to calm down, adjust, and find a new way to help our students or our school find success. It may be a little harder, be not as convenient, take longer than expected and definitely cause more perspiration.

We will handle it, we will find a different way that works and we will do whatever it takes to make everything we do and everyone we work with as successful as possible.

Have a great week!

John

Thought for the Week – August 26, 2013

While I was walking the dog the other afternoon, I couldn't help but overhear a conversation that a middle school age child was having over the phone with his parent. (He was sitting on his front porch and talking loudly. That is why I knew it was a middle school age child.)

He was telling his parent, "I have to defend myself if she touches me because otherwise I will show weakness and no one will respect me." I could also tell that the parent was telling him what he or she expected from a son and I could tell by his facial expression that he was not happy with what he was hearing.

Two cultures were colliding.

It is tough for sons to know what it means to be a gentleman in an age when you don't get points for that or you may have to take too much garbage off of people. It is tough on parents because they don't want to see their children stepped on but have to make it clear what they expect of their sons as they slowly become men. It is tough on both when they live in a culture where confrontation is admired over courtesy and walking away from rude people is considered cowardice.

I said a quick silent prayer for the parent and the child. It is a major undertaking to create, encourage and build up a boy so he will become a gentleman. I think he will do just fine. He will have to swim against the current, listen to some name calling, lean on his parents and learn to endure. We need more gentlemen. I am glad we will be getting at least one more.

Have a great week!

John

Thought for the Week – September 10, 2013

I went to a writing conference at AASU last Saturday. I saw some people I know and used to work with, and made some new friends.

You may wonder why, as a writer, did I sign up for a writing class? I signed up to learn about how to help students write more, to improve our writing scores and to practice what I preach. (We are all scholars and we need to learn new things and study our craft all the time.)

I was reminded of more than that.

I was reminded that we are all writers. We all need to reflect and think and write about things that are meaningful to us. We need to find our voice and not be afraid to share what we write. We can also change our minds and edit and revise and then share our writing once again. I was reminded that good writing takes time and should not be delegated to just a short duration each day.

I was reminded of why I write.

I have said for years that writing is my therapy. It is cheaper than professional help and a great deal more satisfying. It has given me the strength to work through the deepest agonies, share feelings of the greatest joy, and reminisce about past lives, friends who have passed on and events and adventures that occurred when I was a younger and dumber man.

This is why I write – I want to share and this act of sharing fills a heart, clears a mind, strengthens a backbone and heals a soul.

That is why we should all write. So pick up your favorite writing utensil and give it a try. It is not hard...it just might be that you are out of practice!

Have a great week and write something down!

John

Thought for the Week – October 1, 2013

About a week ago, after a very stressful day, (which days aren't?), I finally made my way home. I felt very tired from the day and had hundreds of things flying through my mind. I had the to-do list, the need to do list, the really need to do list and…. I really should have done something else list. So, I was ready for some quiet time listening to my dog scratch and the occasional whirr of the air conditioner. I put the phones down, left the computers off, the stereo quiet and the IPAD sitting on the table.

As I sat on my back porch trying to de-stress, I noticed three swallow tail butterflies all flying together in a chaotic yet beautiful formation. It looked like they were playing tag and when one left the group, the other two would find it and if two of them went one way, the one left behind caught up quickly. I do not know how long I watched them, but they stayed in my little backyard for a long and grateful period. Finally, I watched the trio move steadily south through other backyards until they were too distant for me to see.

Afterwards, I felt that the weight of the day was off me. I was able to take a deep breath and gather my thoughts and tackle some things that really needed to be done.
It is amazing how something so small, ethereal, and seemingly inconsequential can focus our minds on what is important. The butterflies simple beauty doing nothing more than what butterflies do, can make us stop, take a break, breathe in aesthetically and emotionally and recharge our batteries for another round of life.

It is not the stress we have to fight. We have to fight the urge not to look for the butterflies playing tag because we think we are too busy to look and then we will miss the true beauty of the world.

Have a great week!

John

Thought for the Week – October 18, 2013

In the book, <u>Never Underestimate Your Teachers</u> Robyn Jackson states: "Teachers who need purpose, need to believe that what they are being asked to do matters and they need to understand how it matters before they can get going."

Teachers are feeling more stressed than ever with new testing, new curriculum, new tasks, new requirements, and new strategies and even new security systems, anti-bullying protocols and the always present staff development.

Our focus needs to be on reassuring all these fine people that what they are doing is making a difference and does matter. We need to remind them to take a deep breath and just do the next thing and help the next kid and keep plugging along. We don't need to remind them of the big picture; that is already on their minds and in their worry zone.

We should never underestimate our teachers and we should never forget that what we say and how we support each other can help us find the purpose, see what matters and do what is right.

Teaching is a purpose-filled life. We just need to remind each other and ourselves of that fact as we start each and every challenging and yet rewarding day.

Have a great week!

John

Thought for the Week – October 30, 2013

Two former students came by to visit yesterday. They weren't 13 year-old sixth graders and they weren't 18 year old seniors. They attended the school decades ago and came from out of town to take a stroll down memory lane.....and to remember better times.

One of the ladies had lost her husband 6 month ago; the other lady lost her husband last month. One had recuperated during the last year from cancer; the other one had a brain tumor removed a few months ago.

Both decided that they would come back to their elementary school because they wanted to remember the fun times, their teachers' names, and their fellow students. They wanted to take the time to pretend, for just a little while, that they were innocent little kids again. Little ones who were too young to feel the pain that inevitably comes as your age turns into crooked numbers.

When they left, the ladies had smiles on their faces and thanked us repeatedly for allowing them access to a past time.

That is what schools do. They create memories that cannot be worn away by time because they reside in a special place in one's heart. The experiences that we offer our students not only mold them into scholars and citizens it also helps create who they are. It is not only the challenging academics. It is the laughs, the special events, the concerts, the games, the homecomings, and our best friends.

Those two wonderful ladies remembered and relived a wonderful time in their lives. I hope all our students will keep equally marvelous memories. We will find out....it is just a matter of time.

Have a great week!

John

Thought for the Week – November 18, 2013

Several weeks ago my dog and I were scheduled for our yearly checkups on the same day (different doctors…I know what you were thinking!). Both of us were found to have something that needed further investigation. So, we scheduled our respective biopsies on two different days (still different doctors).

After living through that fun experience, I had to wait for the results. I actually received the results about Roxie the Wonder Dog before I received my own. Unfortunately, my results were better than hers.

I was given a big negative and was relieved that I could go another six months confident that my aches and pains were due to my age and genetics and not due to something else. Roxie was diagnosed with cancer and given from two to six months to live. She is walking with a pronounced limp and gets tired more easily. In fact, our walks which used to take 15 minutes are now taking 25 because she has slowed down. But, she is happy and eating and her bodily functions are working so we are just going to take one day at a time (a cliché but true).

Roxie has always had a big personality. She cannot be called affectionate but she has been a loyal, understanding friend even when everything around her was changing. Yes, she freaks out every now and then but don't we all.

So some bitter sweet results from the biannual physicals. Hard to hear but now we can prepare and enjoy the days and pray.   More to come………….

Have a great week!

John

Thought for the Week – December 4, 2013

All over my neighborhood, people are leaving their holiday lights on all night. No matter what time of night or early morning I decide to walk Roxie, (or she tells me), there are houses that are lit up not only like a Christmas tree but because of Christmas trees.

It reminds me of old sayings like: "Keep the home fires burning." And "Light a candle in the window." The houses look welcoming and hopeful as if they are waiting for loved one to finally arrive or a safe haven for travelers looking for hospitality.

The lights are a way to show that it is a different time of year. That it is a special time; something out of the norm. We think of a particular story, a special song, an important memory, or a person now gone. We think more about helping or forgiving others or focusing on kindness and prayer. We think more about those that are not as fortunate and those that have houses not as brightly lit or as happy as our own.

Is our own work neighborhood as bright as they could be? Are we the beacon of hope, the example of kindness and understanding, and the person your student and staff can rely on? Can we, by our actions, demonstrate the reason for the season? Can we create a bright and positive place that tries to balance out the dark parts of other people's lives?

During this wonderful season where we decorate and change the ways our houses look for one month out of the year, let's work on decorating our own personalities to lift others up in every way we can. If we can't do it in the month of December, when can we?

Have a great week!

John

Thought for the Week – January 30, 2014

We spend a great deal of time looking at test scores and assessment numbers. We compare them to a set goal and determine what each number means. We analyze and codify and log each one carefully either online (the 21st century way), or in a notebook (the old fashioned way). We look at individuals, classes, grade levels, growth bubbles, Student Learning Objectives, IEP data, IQ's, Rubrics, attendance rates and free and reduced percentages.

We should and all these numbers are important......but.....

Every test score has a face and back story. Each individual score is a child who may be dealing with a myriad of problems, challenges, disabilities, and hardships. Many are succeeding because the constant in their lives is you, their classroom, and their school. This is their safe haven, the place without fear and a place they can relax for just a few hours. They are fed, loved and taken care of...in some cases even with food over the weekend.

Yet, with all that going on, they show some improvement and some growth due to you. They may not be where we want them to be but, where they have come from and what they have accomplished so far should be acknowledged, celebrated and recognized.

Every number we look at has a story and that makes the number less of a destination and more of a mile marker indicating where they have come from and not their final destination.

Have a great week!

John

Thought for the Week – February 6, 2014

This is a late thank you too all our counselors during this 2014 National School Counselors Week.

Our school counselors have become much more than professionals that help students begin their year, deal with the loss of a loved one or pet, and teach "guidance lessons". They are now in charge of divorce groups, children of deployed soldiers groups, test anxiety sessions, children with ADHD sessions, and "I don't know what to call it but I hope it helps" sessions.

They are also responsible for facilitating Peer Mediation training, Career and College Readiness Lessons, assistance with Response for Intervention, connecting parents to other service organizations, leading the Backpack Buddy Program so our neediest of families have food every weekend and helping our homeless students have uniforms that fit so they can fit in.

In their spare time, they deal with the day-to-day crises that happen every day when students walk in our doors. They also calm down over anxious parents and/or overwhelmed grandparents who are doing their best to raise their grandchildren.

Thank you to all school counselors and let's remember them and thank them the other 51 weeks of the year. Let's also pray for them. They are to our kids another mom, an analyst, a therapist, a confidante, a supporter, an advocate, and counselor.

They where many hats but they have just one huge and wonderful caring heart!

Have a great week!

John

Thought for the Week – February 15, 2014

This will be the last missive about Roxie the Wonder Dog. She passed last Friday morning after a short but brave battle with cancer. Back in October, I was told that she had between 2 and 6 months left and she endured it for almost that full duration. She was a brave, wonderful dog and the last connection I had to a past life. She is and will be missed.

I do not want to focus on her passing but on her separate and distinct phases of her life.

First, she was a rescue dog that I adopted from the Savannah Humane Society. She was six months old and no one wanted her because some said she was ugly. She was actually quite pretty. She was not affectionate but she was loyal and wanted to be in the same room breathing the same air.

Secondly, she was a true Pointer/Labrador mix. She would go out into the big back yard in Thunderbolt and slowly and stealthily track a bird or squirrel and raise her front leg and extend her tail just like a Pointer. She would occasionally catch one and be proud of her kill. She once scared a squirrel into a plastic cylindrical bird feeder. I had to try to get the poor thing out without having Roxie attack me and the poor animal. (The squirrel and I survived.)

Third, she was an escape artist. I didn't know for months that she was able to go under the fence in the yard and sojourn around the neighborhood. She knew more neighbors than I did. She would sneak back in the yard before I got home. I found out what she was doing when I began training her to walk with a leash again around the neighborhood. I was planning on moving to Pooler so I needed her to be ready to walk properly through the new homestead. As I walked her through Thunderbolt, neighbors began to yell out asking me if she was my dog and saying, "We see her around here all the time." I looked at her and she just looked down and kept on walking.

Fourth, she was the Prozac dog. When I moved to Pooler and left her alone, she had several moments of panic. She tore up my bathroom and chewed up a cabinet drawer in the kitchen so badly (or so well), that I had to have it replaced by a cabinet maker. Thunderstorms were equally interesting. I never knew if she would drool, jump in my lap or both. At one point she was taking more medication than I was.

Lastly, she was the elderly regal dog her took her cancer in stride and just accepted walking with a limp and taking shorter walks and sleeping in the one position that was not too painful. She did that as long as she could. She didn't want to leave and I didn't want to say goodbye.

I have learned many things from being blessed with Roxie the Wonder Dog. To take the stages in life that come to us as a blessing and takes them in stride; to enjoy them and accept them. I have learned to deal with age in a regal and dignified way. Finally, I have reluctantly learned, once again to accept death as an eventuality to bear and move on from. It makes you appreciate all you have in the present because it can change so quickly and will change inevitably.

I thank God for Roxie and will remember her and miss her for a long time. She is the first dog I have ever had cremated. I am going to spread her ashes all over Thunderbolt. She would appreciate it and it seems like the right thing to do.

John

Thought for the Week – February 25, 2014

Last week several schools had to deal with the loss of a student. It is always a painful situation made more tragic by the young age of the departed. We expect to read or hear about someone's passing after a long productive life; after years of work, growth, maturity and aging.

We never are ready for this kind of loss. We gear up as a faculty and make food, buy flowers, visit the family, send cards, and add them to our prayer list. Even with all that effort we still feel a deep, intense pain in our hearts. We feel for the family and know that the hard part will start when we all go back to our own individual normal.

Their normal is no more. They have to find a new normal and that will take time. Even when the new normal is found, the dull pain will never leave. They will learn to cope but they will never get over the loss. Their eyes will eventually dry but their hearts will never fully heal.

As we go on with our normal, we need to reach out and check on the family and make sure they know that we still think of them, pray for them and feel for them. It is okay for us to go back to our normal. It is the only way to keep our sanity. It is also okay to keep checking on the family. It is the only way that they may make it out of that very painful, deep hole created by the loss of a child.

Keep praying.

John

<u>Thought for the Week – April 1, 2014 (No not an April Fool's joke.)</u>

The words "fourth quarter" induce different thoughts and feelings to different people. To a retail worker or owner, the fourth quarter could make or break their year financially. To an economist it is the last bit of data he will need to evaluate what happened last year and predict what may happen next year. To a football fan, it is a time for the last effort; that one big play to assure the victory. Students in stadiums everywhere hold four fingers up when the fourth quarter starts to show that they know the importance of this moment. They believe if they cheer loud enough and pray hard enough victory will be inevitable – they can't lose!

It is the same for us fighting in the educational trenches. We know it is the fourth quarter. We know it could make our year instructionally. We may not hold any fingers up (and shouldn't) but we do cheer and show our support and we definitely pray.

Let's continue to work and to believe and help and support and try new things and cheer and pray. If we do, we can be just as assured as our students in the stands – victory will be inevitable!

Have a great week!

John

Thought for the Week – April 15, 2014

    Last year on this date, the people of Boston were attacked by pressure cooker bombs placed along the route of the Boston Marathon. This has been a year of rehabilitation for some who lost limbs, a year of mourning for those that lost their lives, and a year of healing both head and heart for all Bostonians.

    Today, several victims with new space-age limbs will run the marathon again! Many survivors who lost loved ones will also be there to say emphatically, "We survived the worst anyone can throw at me! You have not destroyed me!"

    To have the courage to go back to the Boston Marathon is necessary, according to psychologists, for the victims and their families to get more of their lives back; regain some sanity; put away the pain and anguish of that day!

    I am in awe of all of them: The runners, the watchers, the families and the survivors.

    Today let us compare our daily challenges and battles to what the survivors had to endure this past year. We have our daily frustrations; they had to learn to walk again. We have our aches and pains; they had skin graphs and operations. We have things we have to overcome; they had to overcome fear, painful memories and loss.

    To us life is not so bad. I hope later on today, they feel the same way!

    Have a great week!

    John

<u>Thought for the Week – April 30, 2014</u>

My neighborhood is a very active one. There are usually people walking dogs, jogging, running, walking without dogs and bike riders. Yesterday, one of my younger neighbors stopped his bike in front of me. He had a big grin on his face. He announced to me, "Today is the first day that I am riding my bike by myself without training wheels!" I congratulated him and told him I was very proud of this important accomplishment. He said, "Thank you Mr. John!" and rode off.

I had to smile and remember the day that I taught each of my sons how to ride a bike on their own. They were proud and happy too.

In many ways that is what you done with your students this year. You have given them the support and assistance they needed. You have individualized it and differentiated it for the students that needed more help and bigger training wheels. You let each one improve and mature until you knew they could ride on their own. Not all are there yet. Some may still need help from falling down or sliding back but, many have improved enough for you to let them go solo. (Even though you keep your eye on them anyway).

It is hard to see the successes and the growth when we are in the trenches trying to make a difference. Please know that you have. Please know they it shows. Please know that they are as proud as a young child riding his bicycle with no other support attached!

Have a great week! Happy Teacher Appreciation Week May 5th – 9th.
John

Thought for the Week – May 23, 2014

The Webster's Dictionary defines a legacy as: "Something of value that is handed down from an ancestor or to a descendant." What we have strived to do this year is to take what we have learned from our parents and from our teachers and mold it into a philosophy that helps our students. We wanted them to find what we found in schooling – a place that enriched our lives, encouraged our efforts, loved us even when we didn't deserve it and helped us to become more knowing, caring and tolerant.

That is quite a legacy! What we expect schools to do and teachers to do and principals to do is almost unreachable. Yet, all of us strive to do that every day when we help a child and walk in their shoes and dry their eyes and lift them up.

All of us have to be mentors, advocates, counselors, preachers, philosophers and defenders. We have to get back up when we are knocked down by apathy, anger, and neglect. We have to take a deep breath and try again when the support we receive is weak and we feel we are working alone.

As we finish this school year, let's remember our legacy – every child we helped, every co-worker we supported, every parent we counseled and every gain, (even the smallest), made in the classroom.

That is quite a legacy! Be proud!

Have a great summer.

John

A Final Thought – June 2014

I found out in May 2014 that I was going to be the new principal of the largest school in the Savannah-Chatham County Public School System. I am leaving one of the smallest – Bloomingdale Elementary and going to Godley Station k – 8 School with 1600 students!

These thoughts were written during my 13 years at Bloomingdale. I hope it has been an encouraging, open, sometimes humorous book. I have tried to share the important and life changing moments of my life. There has been much lost and much gained and that little school has been a very strong constant in my life.

I will write some more in the future. I will take some time to get to know my new school and new staff and learn what I have to do differently with 127 staff members and 1600 students! I will share more stories and hopefully we can laugh and cry together again. Thanks for reading A Principal's Thoughts. Writing has always been therapy for me. I hope you will share the book or sections with a friend who is an educator, a principal or just a guy with an old dog that reminds you of Kingdog or Roxie the Wonder Dog.

As I have said on every page – Have a great week! Have a great life!

John

www.ingramcontent.com/pod-product-compliance
Lightning Source LLC
Chambersburg PA
CBHW050641150426
42813CB00054B/1151